W0009108

This work is dedicated to the General Electric workers
who labored to design and build the locomotives that occupy these pages
and to the generations of railroaders who have worked with them.

U·BOATS

Greg McDonnell

Stoddart · A Boston Mills Press Book

McDonnell, Greg, 1954-
U-Boats: General Electric diesel locomotives

Includes bibliographical references.
ISBN 1-55046-1125

1. Diesel locomotives-United States-History.
2. Diesel locomotives-United States-
   Pictorial works.
3. Electric locomotives-United States-History.
4. Electric locomotives-United States-
   Pictorial works.
5. General Electric Company- History.
6. General Electric Company-Pictorial works.
I. Title.
TJ625.G45M33 1994   625.2'66'0973
C94-931962-7

Copyright © Greg McDonnell, 1994

All rights reserved. No part of this work covered by
the copyright hereon may be reproduced or used
in any form or by any means–graphic, electronic,
or mechanical, including photocopying, recording,
taping, or information storage and retrieval
systems–without the prior written permission
of the author.

Book Design and Typesetting,
Chris McCorkindale and Sue Breen
McCorkindale Advertising & Design

Copy Editing,
Gordon Turner

Printing and Binding,
Printed in Singapore

First published in 1994 by
Stoddart Publishing Co. Limited
34 Lesmill Road
Toronto, Canada M3B 2T6

The Boston Mills Press
132 Main Street
Erin, Ontario N0B 1T0
1-800-565-3111

JACKET PHOTOGRAPHS:
SP U50C 9950
GE U33C 405 (ex-Southern 3810)
EL U33C 3306
GE Builder's Plate: PC 2902
Greg McDonnell

PAGE 1:
Buffalo-bound during the last days of the Lehigh Valley,
U23B's 504 and 510 cast their reflection in the still waters of a
swamp near Van Etten, New York, at 0925, March 26, 1975.
Greg McDonnell

PAGE 2:
Silhouetted in the cab light, the engineer aboard Conrail U25C
6810 patiently awaits the highball on the eastbound NFSE at
Buffalo, New York, at 0130, July 15, 1981.
Greg McDonnell

PAGE 4:
GE Builder's plate: LS&I 2501
Greg McDonnell

CONTENTS

In the midst of their historic 1960 tour, GE U25B test-bed demonstrators 751 and 752 pose for the company photographer on the head end of a freight. *General Electric photo; Robert Lambrecht Collection*

THE SHAPE OF THINGS TO COME

Deep within the confines of General Electric Transportation Systems' 350-acre facility in Erie, Pennsylvania, a derelict locomotive rusts away, just yards from the famed GE erecting shop known simply as Building 10. Propped on shop trucks and sprayed with test shots of experimental paints, the sorry-looking relic stands quietly as Building 10 echoes the heavy metal symphony of diesel builders assembling 4400-h.p. Dash 9 series locomotives in one of the most hallowed halls of American dieseldom. The decrepit condition of the ancient engine belies its importance, for the heavily cannibalized hulk is none other than GE U25B prototype 752, one of the most significant diesel locomotives in the country.

Sole survivor of the heroic campaign that established General Electric in the domestic road diesel business, GE 752, along with long-scrapped sister 751, changed the course of American motive power development and laid the groundwork for GE's hard-fought rise to number one locomotive builder in North America. The 752 was outshopped from Building 10 in 1959, but the seeds of its origin were planted six years earlier.

In 1953, following the dissolution of the Alco-GE partnership, General Electric quietly began developing its own line of domestic road diesels. The first outside evidence of this program appeared in September 1954, when GE rolled out a 6000-h.p. A-B-B-A set of experimental test-bed locomotives. Fluted side panels and the absence of the distinctive grilled headlight casing could not disguise the similarity between the experimental cab units and the Alco-GE FA, not surprising, considering that the handsome FA styling was also the work of GE designers. Internally, though, the Alco-like experimentals were radically different, and the four- cycle beat of the Cooper-Bessemer diesels throbbing inside their carbodies forecast a revolution that would alter the face—and the future—of American motive power.

Dressed in full Erie colors and numbered Erie 750A-750D, the four- unit test set was leased to the railroad for mainline freight service, but its true role was that of a rolling laboratory. For five years, the black-and-yellow A-B-B-A

racked up revenue miles on the Erie Railroad, while GE engineers reaped invaluable test results and applied lessons learned in the rigors of road service to the design and development of the Universal-series locomotives.

Engine development was a key element of the 750's exhaustive testing and the four-unit set employed two new versions of the Cooper-Bessemer diesel engine. The 750A and 750B were powered by 12-cylinder, 1800-h.p. FVA12LT engines, while 750C and 750D were equipped with 8-cylinder, 1200-h.p. FVA8LT prime movers. GE already had considerable experience with the Cooper-Bessemer power plant, especially the FWL6T, which was used in hundreds of earlier GE locomotives from export units to domestic 70-tonners and 90-tonners. However, GE's new domestic ambitions demanded a larger, more powerful prime mover. In concert with the 750 trials, GE established an engine test laboratory at the Erie, Pensylvania, facility in 1955 and began work on a V16 version of the Cooper power plant.

Without so much as a whisper of the grand scheme to break into the domestic road-unit market, GE introduced the Universal series in 1956 as a line of export locomotives. A pair

of 1800 h.p. UD18 "export demonstrators" outshopped in June 1956 drew little attention from U.S. roads preoccupied with dieselization and committed to the GP9's, SD9's, RS11's and RSD15's of mainstream builders EMD and Alco. Baldwin had built its last locomotive and Fairbanks-Morse was barely hanging on; as the boom years of dieselization wound down, few observers expected a new entry in the shrinking U.S. locomotive marketplace. So, despite their eye-catching red-and-white paint scheme and conventional road-switcher configuration, GE UD18 demonstrators 1800 and 1801 raised little, if any, suspicion as they performed road tests on the Erie Railroad. At the time, the most remarkable aspect of their shakedown trips was their operation in mixed-builder lashups with Erie RS3's. Confirming the advertised export-aimed marketing of the Universal line, GE 1800 and 1801 soon departed for Mexico and an NdeM demonstration tour. NdeM purchased the two demonstrators, as well as eight additional units delivered in November 1956, and America forgot about the UD18. Though they toiled in anonymity, the unheralded Mexican locomotives were harbingers of the technological revolution that would be sparked by the introduction of the U25B in a few short

Perhaps the most important unpreserved diesel in America, General Electric U25B prototype 752 languishes in the shadow of its birthplace in Erie, Pennsylvania, on May 16, 1991. *Greg McDonnell*

Still in her original demonstrator-inspired paint scheme, NdeM UD18 8004 leads sister 8007 in standard NdeM paint at Irapuato, Guanajuato, Mexico, on February 12, 1962. *B.L. Bulgrin*

years. In retrospect, it's obvious that there was far more to the UD18 than met the eye.

Back at Erie, work continued on the V16 engine and the locomotive it would power. In July 1958, the first V16 FDL engine roared to life. Ten months, and uncounted engine hours later, that same FDL16 prime mover was lowered onto the frame of a new locomotive and in May 1959 a clean-lined, unlettered hood unit carrying the number 751 on its numberboards emerged from the Erie works. Shortly thereafter, a second unit numbered 752 was completed. Continuing to disguise the Universal series as an export-only line, GE dubbed the two new units XP24's (export test units, 2400-h.p.) and like previous test beds, dispatched them to the Erie Railroad for a round of rigorous road tests.

More than 100,000 miles later, the 751 and 752 were called back to the plant for modifications, and in early 1960, the veil of secrecy was finally lifted. Upgraded to 2500-h.p. and decked out in blue-and-off-white demonstrator colors, the 751 and 752 re-emerged from the Erie works with their true identity revealed. The XP24 test beds were in fact prototypes for a new GE locomotive, the U25B. These Universal-series debutantes were no export diesels, though: the

new General Electric U25B mainline locomotive was aimed directly at the American market. The U25B, GE boasted, was born of "a carefully integrated design to meet the requirements of a new era of fast freight railroading." For American railroads—and locomotive builders —it was a new era indeed.

Beyond the gates of GE's sprawling Erie facility, a hostile world awaited the shiny blue-and-white U25B demonstrators. With dieselization complete and the country in the midst of a recession, the American locomotive business was more competitive than ever. Baldwin-Lima-Hamilton and Fairbanks-Morse had been knocked out of contention, while Alco and EMD slugged it out in an intense battle to dominate a shrinking market. For diesel builders, the boom times were over. Replacement of aging first generation and minority-builder diesels was the order of the day and, thanks to increased horsepower and reliability, the new models could achieve that at the rate of two-for-three, or better. This was no time for a newcomer to enter the marketplace.

True, the U25B was the new kid on the block, yet GE was anything but a newcomer. Indeed, General Electric had been building

locomotives since 1893. Furthermore, the company produced America's first diesel-electric locomotives in 1918: a 200-h.p. steeple-cab switcher built for the Jay Street Connecting Railroad in New York, an identical unit for the City of Baltimore, and an armored engine for the U.S. Army. Locomotive historians are quick to point out that GE played a key role in almost every major diesel-electric locomotive development in the U.S. between 1918 and 1934. Even Electro-Motive relied on GE for almost all of its electrical equipment until 1938.

Well known as a supplier of electrical equipment and an active participant in the famed Alco-GE partnership, General Electric was a locomotive builder in its own right long before the introduction of the U25B. From the popular 44-ton center cabs and 70-ton switchers that were shortline staples, to monster UP gas-turbines; from virtually unnoticed export diesels to legendary electrics such as Pennsylvania GG1's, Milwaukee boxcabs and "Little Joes," New Haven EP3's through EP5's, massive Great Northern W-1's and million-pound Virginian EL-2B's, thousands of locomotives rolled out of the Erie works in the pre-U25 years. In the trade press and in sales materials, GE emphasized its historic contributions. "Over 23,000 locomotives later...the GE U25B," proclaimed one advertisement. Still, the U25B was a neophyte in the eyes of many railroaders.

Neophyte or not, the U25B, backed by nearly a half-century of GE diesel experience, was the product of seven years of innovative design work, intense development and exhaustive testing. Through several hundred thousand miles of test-bed road trials, design concepts and experimental equipment evolved to become proven technology. The end result was a locomotive that pioneered a number of technological innovations, including pressurized engine and control compartments, a central air system and advanced wheel-slip detection, all centered around the newly developed GT598 main generator and FDL16 engine, conservatively rated at 2500-h.p.

"New from the rails up," GE claimed, but just inches above the railhead, the U25B's AAR type-B trucks cradled four GE 752 traction motors. The 752 motor was hardly new, but GE owed no apologies for equipping its new-age freighter with postwar-era traction motors. With millions of miles of reliable service under everything from straight electrics and gas turbines to virtually all postwar Alco-GE road locomotives, the GE 752 was highly respected as the best traction motor on the market. As they rolled out of Erie on their debut tour, demonstrators 751 and 752 were confronted with no less of a challenge than to prove that the U25B was a locomotive as rugged and reliable as the 752 traction motors slung on the axles of their B-B trucks.

It was a hard sell. While Southern tried out the U25B's on just a single Cincinnati-Chattanooga round trip (after originally offering to test them for up to two months), Pennsylvania put more than 11,000 miles on the demos, working them on everything from Erie-Renovo shakedown runs to hot Chicago-Harrisburg TrucTrains. On Illinois Central, GE 751 and 752 accumulated over 5,000 miles working out of Chicago on hotshot freights to New Orleans, Birmingham, St. Louis and Omaha. Proving their advertised unit-reduction capabilities, the two U25's handled tonnage normally assigned three GP9's on all but the grueling Jackson, Tennessee-Birmingham, Alabama, run. Norfolk & Western put the U25B

demonstrators through more than 7,100 miles of demanding road trials on time freights and heavy drags and Great Northern did likewise, racking up 7,356 miles on the blue-and-white demonstrators. Barnstorming throughout the eastern half of the nation, the U25B demos did extensive duty on C&NW, Wabash and Frisco, Rock Island, L&N and NYC, while D&H, GM&O and Florida East Coast sampled the new units only briefly.

The ten-month, 61,006-mile tour wrapped up on the Frisco on December 27, 1960, and the 751 and 752 came home to Erie. Though the U25B order books were still blank, the test beds-turned-demonstrators had done their job, spearheading GE's campaign to break into the domestic road diesel market. Just a year-and-a-half old, the 751 and 752 went into seclusion at Erie, while their successors, U25B demonstrators 753-756, were completed in preparation for a nationwide tour.

The first production U25B's, GE 753-756 were outshopped in January and February 1961, incorporating modifications and improvements resulting from experience gained from the original demos. Most noticeable was the slightly restyled (but still high-nose) carbody and the adoption of a more conventional road switcher-style pilot and step configuration with end platforms and walkways. Conservatively attired, the quartet wore a simple red-and-gray garb, with "U25B" stenciled on the nose and "General Electric" spelled out

on the hood.

Still searching for the first U25B sale, GE dispatched the four-unit demonstrator set on a nine-railroad, 74,000-mile tour in March 1961. Following in the wake of America's worst year for diesel sales since 1938, GE pushed even harder to break into the marketplace. In the Monzano Mountains and the Tehachapis, the San Gabriel Mountains and the Sierras, ancient hills reverberated to the new sound as the gruff bark of V16 FDL's introduced the west to the U25B.

Meanwhile, back in Erie, the long awaited call came in. Champagne surely flowed at 2901 East Lake Road, as GE inked the first U25B order in the books: four units for Union Pacific. There was plenty to celebrate as Union Pacific 625, the first U25B sold, emerged from the Erie works in August 1961, but this was just the beginning. Frisco also signed up for four U25B's, as well as placing a purchase order for the 753-756 demonstrator set. Within months, Southern Pacific, Santa Fe, Wabash and Pennsylvania would all place U25B orders and UP would come back for more. Eight years of hard work and uncountable man hours, millions of dollars, tens of thousands of miles of test runs—and tens of thousands more demonstrator miles—had finally paid off. The U25B had broken the sales barrier and was gaining momentum. General Electric was in the domestic road-diesel business for good.

So new that their builder's plates have not yet been riveted on, Union Pacific 628, 626, 625 and 627, the very first order of U25B's, proudly pose for their official portrait beneath test track catenary at Erie, Pennsylvania, in August 1961. *General Electric Photo; Robert E. Lambrecht Collection*

UM20B

Horsepower	2000
Engine	FVBL12T
Production Dates	9/54*
Total Built	UM20B-A 2
	UM20B-B 2

* Built as A-B-B-A test beds ERIE 750A-750D. Rebuilt and repowered for sale to UP as UM20B's in 1959.

Original Owners:

General Electric.........................(4)
Union Pacific 4

Separated from her GE test-set companions 750A-750C, Erie 750D poses with F3B 805B and another F3 at Hammond, Indiana, at 12:19 P.M., April 8, 1958.   *R.P. Olmstead; R.R. Wallin Collection*

Although fully painted, lettered and numbered as Erie Railroad 750A-750D, the A-B-B-A test set outshopped in September 1954 was owned by GE and operated in revenue service on the Erie as a rolling laboratory. The 750A and 750B were powered by 1800-h.p. Cooper-Bessemer FVA12LT engines and 586 generators, while 750C and 750D had 1200-h.p. FVA8LT engines and 581 generators. Test beds for the program to develop the FDL16 engine and the domestic Universal- series road locomotive that would become the U25B, the four units operated on the Erie until mid-1959, when they were returned to GE. Rebuilt and repowered with 2000-h.p. FVBL12T engines and 586 generators, the four units were given model designation UM20B and sold to Union Pacific in October 1959. Numbered UP 620, 620B, 621 and 621B, the unique units saw just four years of irregular service before their October 1963 retirement.

Nearing the end of their careers, UP UM20B's 620, 620B, 621B and 621 stand in the snow at Council Bluffs, Iowa, on February 24, 1962.   *Dave Ingles*

UD18

Foreshadowing General Electric's dramatic entry into the domestic road locomotive business, NdeM's UD18's were the first heavy-duty GE diesels built for a North American railroad. In keeping with GE's implied export ambitions for the Universal line, the first two units were tested on the Erie as GE 1800-1801, then headed for Mexico on a demonstration tour. NdeM purchased the two demos, along with eight more UD18's built in November 1956. Though lacking the advanced technology introduced by the U25B, the UD18's physical appearance forecast the shape of things to come. Class engine 8000 was wrecked in 1961, but most of the NdeM UD18's remained in service until the mid-seventies, ironically outlasting many early U25B's.

Horsepower	1800
Engine	FDL12
Production Dates	6/56-11/56
Total Built	10

Original Owners:

General Electric.........................(2)
Nacionales de Mexico...............10

Although equipped with steam generators for passenger service, NdeM's UD18's evidently spent most of their careers in freight service. Wearing the red-and-white colors introduced by UD18 demonstrators 8000-8001, NdeM 8004 leads sister 8007, in standard dress, on the head end of a drag freight at Irapuato, Guanajuato, Mexico, on February 12, 1962. *B.L. Bulgrin*

With a crewman's bicycle safely stowed on the gangway, NdeM UD18 8007 switches the passenger station at Guadalajara, Jalisco, Mexico, on April 9, 1971.
Gordon Lloyd, Jr.

U25B

Horsepower	2500
Engine	FDL16
Production Dates	4/59-2/66
Total Built	478

Original Owners:

New York Central	70
Southern Pacific	68
Pennsylvania	59
Rock Island	39
Chesapeake & Ohio	38
Frisco	32
Erie Lackawanna	27
Louisville & Nashville	27
New Haven	26
Great Northern	24
Santa Fe	16
Union Pacific	16
Wabash	15
Milwaukee	12
Burlington	6
General Electric	2
Norfolk & Western	1

In the post-dieselization doldrums of recession-racked 1960, the U25B burst on the scene with an audacity and excitement unseen in railroading since the introduction of the Electro-Motive FT in 1939. The brash new locomotive packed the newly introduced 2500-h.p. FDL16 under the hood and pioneered such technological advances as a central air system, pressurized engine and control compartments, advanced wheel-slip control and an improved cooling system.

GE backed the U25B with an aggressive marketing campaign and no less than four sets of U25B demonstrators. Following their ground-breaking 14-road, 61,006-mile tour of 1960, U25B prototype demonstrators 751 and 752 were succeeded by GE 753-756, completed in January-February 1961. The first production U25B's, the high-nosed quartet featured refined styling and redesigned front platforms, steps and walkways. From March to October 1961, the red-and-gray demos racked up 74,071 miles on Santa Fe, SP and WP, Frisco, Burlington, Milwaukee and SOO, Northern Pacific and New York Central. Union Pacific and Frisco signed up for the first U25B's sold, taking delivery of four each during 1961. Frisco also purchased GE demonstrators 753-756 in December of the same year.

The first low-nose U25B, GE 2501 emerged from Erie in February 1962 along with high-nosed sisters 2502-2504. While the brightly painted foursome toured the country, covering 51,305 miles on ten railroads, the U25B began to sell in earnest. In late March 1962, Southern Pacific 7500 debuted the classic U25B styling. The first of an eventual 68 SP U25B's, the 7500 featured a flat-profile low nose, single-piece windshield and conventional road switcher-style steps on both ends. By May, Santa Fe and Wabash had also received low-nose U25's, while Pennsylvania had 29 units on order. High-nose U25B production ended that same month with the delivery of UP 629-632. Prior to the late-summer delivery of low-nose U25's 637-640, UP purchased GE demonstrators 2501-2504, giving the road 11 of the 19 high-nose U25B's sold (Frisco had the other eight).

The order books were bulging and Building

Illustrating the evolution of the U25B, Frisco 827, one of the last U25B's built, and high-nosed SL-SF 803, one of the earliest production U25B's back onto their train with a pair of black GP35's at Birmingham, Alabama, on August 31, 1968. *Ken Douglas*

10 was crowded with U25B's under construction when GE 51-54, the final U25 demonstrator set, were dispatched from Erie in December 1962. While the low-nosed demos battled heavy drifting snow with Rock Island tonnage on the Kansas plains, worked Southern Railway time freights over the Rathole and mingled with New Haven FA's in Maybrook, new and repeat U25B orders poured in. In the summer of 1963, Frisco purchased the four demos, as well as four new U25B's, and by year's end C&O, L&N and Rock Island had taken delivery their first U25's; Santa Fe and SP had placed repeat orders and New York Central had a $6 million, 30-unit order on the books.

Trade-ins, from Santa Fe Erie-builts to SP Baldwins and Wabash FA's, crowded the scrap dock in GE's Erie backyard, while brand new U25B's posed for builder's photos beneath test-track catenary. Although statistically eclipsed by record-breaking GP30 sales, the U25B was an unqualified success. After just three years in the domestic road-diesel business, GE posed a serious threat to former partner Alco, and was causing concern in the board rooms and back rooms in La Grange.

While sales were impressive, the U25B's remarkable success was tempered by teething pains, particularly those experienced by the new FDL16 engine. GE stood behind its product,

though, with field support and warranty work covering everything from minor modifications to complete engine changes. If anything, GE's effective response helped strengthen its market position, and the U25 kept on selling.

As production increased and sales gained momentum, GE continued to refine the U25B inside and out. Internal modifications were not obvious, but the evolution of the U25B carbody was. In December 1964, the esthetically pleasing, but expensive to replace, single-piece windshield was eliminated in favor of a more practical two-piece split windshield. Only 50 units were produced with this transitional appearance before Great Northern 2513 was outshopped in May 1965 with what would be the final U25B carbody. In addition to the recently adopted split windshield, the familiar U25B face was further altered as a slightly sloped nose replaced the original flat profile.

In February 1966 the last U25B rolled out of Erie. Coincidentally, the locomotive belonged to Frisco, owner of the first production U25B: SL-SF 804, formerly GE demonstrator number 753. Riding on the rebuilt trucks of an Alco trade-in and carrying GE serial number 35768, Frisco 831 marked the end of production for a legendary locomotive, but was just the beginning of GE's climb to the top.

WHAT'S IN A NAME?

Kicking up the dust on the Route of the Rockets, Rock Island U25B's 205, 234 and a GP35 highball through Morris, Illinois, in November 1965. As the December 1965 issue of *TRAINS* hits the newsstands, America will discover a new name for the GE diesels, one already well known to the crew in the cab of the 205: U-boats. *Paul Meyer*

Conservatively attired in tuscan dress, Rock Island's U25B's were not the most attractive of their kind, nor were they particularly notable or high-profile locomotives. However, the chance meeting of a young college student, a Rock Island train crew and a trio of U25B's at Silvis, Illinois, on January 24, 1965, changed all that, as the Rock GE's earned national recognition and made a lasting contribution to the legacy and the identity of all General Electric U-series road diesels.

Taking advantage of a semester break from MacMurray College, Dave Ingles and Charlie Mote headed west to track down a rare Chicago Great Western RS2 assigned to a remote branch on the Iowa prairie. En route, the two stopped in at Silvis, where a westbound Rock Island mainliner, with U25B's 208, 216 and 222, had paused to change crews. Always friendly, the RI crew struck up a conversation with the young photographers, asking "How do you like our new U-boats?" Ingles included the colloquialism in

his text of "Christine and the Mongeese," a Rock Island diesel piece published in the December 1965 issue of *TRAINS* magazine. The Rock Island localism caught on and soon gained universal acceptance among railroaders and railroad observers who applied the U-boat moniker to all GE U-series diesels. The Rock, the 208, 216 and 222 are long gone, but thanks to an unknown crewman and a young writer, the name lives on.

13

The first production U25B, GE demonstrator 753 eases down the lead tracks at Burlington's shop in Denver, Colorado, in August, 1961.   *Ken Douglas Collection*

Nearing the end of a multi-million-mile career, Frisco U25B 804, ex-GE demonstrator 753, rests at Memphis, Tennessee, on Christmas Eve 1976. In the New Year, SL-SF 804, the first production U25B, will be traded in to GE on the first production B30-7's.   *David M. Johnston; R.R. Wallin Collection*

Dressed in black, Frisco U25B 803, a pair of GP35's and a mandarin-red U25B storm out of Topeka, Kansas, on UP iron, leading a Frisco-UP runthrough to North Platte, Nebraska, on November 5, 1966.   *Steve Patterson*

On lease to Colorado & Southern in June 1970, UP U25B's 625 and 633 idle on the shop tracks at Denver, Colorado, in the company of Rio Grande GP35 3029, a GP30 and another GP35. The first U25B sold, the 625 is on borrowed time and will be retired by September 1972. While most UP U25B's were rebuilt by Morrison-Knudsen, albeit to 567-engined hybrids and slugs, the 625 was not. M-K crews cut the historic unit up for scrap at Boise in 1981.   *Keith E. Ardinger Collection*

Freshly overhauled Union Pacific U25B 632, sisters 639, 627 and ex-EMD GP35 demonstrator 763 stand ready to depart Topeka, Kansas, with an Extra West on March 13, 1966. In April 1969, UP 632 was re-engined with a 12-cylinder 2500-h.p. FDL as part of the program to develop the U50C. After removal of the test engine in the summer of 1972, the 632 was sold to Rock Island for parts and later rebuilt to RI road slug 283.   *Steve Patterson*

Nearing the end of their 51,305-mile demonstration tour, GE U25B's 2501-2504 pause at C&O's Rougemere Yard in Dearborn, Michigan, in June 1962. Within a month, the demos will be sold to Union Pacific. GE 2501, the first low-nose U25B, will become UP 633, while high-nosed sisters 2502-2504 will become UP 635, 634 and 636. As UP 633, the former demo will remain distinctive as the only low nose U25B built with the XP24/early U25-style one-piece pilot with steps notched in the sides. *Emery J. Gulash*

Less than four months later, dressed in pristine armor yellow and reborn as UP 633, ex-GE 2501 and UP GP9B 314B lead the 98-car PFE into North Platte, Nebraska, at 11:16 A.M., October 3, 1962. While the 633 lives on, albeit re-engined with an EMD 567 and rebuilt as an M-K TE53-1-4E, the rattletrap stock cars, 40-foot boxcars and Pennsy wagon-top in the PFE's consist are surely history. *Robert R. Malinoski*

While a silver-faced Baldwin road switcher and zebra-striped EMD switcher look on, brand new SP U25B 7541, GP35 7454 and DD35B 8402 exit San Antonio, Texas, with a westbound drag in August 1964. With a flat-profile low nose, single-piece windshield and conventional steps, SP 7541 shows off the "classic" U25B styling debuted by SP 7500 in March 1962.
J. Parker Lamb

In the time-honored, but soon-to-disappear, Southern Pacific tradition, SP U25B 6702 carries train number 373 in her train-indicator boards as she leads freshly renumbered sisters 6762, 6732 and GP35 6627 through Glendale, California, in July 1966.
Alan Miller

Runthrough pool service was a common assignment for U25B's on many railroads and Santa Fe was no exception. No longer new, but still in runthrough service, Santa Fe U25B's 1602, 1609 and NYC F7B 3431 pose on the service tracks at Penn Central's West Detroit, Michigan, facility in May 1968. *Harry L. Juday; Keith E. Ardinger Collection*

Working a favorite U25B haunt, Santa Fe 1605 and 1612 lead PC U33B's 2909 and 2859 on an ATSF/PC runthrough on the Kankakee Belt at West Kankakee, Illinois, in March 1969. Still in full NYC paint, the 2859 is one of the first two production U33B's, built in the midst of NYC U30B's 2830-2889 in September 1967. *Paul Meyer*

Eastbound in former Nickel Plate territory, N&W U25B's 3515, 3525 and GP35 1317 work through Silver Creek, New York, with 91 cars at 11:11 A.M., May 4, 1969. A wreck rebuild constructed with some components from Wabash 512, destroyed in a head-on collision at Hannibal, Missouri, just before the merger, the 3515 is the only U25B built for N&W. The second unit, N&W 3525, is ex-Wabash 510, rebuilt by GE-Erie in December 1965. Between July 1965 and February 1966, all 14 surviving Wabash U25B's were rebuilt at Erie and outshopped as N&W 3516-3529.
Robert R. Malinoski

Proudly wearing the Wabash flag, U25B 510 leads F7A's 722 and 649 on westbound train ADK-1 at Jacksonville, Illinois, on March 10, 1965.   *Dave Ingles*

Slogging up the legendary Allegheny grade, PRR U25B's 2530, 2506, 2523 and 2511 drag Chicago-bound TrucTrain TT3 around Horse Shoe Curve, west of Altoona, Pennsylvania, on June 5, 1965.   *Robert R. Malinoski*

Just over six weeks old, but looking more like six years old, Pennsy U25B 2541 leads GP35 2255 and GP30 2225 out of Altoona, Pennsylvania, passing Slope Tower with a westbound symbol freight on April 4, 1965. Part of Pennsy's fourth U25B order, the 2541 features the transitional carbody with the flat-profile low nose and split windshield.
Ken Douglas

Thirteen years and two mergers later, Conrail U25B 2641, ex-Penn Central 2641, nee-Pennsylvania 2541, leads U23B 2703 and a westbound drag through Waverly 4 in Newark, New Jersey, at 1020, August 23, 1978. *Greg McDonnell*

Under sunny summer skies, Rock Island U25B 233 and U28B 256 head up the Royal American Shows circus train at Como Shops, St. Paul, Minnesota, on September 3, 1974.   *Steve Glischinski*

Only one day after being delivered, Rock Island 225, the first unit of RI's final U25B order, poses at Blue Island, Illinois, on September 12, 1965. Featuring a sloped low nose and split windshield, RI 225 illustrates the late U25B styling that carried over into early U28B production.
K.C. Henkels; Keith E. Ardinger Collection

Following the Rock Island shutdown on March 31, 1980, RI U25B's 225-238 were sold to Maine Central. Retaining their Rock road numbers, all but five units were put in service and eventually repainted in MEC orange and green. At least two units were later repainted in GTI gray and orange. Working a D&H/N&W runthrough freight, Guilford-painted MEC U25B 225, B&M U33B 190 (ex-CR/PC 2916) and faded-blue D&H GP38-2 7316 (ex-LV 7316) thread the crossovers at Puzzle in Cleveland, Ohio, on June 2, 1984. *Thomas Seiler*

Longevity was the claim to fame for Louisville & Nashville's U25B's. Long after the demise of several U25 fleets, Louisville & Nashville 1600-1626 soldiered on, ranking as the last intact U25B fleet as late as 1982. Replacing Alco RS3's in the late seventies and early eighties, many L&N U25B's were posted in yard and transfer service operating out of DeCoursey, Kentucky. Assigned to yard duty with slugs built from RS3's, L&N U25B's 1608 and 1620 pose side by side under the yard lights at DeCoursey at 2230, April 3, 1980.
Greg McDonnell

Fifteen years old and still performing as GE promised she would, L&N U25B 1619 thunders out of Verona, Kentucky, leading C628 7517, leased SP U33C 8722 and U25B 1602 on an eastbound freight on May 20, 1979.   *Jeff Mast*

Like many aging GE's, 15 Chesapeake & Ohio U25B's found refuge in Mexico in the early 1980s. A long way from the West Virginia coal fields (and even farther from the former Pere Marquette Canadian Division), NdeM U25B 6713, originally C&O 2533, rests at Valle de Mexico, Mexico, in the company of a leased SP U33C on March 23, 1980.
V. Delgado; Matthew J. Herson, Jr., Collection

Headed for Canada, Chesapeake & Ohio U25B's 2536, 2522 and 2510 roll past the semaphores at Delray Tower in Detroit, Michigan, in September 1966.   *Emery J. Gulash*

The crew of Second XN-2 is out for the camera as the New York-bound symbol freight, led by NYC U25B's 2500, 2538 and 2521, works in electrified third-rail territory at Croton-Harmon, New York, on March 21, 1965. Class engine of the largest original U25B fleet, NYC 2500 was restored at GE Erie in 1993 and has been preserved at the National Railway Historical Society Lake Shore Chapter Museum in North East, Pennsylvania. Conrail 2510, ex-NYC 2510, has been saved by the Mohawk & Hudson River Chapter of the NRHS. *Robert R. Malinoski*

Headed up by NYC 2518, a quartet of Central U25B's hammer the CNR diamond at Hagersville, Ontario, as they race a westbound hotshot over the Canada Southern on May 28, 1966. *Peter Cox*

Nearly a decade after Peter Cox caught her at Hagersville, the 2518 wears Penn Central paint as she and ex-New York Central U30B 2830 work the homeward-bound Massena, New York-Montreal, Quebec turn job through Montreal West, on CP Rail's Adirondack Subdivision at 1417, December 7, 1975.   *Greg McDonnell*

The first of 22 New York Central U25B's built with the transitional carbody, Conrail 2538, ex-PC/NYC 2538, leads solid-black SD40 6248 on a westbound TV train at Iona Island, New York, in June 1979.   *Hal Reiser*

Years and miles removed from their Great Northern days, BN U25B's 5407 and 5418, ex-GN 2507 and 2518, are deep in Burlington country as they work the Buckwheat Local, with eight cars and a silver Burlington waycar, near Denver, Colorado, on November 30, 1977.   *Philip Mason*

Transitional-carbodied Great Northern U25B 2510 rests at Minneapolis Jct., Minnesota, in the company of classic U25B 2500 and big sky-blue U28B 2527 on May 30, 1968. *Alan Miller*

The head-end brakeman is out to get the mainline switch as BN U25B 5409 (ex-GN 2509), Burlington GP40 3025 and a pair of Chinese-red SD's depart Pueblo, Colorado, in August 1971. *Tom Brown; Dan Pope Collection*

The staccato bark of laboring GE FDL's and Alco 251's echoes in the hills as Erie Lackawanna U25B 2516, C424's 2412 and 2407, U25B's 2515, 2524 and C424 2411 thunder over the Delaware River at Mill Rift, Pennsylvania, with 68-car #97 at 2:51 P.M., July 16, 1966.   *Robert R. Malinoski*

Tracing the Canisteo River, Erie Lackawanna U25B's 2514 and 2520 roll westbound tonnage through the scenic Canisteo Valley west of Rathbone, New York, at 1755, April 4, 1976.   *Greg McDonnell*

General Electric scored a major coup with the 1964 sale of six U25B's to loyal EMD customer Chicago, Burlington & Quincy. Burlington's first non-EMD road power, U25B's 100-105 were commonly assigned to runthrough pools with Union Pacific and New York Central. Working a Burlington-UP runthrough, CB&Q U25B 105 leads three UP GP30's and a Q GP30 through Cheyenne, Wyoming, on September 25, 1966.
Matthew J. Herson, Jr.; Keith E. Ardinger Collection

Kicking up the snow on Burlington's famed racetrack, CB&Q U25B 104, U30B 141, U25B 101, GP30 974 and a UP GP30 wheel a CB&Q/UP pool train through Eola, Illinois, in January 1968.   *Paul Meyer*

Her UP pool days are long gone, and her handsome Chinese-red paint and nose lights are history, but nine-and-a-half years later, former CB&Q 104 is alive and well and back in Eola, Illinois, in June 1977. Now Burlington Northern 5428, the aging U25B works the racetrack in the company of another Q veteran: BN U30B 5480, ex-CB&Q 150.   *Robert Lambrecht*

Running cab hop through former New Haven electrified territory, PC train NO-9, with unrenumbered U25B 2524 and PC renumbered 2660, 2670 and 2665, passes a set of short-arm semaphores at West Haven, Connecticut, in August 1969. *Jim Reddington*

New Haven has been part of Penn Central for six months, but there is little evidence of change as U25B 2506 poses with an A-B-B-A of FA1's and McGinnis-painted FL9 5031 at Dover Street Yard in Boston, Massachusetts, in June 1969. *Jim Reddington*

Sporting distinctive New Haven region "ghetto grates" over her windshields, Penn Central U25B 2661 (ex-NH 2501), former NH FA1 1331 and a New Haven painted U25B hurry OB-4 through Hebronville, Massachusetts, in January 1971. *Jim Reddington*

A long way from New Haven, Conrail 2679, originally NH 2519, storms through Oak Harbor, Ohio, leading a westbound Water Level Route TV train with a rare back-to-back set of U25B's in May 1978. *Jeff Mast*

Working Milwaukee Road's Coast Division, a traditional GE haunt, U25B's 5052, 5056, 5057 and U30B 5609 lead a 47-car 901 through Western Jct., Washington, at 4:00 P.M., June 3, 1979. Milwaukee 5056 has been preserved at the Illinois Railway Museum in Union, Illinois, while the 5057 is at the Feather River Rail Society Museum in Portola, California. *J.D. Schmid*

Standing under Coast Division catenary that has fed legendary GE-built box-cabs and Little Joes for generations, Milwaukee Road U25B 5000 and two companions pause at Avery, Idaho, with an eastbound Dead Freight in August 1970. Before continuing eastward, the U25's will be joined by a Little Joe helper that will lead the all-GE lashup over St. Paul Pass. *Keith E. Ardinger*

Dropping off the 2.2 percent Boylston Hill, Milwaukee U25B 5000 and two sisters put the Saddle Mountains behind them as they cruise across the spectacular 3,016-foot bridge over the Columbia River at Beverly, Washington, in August 1970.
Keith E. Ardinger

Trailing log gons piled high with fresh-cut timber, Oregon, California & Eastern 7604 and 7605 negotiate the Bly Mountain switchbacks near Squaw Valley, Oregon, in August 1978. At a glance, the OC&E units, ex-UP 628 and 638, appear to be run-of-the-mill U25B's; however, twin exhaust stacks and the rhythmic beat of EMD 567's indicate otherwise. Along with four other ex-UP U25B's; the 7604 and 7605 were rebuilt by Morrison-Knudsen in 1975-76. Designated TE53-1-4E's and repowered with 567 engines and generators from B&O F7's, the ex-UP U25B's became Weyerhauser 310 and OC&E 7601-7605. Former UP U25B's 629 and 636 were rebuilt as OC&E slugs 7606-7607 and operated in road service with their repowered mates. Oregon's last logging railroad, OC&E quit in 1990 and the M-K rebuilds were sold to Texas-based Econorail.
Keith E. Ardinger

Southern Pacific, owner of the second largest U25B fleet, was the only railroad to initiate a capital rebuild program for the pioneer GE road units. Completely rebuilt and rewired, christened "Spirit of 1776" and decked out in brilliant red-white-and-blue colors, former SP 6708 was outshopped from the road's Sacramento Locomotive Works in September 1975 as U25BE prototype 6800. Unfortunately, the future of the U25BE program was not nearly as bright as the 6800's bicentennial colors. SP 6801, formerly SP 6724, was the only other unit completed before the program was canceled. Resplendent in bicentennial paint, SP 6800 slumbers beneath the full moon at San Luis Obispo, California, on August 10, 1976. Renumbered SP 3100 and repainted to standard crimson-and-gray in 1979, the U25BE's were retired in December 1984. While the 3101 was scrapped, the 3100 has been preserved along with SP U28B 7028 at the Orange Empire Railway Museum in Perris, California.
Brian Jennison

Exploring every option to extend the life of its aging U25B's, Southern Pacific had Morrison-Knudsen rebuild retired units 6745, 6717, 6733 and 6752 as Sulzer-powered TE 70-4S's. Outshopped from Boise in experimental Daylight colors on February 24,1978, SP 7030-7033 were less than successful. The Little Sacramento River canyon echoes the strange sound of Sulzer diesels as SP 7030, 7031 and 7033 coil through Gibson, California, on their maiden run with the BRLAT at 3:10 P.M., March 1, 1978. A foreboding indication of what's to come, the 7032 is absent from the consist, having failed en route and been set out at Black Butte. *J.D. Schmid*

Among the last U25B's in service anywhere, Maine Central's ex-Rock Island U25B's labored in the employ of Guilford well into the second half of the eighties. Heading a D&H southbound in the last days of Penn Division operation, MEC U25B's 231 and 234, along with D&H GP38-2 7320 and GP39-2 7420, rumble beneath Starrucca Viaduct at Lanesboro, Pennsylania, on October 4, 1985. *Philip Mason*

Inheriting U25's of New York Central, New Haven, Pennsylvania and Erie Lackawanna heritage, Conrail took title to no less than 179 U25B's upon its creation on April 1, 1976. Not surprisingly, Conrail became one of the last major operators of the trend-setting GE freighters. Near the end of the U25B era, Conrail 2582, ex-Erie Lackawanna 2513, receives servicing in the DeWitt shop in East Syracuse, New York, on August 12, 1979. The 2582 was cut up at Midwest Steel & Alloy in Hubbard, Ohio, in 1981. *Greg McDonnell*

Working out what many figured to be their final days, L&N U25B's 1616, 1625, 1626, 1611 and an ex-RS3 yard slug drag a heavy Cincinnati-bound transfer through Covington, Kentucky, at 1720, March 31, 1980. While many notable diesels, including NYC Limas and Baldwin Sharks, Pennsy FM's, C&O Baldwins and L&N FA's, made their last stand in Cincinnati transfer service, the L&N U25B's broke with tradition and returned to road service. Longevity was indeed their strong suit and the 1616 hung on to become the last U25B in service anywhere. Renumbered CSX 3416, the never-say-die GE made its last run on train R409, arriving at Waycross, Georgia, on April 1, 1989. Appropriately, CSX donated the historic diesel to the B&O Railroad Museum, which in turn loaned the unit to the Tennessee Valley Railroad Museum in Chattanooga for restoration and display. *Greg McDonnell*

U25C

Horsepower	2500
Engine	FDL16
Production Dates	9/63-12/65
Total Built	113

Original Owners:

Northern Pacific	30
Atlantic Coast Line	21
Pennsylvania	20
Louisville & Nashville	18
Burlington	12
Oro Dam Constructors	10
Lake Superior & Ishpeming	2

Bracketing SD45 3621, Northern Pacific U25C's 2516 and 2523 work at Garrison, Montana, on July 23, 1969. *Joe McMillan*

As the U25B demonstrators toured the country, a number of railroads expressed interest in a six-motor version of the nation's newest freighter. Introduced in September 1963, the U25C was the result. Just over four feet longer than the U25B, the 64-foot 6-inch U25C packed the same 2500-h.p. FDL16 engine, but rode on six-wheel double-equalized trimount trucks and weighed in at 348 tons, compared to the 130-ton weight of its B-B companion. Interestingly, though, the first U25C's went, not to a railroad, but to the contractor building the Oro Dam on the Feather River near Oroville, California.

Oro Dam Constructors put seven U25C's to work, using back-to-back pairs to haul 4400-ton trains of fill over a 12-mile railroad (part of it

a remnant of the relocated Western Pacific mainline) built to facilitate construction of the largest earth-filled dam in the world. A head-on collision in October 1965 killed four crewmen and totally destroyed two of the four U25C's involved in the wreck. Replacements 8017-8019 delivered to ORO in December 1965 were the last U25C's built.

The two ORO orders bracketed deliveries to six railroads during the U25C's brief production run of just over two years. Sampling the wares of all three builders, six-motor advocate Atlantic Coast Line placed four-unit orders for Alco C628's, EMD SD35's and the first U25C's delivered to a common carrier. Repeat orders boosted the ACL U25C fleet to 21 units, second only to Northern Pacific's 30. The ACL and NP

orders marked a significant victory for GE, as both were new customers. Another new GE customer, Michigan ore hauler Lake Superior & Ishpeming, purchased two U25C's, while U25B owners Burlington, L&N and Pennsy exercised the six-motor option, bringing sales of the first C-C U-boat to a total of 113 units.

Styling changes implemented during concurrent U25B production were not applied to the U25C. All 113 units were built with single-piece windshields and the level profile of their pug noses was not altered. What was changed, though, was the 2500-h.p. rating of the FDL16. A number of U25C's were successfully uprated to 2800 h.p., hastening the formal introduction of the U28C.

LAST OF THE MOHICANS

LS&I 2501, 2404 and 2403 at Eagle Mills, Michigan, July 9, 1986. *Greg McDonnell*

Idling on the shop track at Eagle Mills, Michigan, LS&I U25C 2501 keeps company with a pair of Alco RSD15's on a warm July night in 1986. Chanting a throaty four-cycle serenade, the big GE and her Alco companions patiently await dawn...and the call to work the 7 A.M. "Hill Job" to the ore docks at Marquette. Long past their prime, the aging members of this six-motor trio have found sanctuary here in Upper Peninsula ore country, where diesel dinosaurs have ruled since Baldwin DT-6-6-2000 centercabs replaced elderly Brooks-built Consolidations on DSS&SA ore trains.

Freshly overhauled and wearing LS&I's bright new colors, U25C 2501 hardly looks her years, but glistening paint and a finely tuned FDL16 belie the fact that the 2501, like the RSD15 "Alligators" in her company, is an endangered species. Indeed, the ancient U-boat is even rarer than the Alcos coupled behind her. From Conway to Corbin, Tacoma and Tepic, virtually all other U25C's have fallen victim to old age and trade-in incentive programs. Just seven days shy of her 22nd birthday, Lake Superior & Ishpeming 2501 is the last U25C operating anywhere.

Not that long ago, the 2501 languished outside the Eagle Mills shops, a fire-damaged and rusting hulk. Out of service for several years, the unfortunate engine was a certain candidate for the torch until fate intervened and she was granted an unexpected eleventh-hour reprieve. Looking better than the day she rolled out of Erie, and ready to haul 120-car ore trains with her elderly Alco partners, LS&I 2501 is the last of the Mohicans.

The fourth U25C built, Louisville & Nashville 1519, ex-Oro Dam Constructors 8013, rests at DeCoursey, Kentucky, on January 11, 1977.
John A. Cloutier; Brian Jennison Collection

Passing the relocated Western Pacific mainline east of Oroville, California, Oro Dam Constructors U25C's 8016 and 8012 head for the Oroville Dam construction site on the Feather River north of town with a trainload of fill on May 20, 1964. On October 7, 1965, the 8016 was wrecked near this location in a head-on collision that claimed the lives of four railroaders. Destroyed along with the 8016 was ORO 8010, the first U25C built. Upon completion of the project, the eight surviving ORO U25C's were sold to Louisville & Nashville, becoming L&N 1518-1525 in October 1967. *Ken Douglas*

Fighting upgrade under a towering column of exhaust, L&N U25C's 1510, 1509 and U30C 1563 work a northbound drag out of Corbin, Kentucky, at 1830, April 1, 1980.
Greg McDonnell

Spliced by GE U30B demonstrator 301, Atlantic Coast Line U25C's 3011, 3019 and a GP7 wait to couple to their train at Waycross, Georgia, on April 16, 1967.   *Keith Ardinger*

Part of the late seventies and early eighties exodus of aging GE's, NdeM U25C 7708, ex-SCL 2108 (originally ACL 3008) rests in the sun at Tepic, Nayarit, Mexico, on November 6, 1980. All but two of SCL's 21 ex-ACL U25C's were rebuilt at GE's Hornell, New York, shop and sold to NdeM in 1980. *Paul Hunnell; Matthew J. Herson, Jr., Collection*

Veterans of ACL's second generation six-motor splurge, SCL U25C 2118 and C628 2207 head #376 out of Waycross, Georgia, in September 1970. *Ken Goslett Collection*

Easing through the washers, Northern Pacific U25C 2525 and GP9 272 get a well-deserved bath at Livingston, Montana, in August 1968. *L. Norman Herbert*

Stopped at a red signal, a Milwaukee Road F7 waits patiently while BN U25C 5636, still in full Burlington paint, and a trio of ex-NP GE's roll a coal train through the interlocking at Hoffman Avenue in St. Paul, Minnesota, in June 1971. *Jim Reddington*

Swinging through the S-curves near Cooks, Washington, BN U25C 5624 (ex-NP 2524) and three SD's work an eastbound freight along the Columbia River in June 1978.   *Jim Reddington*

With a sure-footed grip on sanded rails, Pennsy U25C 6502 and Penn Central-painted 6501 grind past MG Tower with CB-9, just west of Horse Shoe Curve, Pennsylvania, on October 1, 1968.   *Robert R. Malinoski*

At 0130, July 15, 1981, Conrail NFSE-4, with former Pennsy U25C 6810 and ex-EL SD45 6095, awaits the highball to head east from Frontier Yard in Buffalo, New York. *Greg McDonnell*

U50

Horsepower	5000
Engine	FDL16 (two)
Production Dates	9/63-8/65
Total Built	26

Original Owners:

Union Pacific 23
Southern Pacific 3

Trailing high-nose U25B's 629, 632 and a string of 40-foot grain boxes, UP U50 32 blasts through a deep cut on Aikins Hill, near Aikins, Kansas, on July 1, 1967.   *Steve Patterson*

Union Pacific's early acceptance of the U25B came as little surprise, considering the railroad's historic relationship with General Electric. UP had been dealing with GE since the experimental steam turbines of 1938-39 and rostered 58 GE-built gas turbines, as well as the four UM20B's and a single GE 44-tonner. However, after purchasing 16 U25B's, UP ordered no more; motive-power chief David S. Neuhart had something bigger in mind.

Neuhart, the man responsible for UP's acquisition of the 4500-h.p. and 8500-h.p. GE gas turbines, wanted a diesel capable of producing 15,000-h.p., in two- or three-unit lashups. In 1963, he took his proposal to the builders, and GE responded with the twin-engine, 5000-h.p., four-trucked U50. Mechanically, the U50 amounted to two U25B's built on a single platform, but in person, the 83-foot 6-inch, 558,000-pound brute was dieseldom's answer to the Big Boy.

Utilizing the span-bolstered B-B trucks from

4500-h.p. "Veranda" turbine trade-ins, UP acquired 23 U50's between October 1963 and August 1965. Experimenting with everything from 4000-h.p. German-built Krauss-Maffei hydraulics to Alco C643H hydraulics, Southern Pacific purchased three U50's in the spring of 1964. While the U50's were far more successful than the ill-fated and short-lived hydraulics, SP later reverted to more conventional power and the three U50's remained roster uniques.

BIG BOYS

UP 46, 95B and 75B exit Rawlins, Wyoming, June 1967.   *Emery J. Gulash*

Rattling the windows of the Ruby Hotel, the Wyoming Bar and the historic storefronts facing the UP main, U50 46 and a pair of DD35B's urge westbound tonnage out of Rawlins, Wyoming, in June 1967. The manifestation of David S. Neuhart's dream of three-unit, 15,000-h.p. lashups, the double-engined diesels work the Overland Route in the footsteps of legendary Union Pacific 4-8-8-4 Big Boys.

For power of presence, immensity and sheer spectacle, the Big Boy is unequaled in the diesel domain. However, the U50 and DD35 were born of the same "bigger is better" UP motive power doctrine that sired the Big Boy and the 8500-h.p. "Big Blow" turbines. Departing Rawlins, Extra 46 West digs in, with six V16's, 96 cylinders and 24 traction motors putting on a fuel-injected, turbocharged performance that carries on the spirit and tradition of the great 4-8-8-4's. Until the advent of the DDA40X, the U50's and DD35's will reign as the dieseldom's Big Boys, and those fortunate enough to encounter the eight-axle, twin-engined monsters will not forget.

Following the Los Angeles River, Southern Pacific U50 9552, DD35 9500 and a GP20 pass North Main Street in Los Angeles, California, with an SP drag on March 30, 1967.   *Alan Miller*

Kicking up the dust, westbound UP U50's 48 and 32 slam past Extra 34 East at Odessa, Nebraska, on May 13, 1969.   *James A. Brown*

U28B

Horsepower	2800
Engine	FDL16
Production Dates	1/66-12/66
Total Built	148

Original Owners:

In service for less than a week, SP U28B's 7025 and 7026 pause in the company of older U25B's at Taylor Yard in Los Angeles, California, on February 20, 1966. The first 47 U28B's were built with the U25B carbody. *Alan Miller*

Introduced in January 1966, at the height of the mid-sixties horsepower race, the U28B was little more than a stopgap measure in GE's push to produce a 3000-h.p., four-motor hood to compete with EMD's new GP40. From the very beginning, GE emphasized the high-horsepower potential of the FDL16 and the conservative 2500-h.p. rating of the U25 line. Several U25 owners—ACL, Frisco, NYC and Pennsy among them—had upgraded units to 2750 and 2800 h.p., but further increases were held back by the limitations of the D.C. transmission.

Even as the first U28B's were rolling off the assembly line, GE was working on the A.C./D.C.

drive that would render the model obsolete. By May 1966, NYC U28B's 2822 and 2823 were testing the A.C./D.C. drive and by June, U30B test beds 301-304 were on the road. Late U28B's were delivered with A.C./D.C. transmsions as standard equipment.

A transitional locomotive in every sense, the U28B evolved mechanically and cosmetically during its record short, one-year production run. Except for the increased horsepower, the first 47 U28B's were little different from their U25B predecessors and shared the same carbody. Engineering advances and equipment changes introduced with NYC 2822-2823 prompted the restyling of the familiar U-boat

carbody. The overall clean lines were retained, but the long, sloped nose of the U25B gave way to a pug nose similar to that of the U25C. Equipment-blower intakes were moved forward and positioned immediately behind the cab, while the air compressor was relocated to the rear, the radiator section was enlarged and the distinctive hump (accommodating oil-bath air filters) on the gangways near the rear of the unit vanished. Although equipment changes and minor modifications would alter specific details, the U28 restyling defined the GE look for the duration of U-boat production. Indeed, the same basic U-boat styling endured for the entire Dash 7 construction through 1988.

SURVIVORS

It's long past midnight as TTI U28B 247 (ex-P&LE 2809) slumbers quietly in the old L&N roundhouse in Paris, Kentucky. Her silver-and-blue dress is soiled with lube oil, coal dust and exhaust carbon, and open hood doors expose an exhaust-blackened, oil-streaked FDL engine and GT598 generator. Tools and engine parts clutter the gangways of the aging GE and, come morning, shopmen will resume their efforts to get the 247 back on the road.

Occupying the next stall, U28B 258, still wearing the Cascade green of former owner Burlington Northern, awaits attention, while outside a dozen more U28's doze in the darkness. A distant horn pierces the night air and just after 2 A.M., TTI Extra 243 South rumbles into the yard. Silhouetted in the yard lights, the darkened forms of six dirty U28B's lumber past, FDL's grumbling quietly to themselves, exhaust drifting lazily downward. In their wake, a seemingly endless string of empty black coal hoppers rattle, bang, clatter and squeal their way through the turnouts and into the yard.

In the drizzling darkness of a September 1988 night, Paris, Kentucky, plays host to the last operating U28B's anywhere, 20 TTI hand-me-downs of Burlington, Rock Island and P&LE heritage. While the 247 and her companions continue to slumber at the shop, the six units just in from Maysville rest briefly at the yard office, waiting only for the arrival of a new crew called for 4 A.M.

By dawn's first light, the aging U-boats will tie on to a 7900-ton train of eastern Kentucky coal billed to the "Rail-to-River" transloaders on the Ohio River at Maysville. Lugging coal trains over the roller-coaster profile of the 50-mile Paris-Maysville Branch is hard, dirty work. There's little glamor in the lives of the TTI U28B's, but they're survivors. Over two decades old and still performing as GE promised they would, TTI's venerable U28's are the oldest operating U-boats in the land, and there's honor enough in that.

TTI U28B 247 at Paris, Kentucky, September 18, 1988.   *Greg McDonnell*

Slicing through the evergreen forest, Milwaukee U28B's 5502, 5601 and U30B 5609 haul through Frederickson, Washington, with a Portland-bound freight on July 16, 1979. Built in January 1966, Milwaukee 393-398 (renumbered 5500-5505 in 1968) were the first U28B's built. *John Bjorklund*

Snow complicates a normally simple operation as crews work to turn Rock Island U28B 252 on the turntable at Albert Lea, Minnesota, on December 22, 1977. Outshopped from Erie in May 1966, RI 252 is one of the last U28B's built with the U25B carbody.
Steve Glischinski

Struggling over the road with local freight and at least 150 empty hoppers, Pittsburgh & Lake Erie U28B's 2812, 2809 and 2808 rumble southbound along the Ohio River through Stoops Ferry, Pennsylvania, on November 3, 1984. Although their P&LE days are almost over, the three U28's are destined to be among the fortunate few sold to Transkentucky Transportation for coal-train service out of Paris, Kentucky. *Thomas Seiler*

Still dressed in P&LE black, but in the employ of Transkentucky Transportation, U28B 2802 shares a quiet moment on the shop tracks at Paris, Kentucky, with TTI 242, ex-Rock Island 242 on September 19, 1978. *Greg McDonnell*

Leased to CP Rail, P&LE U28B 2811 looks on as CP FA2 4093 and an RS3 ride the turntable at Cote St. Luc, Quebec, in February 1974. While the FA and RS3 are long gone, P&LE 2811 survives 20 years later as TTI 252. *Stan J. Smaill*

Hauling sugar beets in ancient Burlington hoppers, ex-CB&Q U28B's 5470 and 5472 work the Buckwheat Local past
Church Lake, Colorado, on October 31, 1976.   *Philip Mason*

Basking in the sun at Denver, Colorado, in April 1970, Great Northern U28B 2527 shows off the pug nose and refined lines of the redesigned U-boat carbody. Introduced by NYC 2822-2823 in May 1966, the new carbody replaced the classic U25 styling and defined the GE look until the advent of the Dash 8 more than 20 years later. *R.R. Wallin Collection*

Westbound on the old Wabash, Norfolk & Western U28B 1909 and three U30B's approach the IC diamond at Starnes Tower in Springfield, Illinois, on October 2, 1970. Following a long-standing N&W tradition, all four GE's have high short hoods.
Dave Ingles

U28C

Horsepower 2800
Engine FDL16
Production Dates 12/65-12/66
Total Built 71

Original Owners:

Burlington 16
Pennsylvania...........................15
Northern Pacific......................12
Southern Pacific......................10
Union Pacific 10
Louisville & Nashville................8

Dressed in Burlington's splendid Chinese red, CB&Q U28C 567, U28B 143 and U25C 559 pause by the water tower in Laurel, Montana, in May 1969.   *Jim Reddington*

Like the U28B, the U28C was a transitional model produced for just one year. The first 28 U28C's (Burlington's 16 and NP's 12) were outshopped from Erie with the U25C carbody and double-equalized trimount trucks. In May 1966, GE launched the improved U28C, with the release of L&N 1525-1532. The L&N units and all subsequent U28C's featured the same engineering advances, equipment changes and restyling applied to the refined U28B, along with another significant change: the ungainly trimount trucks used by the U25C were replaced by new floating-bolster trucks.

In the case of the L&N order, the Adirondack casting of the new truck was used, but a General Steel Castings version of the same truck soon appeared under other units. Although the Adirondack and GSC trucks appeared slightly different, they were mechanically identical and GE employed them indiscriminately throughout its six-motor U-boat production. As railroads shopped their six-axle GE's, it was not uncommon to see units riding on one Adirondack and one GSC truck.

By the summer of 1966, the writing was on the wall for the U28C. The U30B test beds were performing well in road service on the

New York Central and GE was already accepting orders for the U30C. In fact, late U28's and early U30C's shared not only the shop floor at Erie, but a common carbody. Southern Pacific 7159, the last U28C, was placed in service on November 29, 1966, just three days before the first U30C, Atlantic Coast Line 3021. Their builder's plates read U28C, but ACL 3021-3024 had been upgraded to U30 specifications. GE records refer to the four ACL units as U30's and they are generally accepted as the first U30C's built.

Snails

SP Extra 7153 East approaching Tunnel 2, east of Caliente, California, June 1, 1974.
Brian Jennison

The parched brown hillsides of the Tehachapis echo the exhaust of laboring FDL's and 645's as SP Extra 7153 East grinds up the 2.1 percent grade east of Caliente, California. Leading the Eugene-West Colton EUWCY on June 1, 1974, the 7153 is one of just ten U28C's on the Southern Pacific roster.

Never very popular with operating crews, SP U28C's 7150-7159 were purchased specifically for ore service and spent their early years working 13,500-ton ore drags between the Eagle Mountain Mine Railroad connection at Ferrum, California, and the Los Angeles Basin. Struggling over Beaumont Hill with one of the heavyweight drags, a crewman called his U28C's "snails" and the moniker stuck. As export ore movements dwindled, the six-motor U28's were transferred to the Bakersfield-Tehachapi Freight Pool and their name and reputation followed.

Her ore-hauling days behind her, SP 7153 hasn't found life in the Tehachapis to be any easier. The lumber-laden EUWCY requires no less than 22,300 horsepower—the 7153, two SD40's and a U33C on the head-end, along with two mid-train SD45 helpers and a three-unit swing helper—to make the grueling climb up Tehachapi's north slope. Although the big GE's 16-position throttle is notched wide open, the upgrade progress of Extra 7153 East resembles no more than a snail's pace.

Eastbound in Big Sky country, BN U28C 5650, U33C 5740 and F45 6629 work through Bison, Montana, on August 6, 1979.
While the 5740 and 6629 were built for BN, 5650 is former Burlington 562.   *Richard Yaremko*

Trailing a cut of stock cars and nearly a mile of mixed freight, Northern Pacific U28C 2801, U25C 2507 and an SD45 roll B603 through Mission, Montana, in September 1967.   *Robert R. Malinoski*

Kicking up the snow, UP U28C 2804, U25B 635 and U50 53 storm through Menoken, Kansas, Nebraska-bound on February 15, 1969.
Joe McMillan

Bound for the Berkshires on the old B&A, PC U28C 6522, Pennsy-painted SD40 6081 and PC U33C 6550 roll a westbound freight past the station at Springfield, Massachusetts, on October 12, 1969.   *Philip Mason*

Hurrying the DeWitt Steam Crane to the derailment of TV5&7 west of Palmyra, Conrail U28C 6520 and U33C 6563 pass the VNF-7 at Clyde, New York, at 1735, July 10, 1977. Headed by U25B's 2533, 2525 and GP40 3083, the VNF-7 is one of many trains tied up by the wreckage blocking both tracks of the Water Level Route.   *Greg McDonnell*

U28CG

Horsepower	2800
Engine	FDL16
Production Dates	7/66-8/66
Total Built	10

Original Owner:

Santa Fe 10

Santa Fe U28CG's 355 and 357 exit Topeka, Kansas, with #24, the *Grand Canyon,* on September 2, 1968.   *Steve Patterson*

In the sixties, while piggyback boomed and railroads won an increasing share of the nation's auto traffic, passenger trains—victims of declining patronage and lost mail contracts—were discontinued by the dozen. Demoted E-units and PA's were pressed into freight service or retired and there was little call for new passenger locomotives.

To satisfy what demand there was, locomotive builders offered dual-service options on a number of second-generation models. Alco built high-nosed, steam generator-equipped C420's for Long Island and Monon and the C628 could accommodate an optional steam generator in its long hood. EMD catalogued

passenger-service options for most of its GP models, built boiler-equipped GP35's for NdeM and GP28's for CH-P, and even installed steam generators in the front end of eight UP GP30B's. When the 35-series was introduced in 1964, La Grange included the steam generator-equipped SDP35 among the models available, and sold a total of 35 units to Atlantic Coast Line, Seaboard, L&N and UP. Instead of boilers, L&N SDP35's 1700-1703 utilized the steam generator compartment to house remote control equipment for mid-train helpers.

Although there were no takers, General Electric offered steam generators and passenger-service options on the U25B and U25C. In

1966, though, Santa Fe commissioned boiler-equipped U28's and the U28CG was born. Outshopped from Erie in July and August, the ten AT&SF U28CG's were dressed in red-and-silver war-bonnet paint and carried passenger-series road numbers 350-359. But for their passenger colors and roof-top steam generator stacks, the 28CG's bore little outward evidence of their uniqueness. To the chagrin of the purists, Santa Fe put the big C-C's to work on the *Texas Chief,* where they replaced multiples of aging F-units on the Chicago-Houston streamliner.

WAR BONNETS AND CHAIN-GANG BLUES

Simmering in the hot Texas sun, a brace of battered Santa Fe F7's idle in the siding at Hoyte, as the *Texas Chief*, with U28CG's 355 and 356 bracketing U30CG 403, overtakes Extra 205C West on July 26, 1969. Humbly attired in freight-service blue, the veteran cabs stand clear as #15 slams past in a blur of war-bonnet paint and glistening stainless steel.

In the grand tradition, #15's GE's wear the war-bonnet colors of legendary Santa Fe passenger diesels from slant-nosed E1A's and handsome PA's to legions of stainless steel-flanked F-units. Unfortunately for the big GE's, the glory days are all but over. Cited for a number of derailments, the passenger U-boats have been restricted from high-speed operation and will soon be banished to freight duty.

Far removed from the glamor and stainless-steel splendor of the *Texas Chief* and the *Grand Canyon*, renumbered U28CG 7908 and U30CG 8002 have traded war bonnets for work clothes as they gang up with U33C 8519, U36C 8745, GP35 3313 and GP30 3250 to drag the 76-car 953-BG-1 east of Seligman, Arizona, on October 28, 1977. Born to wear silver and to wheel pristine streamliners over the Santa Fe Trail, the deposed passenger engines have been cloaked in workaday blue and will finish their days in chain-gang service, hustling piggybackers and hauling drags in "Uncle John's" freight pool.

Santa Fe #15, the *Texas Chief*, overtakes Extra 207C West at Hoyt, Texas, July 26, 1969. *Steve Patterson*

ATSF 953-BG-1 east of Seligman, Arizona, October 28, 1977. *Steve Patterson*

U30B

Horsepower	3000
Engine	FDL16
Production Dates	5/66-3/75
Total Built	295

Original Owners:

Norfolk & Western	110
New York Central	58
Chesapeake & Ohio	35
Frisco	31
Western Pacific	21
Seaboard Air Line	15
Illinois Central	6
Burlington	5
Louisville & Nashville	5
Milwaukee	5
Atlantic Coast Line	4
General Electric	(4)

Working eastbound NYC hotshot NY-4, GE U30B test bed/demonstrators 303, 301, 302 and 304 pause to change crews at Detroit, Michigan, in July 1966.   *Emery J. Gulash*

In the summer of 1966, the horsepower race intensified as a quartet of solid-black locomotives rolled out the back gate of GE's Erie works and ventured onto the New York Central main line. Wearing just a small GE crest on their cab sides and numbered 301-304, the mysterious black units represented General Electric's drive to regain lost ground. While U28's were being built at Erie, EMD and Alco had pulled ahead with their 3000-h.p. GP40/SD40 and C430/C630 lines, but the menacing-looking test beds were about to change all that.

Though the horsepower and model entries on their cast-aluminum builder's plates were intentionally left blank, their vital statistics were no secret. Throbbing beneath their shiny black hoods were turbocharged FDL16's rated at 3000-h.p. and mated to GE's new A.C/D.C.. drive. Ready to take on the GP40 and C430, the U30B had arrived.

Assigned to NYC Super Van trains and symbol freights, the 301-304 got a vigorous workout on the Water Level Route, while Erie geared up for the first production U30's. There

were still U28's on the erecting floor in Building 10—and more to be built—when work began on NYC 2830, the first U30B. In fact, the first NYC U30B's were outshopped before the last Burlington, Milwaukee and Rock Island U28B's were completed. Externally, the late U28's and early U30B's were identical. Under the hood, mechanical similarities were close enough that a number of late U28's were soon upgraded to 3000-h.p.

Although built as test beds, GE 301-304 were soon assigned demonstrator duties and the solid-black quartet broke some significant sales barriers as they toured the nation. Seaboard Air Line bought its first GE's and established a precedent when U30B's 800-814 were delivered riding on the Blomberg trucks of EMD F3 trade-ins. EMD diehards Illinois Central and Western Pacific broke with tradition to order U30B's. WP imitated Seaboard and specified Blombergs for its U-boats, as did SAL merger partner ACL for its four U30B's.

For several years, New York Central's 58 U30B's ranked as the largest fleet, but in 1970-71, Norfolk & Western placed two large

orders that increased its U30B stable from 35 to 110 units. In the N&W tradition, all 110 were built with high short hoods.

With a production run that spanned more than eight years, from November 1966 to March 1975, the U30B underwent a number of changes. The most visible were those made to the radiator section, which evolved from the original version shared with late U28's, through at least one intermediate style, to the final design with the entire radiator section built out a couple of inches wider than the rest of the hood.

Beneath the hood, U30B refinements were more dramatic. In 1972, GE introduced the XR Series (Extra Reliability) to promote more than 50 technological and quality enhancements of the U-boat line, from upgraded wiring and insulation to new CMR wheel-slip control, improved engine-protection devices and tougher connecting-rod bearings. While EMD launched the Dash 2 line to spotlight similar improvements to its own locomotives, GE made no model changes. However, the Erie builder did paint L&N U30C 1499 in a special XR Series scheme and added XR Series lettering to a few other locomotives. Among them was Frisco U30B 846, outshopped in May 1973 wearing a large XR logo on its mandarin-red flanks. Notable for its XR markings, the 846 was even more significant as GE's 2500th domestic U-series locomotive.

As U30B production wound down in late 1974, C&O 8225-8234 were delivered with a new option, GE's floating-bolster FB2 truck. While the FB2 would become standard on later models, it was offered as an option for several years. U30B production ended in March 1975 with the delivery of SL-SF 858-862. The Frisco units rode on standard AAR-B trucks, leaving C&O's ten units as the only U30B's with FB2 trucks. Frisco also bought the first examples of the U30B's successor, receiving B30-7's 863-870 in December 1977. Included among the eight U25B's traded in on the Dash 7 order was SL-SF 804 (ex-GE demo 753), the first production U25B.

BORN TO WANDER

On UP iron, Western Pacific U30B 770 (ex-General Electric 303) and companions kick up the snow in Utah's Echo Canyon in December 1971. *Keith E. Ardinger*

Shrugging off the snow of a Wasatch winter storm, Western Pacific U30B 770 and three WP sisters kick up a blizzard of their own as they thunder through Echo Canyon on UP's Overland Route in December 1971. The 770 has been in the employ of Western Pacific for just five months, and while her Perlman-green paint is still fresh, the new-looking U30 is a heavily modified, high-mileage veteran of rigorous GE road trials and punishing nationwide demonstration tours.

Built in June 1966 as General Electric 303, the 770 was once part of the four-unit U30B test bed/demonstrator set that toured the nation between 1966 and 1970. Progressively upgraded to U33 and U36B specifications, the quartet logged several hundred thousand miles racing NYC Super Vans over the Water Level Route and lugging D&H tonnage over Richmondville Hill; wheeling SCL hotshots to Florida, hauling North Western symbol freights across the Iowa prairie and, yes, working WP tonnage over Altamont and through the Feather River Canyon.

Retrofitted to her original U30B configuration, reconditioned and retrucked with EMD Blombergs, the 303 and sister 304 finally found a home on Western Pacific in the summer of 1971. Although her demonstrator days are over, the 770 still has wanderlust in her blood. Inside Gateway BN runthroughs and WMX and PBF-UP pools with Union Pacific afford the 770 plenty of opportunities to range beyond the scenic confines of the Feather River Route. Born to wander, the nomadic U-boat just can't stay home.

Only a few weeks old, New York Central U30B 2850 rests with NYC U25B 2551 at Central Terminal in Buffalo, New York, in September 1967. *Eric Clegg*

The crew aboard a Buffalo-bound drag enjoys the breeze as Conrail U28B 2847 and U25B 2524 hammer westward through the Canisteo Valley, passing a set of ancient Erie semaphores near West Cameron, New York, in May 1977. *Stan J. Smaill*

Leaning into Calendar Curve on Burlington's racetrack, near Naperville, Illinois, CB&Q U30B 150 leads NYC U30B's 2837, 2887, a PC GP35 and brand-new Great Northern U33C 2537 on a PC/CB&Q runthrough in July 1968. Illustrating early stages of the evolution of the U30B, the two NYC units have the early carbody, while CB&Q 150 has the intermediate styling, with the small fairing where the engine and radiator sections meet.   *Paul Meyer*

Riding the Blomberg trucks of EMD F3 trade-ins, Seaboard U30B's 809, 805 and 802 pass an idling C420 as they pull into Baldwin, Florida, on May 28, 1967.
Keith E. Ardinger; Alan Miller Collection

Following Seaboard's lead, future merger partner Atlantic Coast Line had its four U30B's built on trade-in Blomberg trucks as well. Leading E8 555, an E6B and an F-unit, ACL U30B 978, soon to be SCL 1703, stands at Waycross, Georgia, on April 15, 1967.   *Keith E. Ardinger*

Trailing a pair of leased Rio Grande F7B's, Illinois Central U30B 5002 leads a train of coal empties through Monee, Illinois, in June 1969. With the exception of the 5003, wrecked in 1979, the IC U30B's were sold to the Iowa Railroad in May 1982.
Paul Meyer

Probing the "dog house" electrical compartment, a diesel maintainer services Iowa Railroad U30B 22, ex-IC 5002, at Council Bluffs, Iowa, in August 1982. The Iowa Railroad's operation of the Bureau-Council Bluffs portion of the ex-Rock Island mainline was short-lived. Iowa Interstate took over the entire RI main east of Council Bluffs in 1984 and U30B's were scrapped.
Paul Meyer

In the eerie glow of a full moon, Western Pacific U30B's 3057 and 3058 idle in the company of EMD's 3017, 3516, 3015 and 3508 at West Oakland, California, on June 26, 1972.   *J.D. Schmid*

Highballing through the desert on paired SP/WP track, Western Pacific U30B 3057, GP35 3015, GP40 3509 and U30B 3068 race a 65-car freight west of Elko, Nevada, at 5:28 P.M., May 10, 1974. Between Alazon and Weso, Nevada, the parallel SP and WP mains have been operated jointly as a double-track railroad since World War I. With home-road rails just yards away, the WP extra is westbound on SP iron.
J.D. Schmid

Snaking through the Feather River Canyon, WP U30B 3055 and BN pool power, Burlington-painted GP35 2534, ex-SP&S C425 4255 and a pair of SD45's, work westbound past the slide-detector fences at Pulga, California, on June 22, 1974.
Steve Patterson

Thundering through Moss Run, Virginia, C&O U30B 8222 leads a pair of B30-7's spliced by a GP40 on a westbound symbol freight in June 1984.   *David Jakubiec*

Dressed in pre-merger colors, CSX U30B 5347, U18B 1917, U30C 7262 and B30-7 5502 descend Crooked Hill, south of Livingston, Kentucky, with train R544 on March 19, 1989. *Ron Flanary*

Part of the first order of GE locomotives built with FB2 trucks, CSX U30B 5362, ex-C&O 8234, emerges from the Falls Cut Tunnel west of Fairhope, Pennsylvania, with GP40 6639 and SD40-2 8062 on a 30-car ballast train at 12:17 P.M., October 14, 1987.   *J.D. Schmid*

Under the watchful eye of UP SD40-2 3413, BN U30B's 5794 and 5799, formerly SL-SF 857 and 862, switch at Cheyenne, Wyoming, at daybreak on October 24, 1988. The last U30B built, the former Frisco 862 was sold to Kyle in May 1991, along with BN 5794-5796.   *George McDonnell*

Heading up a consist that only Burlington Northern could assemble, BN U30B 5787 leads cabless SD40 7600 and B30-7A B-unit 4024 on an eastbound at St. Croix Tower in Hastings, Minnesota, on September 15, 1984. Built as Frisco 849, the 5787 went to scrap in 1992, while the 7600, a wreck rebuild of BN SD40 6302, became SOO 6450 in 1987.   *Steve Glischinski*

Leaving Memphis, Frisco U30B 860, B30-7's 870, 866 and GP38-2 438 cross the Mississipi River into West Memphis, Arkansas, with the QLA on June 2, 1980.   *David P. Oroszi*

U30C

Horsepower	3000
Engine	FDL16
Production Dates	11/66-9/76
Total Built	600

Original Owners:

Burlington Northern	181
Union Pacific	150
Louisville & Nashville	78
Southern Pacific	37
Missouri Pacific	35
Rock Island	18
Chesapeake & Ohio	13
Delaware & Hudson	12
Detroit Edison	11
SOO Line	10
Ferrocarril del Pacifico	8
Milwaukee	8
Chicago & North Western	7
Kaiser Steel	5
Pennsylvania	5
Reading	5
Southern	5
Atlantic Coast Line	4
Colorado & Southern	4
Norfolk & Western	3
Dept. of Transportation	1

One of the first U30C's built, SCL 2123, ex-ACL 3023, stands at Memphis, Tennessee, with U36C 2125, ex-Clinchfield 3600—the first U36C built—and GP38-2 538 on December 15, 1977.   *David M. Johnston; Keith E. Ardinger Collection*

Taken to its lowest common denominator, the success of the U30C, GE's best selling U-boat, can be explained in a single word: coal. In the employ of early owners, the six-motor, 3000-h.p. freighters drew premier assignments, but found their true niche in heavy drag service. MoPac put its U30C's on St. Louis-Kansas City hotshots, but they were preferred power on Granite City ore trains and Labadie coal trains. D&H pitted lightning-striped U30's against legendary Penn Division grades. Southern Pacific assigned its 37 U30C's to the Bakersfield-Tehachapi Pool—one of the toughest jobs on the railroad—while Kaiser Steel put its SP copies to work hauling 10,000-ton ore trains on the Eagle Mountain Mine Railroad. Though early sales were moderate at best, the U30C had a good reputation as a heavy hauler, so sales boomed when coal traffic began to escalate in the early seventies.

Reflecting the evolutionary development of the U-boat line, early U30C's, like their '30B counterparts, were indistinguishable from late-production U28's. Technological advances and related carbody changes made to the U30C roughly paralleled those of the U30B, with intermediate styling of the six-motor model including a small radiator-height fairing where the engine hood met the built-out radiator section.

GE launched the XR Series in September 1972 and displayed brand new L&N U30C 1499, decked out in a special black-white-and-gold paint scheme for the occasion, at the Railway Supply Association show in Chicago. While the highly touted 50-plus Extra Reliable Series enhancements surely helped boost orders, the post-1970 coal boom figured heavily in the success of the U30C. Indeed, BN, L&N and UP, three roads with a major stake in coal traffic, accounted for 409 of the 600 U30C's built. Although the competing SD40/SD40-2 line outsold the GE offering by better than four to one, the U30C's strong showing put the first serious chinks in EMD's armor.

KING OF THE HILL

D&H 702 and 602, northbound at Fuller Road, south of Sanitaria Springs, New York, 0950, September 10, 1975.
Greg McDonnell

The sun has been up for hours but, long past the chilly dawn of a September 1975 day, the lower end of Delaware & Hudson's Belden Hill is shrouded in early morning mist. At Sanitaria Springs, the sun has broken through and the fog ends abruptly in a vertical gray wall. Wisps of mist cut through the tree tops, birds sing softly, and from somewhere deep in the fog-capped valley, the distant thunder of a northbound freight stirs the peaceful morning air.

The staccato bark of laboring four-stroke diesels grows steadily louder as the minutes pass. The sound and suspense intensify with every beat, until a lightning-striped U30C and C628 explode into view. Clawing upgrade, D&H 702 and 602 stomp past, their blue-and-gray flanks layered with sand, lube oil and carbon that bear testament to uncounted battles with storied Bridge Line grades: Belden, Ararat and Richmondville.

Shouting to the heavens, the GE-Alco duo put on a breathtaking, adrenalin-pumping performance, doing what they do best, lugging all the tonnage that the Bevier Street yardmaster in Binghamton dared tie to their drawbars. A mile back, behind 40-foot boxcars of flour, groaning covered hoppers, rattling scrap gons and bi-levels loaded with new Ford trucks, the Belden Hill pushers—C628 617, U30C 710 and U23B's 2308 and 2304—lean hard on a wide-vision caboose.

The big six-motor brutes will rule the hill for just three more years before being dealt to power-short Nacionales de Mexico. Proceeds of the sale will have little impact on the empty coffers of the cash-starved D&H, but their absence will be felt on Belden Hill for years. Belden's loss will be Aguascalientes' gain.

Stretched out on Cuesta Hill, "the distilled essence of the SP," in the words of Southern Pacific dispatcher J.D. Schmid, U30C's 7931, 7926 and 7914 work the Oakland-bound LAOAF through the spectacular mountains just north of San Luis Obispo, California, on April 6, 1980. *Brian Jennison*

Brian Jennison

Trudging through the desert, Kaiser Steel U30C's 1034, 1030 and 1033 drag an ore train out of Eagle Mountain, California, bound for the SP connection at Ferrum on February 4, 1982. From Ferrum, SP will move the ore to the Kaiser Steel mill at Fontana, California. Diverted from SP's initial 30-unit order, Kaiser U30C's 1030-1034 were built in March 1968 to replace tired Baldwin DRS6-6-1500's and AS616's on ore trains making the grueling 52-mile haul from the Eagle Mountain Mine to Ferrum. As Kaiser cut steel production at Fontana, the market for Eagle Mountain ore dried up. The Eagle Mountain Mine Railroad was shut down in March 1986 and the five U30C's were stored at Fontana, where they remained as of January 1994.   *David R. Busse*

Bound for the CP Rail connection at Portal, SOO U30C 800 and SD40 776 rip through Bergen, North Dakota, on September 4, 1977. SOO Line's only GE's since 44-tonner 330, U30C's 800-809 were minority power on an EMD-dominated road and were traded in to La Grange on SD40-2's in 1983-84. *Richard Yaremko*

Outshopped from Erie between May and July 1968, C&O 3304-3312 were the last U30C's constructed with the intermediate-style carbody. Less than a month old, C&O 3306 leads SD35 7431 and a pair of B&O GP38's through Romulus, Michigan, in June 1968. *Emery J. Gulash*

Bracketing GP39-2 3411, Reading U30C's 6300 and 6302 work their train at Rupert, Pennsylvania, in April 1975. On April 1, 1976, the Reading and the "Bee Line Service" U30C's will be absorbed by Conrail, but the nearly new 3411 will become Delaware & Hudson 7411. *Jeremy F. Plant*

Approaching Summit, on Monongahela's Manor Branch west of Waynesburg, Pennsylvania, Detroit Edison U30C's 018, 019 and Conrail SD40-2's 6500 and 6477 labor upgrade with a 140-car coal train, passing milepost 11.6 at 1140, November 3, 1992. Just loaded at Bailey Mine, the Monroe, Michigan-bound train is being assisted by remote helpers, DE U30C's 021, 022 and SD40 013, cut into the train some 85 cars deep.   *Greg McDonnell*

Running long hood forward in the Southern tradition, high-nosed SOU U30C 3801, U33C 3810, a robot car and two SD's roll coal empties through Birmingham, Alabama, on May 9, 1977. While Southern's U30C's were retired by 1982, the 3801 survived as a training locomotive at the McDonough, Georgia, training center until 1992. Traded in to GE in 1987, Southern 3810 found a post-retirement career assigned to GE's Erie test track as GE 405.   *Philip Mason*

Exercising trackage rights on Santa Fe east of Kansas City, N&W U30C 8000 and C39-8 8612 pass the dilapidated depot at Sugar Creek, Missouri, on May 6, 1988, unnoticed by the dog investigating the station platform.   *Bradley McClelland*

Ready to leave Corbin, Kentucky, with southbound coal trains, L&N U30C's 1537 and 1559 wait side by side while C430 2260 and slug 2058 shove past with a cut of loaded hoppers on April 3, 1980.   *Greg McDonnell*

Dressed in Seaboard System paint, CSX U30C 7274 (ex-L&N 1580) and U36C 7302 (originally Clinchfield 3602) stride through Barberton, Ohio, with a westbound Sea-Land doublestack container train on August 23, 1987.   *Thomas Seiler*

Making their last stand in coal service out of Corbin, Kentucky, CSX U30C's 7212, 7254, 7221 and 7271 lead a southbound unit train through Faber, Kentucky, on April 9, 1990. *William D. Miller*

High and dry in the siding at Kilsyth, Tennessee, a southbound CSX coal train, led by aging U30C 7224, waits on a meet with R210, while the B&B Market does a land office business in coffee and Moon Pie sales on April 19, 1991. *Greg McDonnell*

A United Air Lines DC 8 cruises down the runway at Denver's Stapleton Airport, while Rock Island U30C 4587 and GP38-2's 4328 and 4350 roll westbound on UP iron through Duban, Colorado, on March 13, 1980.   *Steve Patterson*

With MoPac's famed Screaming Eagle emblazoned on their hoods, U30C's 3313, 3329 and 3333, along with 3309 in simplified blue, lift the Labadie coal train out of St. Louis, Missouri, on October 5, 1974.   *David R. Busse*

Serving in its intended role, Milwaukee Road U30C 5651 leads BN U30C 5313, Milwaukee SD40-2 197 and BN U28C 5667 on a Wisconsin Electric coal train at Olivia, Minnesota, on June 26, 1977. Milwaukee U30C's 5651-5658 were built to BN specifications for use on pooled BN/MILW Powder River Basin coal trains. In 1990, the 5651 was rebuilt at GE-Montreal, becoming Super 7-C30 GECX 3006.   *Steve Glischinski*

Carrying the road number of the trailing unit, FCP U36C 414, in its train indicator boards, FCP U30C 406 heads an Extra South at Benjamin Hill, Sonora, Mexico, on February 23, 1985. The train indicator boards and crimson-and-gray paint reflect the Ferrocarril del Pacifico's heritage as a one-time Southern Pacific holding, the Sud Pacifico de Mexico.   *Matthew J. Herson, Jr.*

Still dressed in Chicago & North Western colors, NdeM U30C 933, ex-C&NW 933, rests at Monterrey, Nuevo Leon, Mexico, on March 8, 1981. Visible in the background is another American expatriate, an ex-N&W U30B, along with Alco re-engined NdeM GE 70-tonner 5100.
Matthew J. Herson, Jr.

Experiencing her last Minnesota winter, C&NW U30C 936, and SD45 918 trudge past St. Anthony Tower in St. Paul, Minnesota, on January 8, 1978. In September, the 936 and sisters 930-933 and 935 will emigrate to sunny Mexico, becoming NdeM 930-933, 935 and 936.   *Steve Glischinski*

Leaning into the curve at Otto, Wyoming, Union Pacific U30C 2855 and a pair of DDA40X Centennials climb Sherman Hill on April 5, 1975. *Steve Patterson*

Under threatening skies, battle-scarred UP U30C 2919 and a trio of C30-7's snake through the S-curves with a coal train at Dale Jct., Wyoming, on June 25, 1984. *Jerry Palmer*

In the snow-capped majesty of the Wasatch Mountains, UP U30C 2889 and two SD40-2's thunder through Peterson, Utah, in February 1986. *Doug Harrop*

The gruff bark of five FDL16's is swallowed by the vast open plains as BN U30C's 5940, 5303, two Santa Fe C30-7's and a BN U33C accelerate a southbound coal train near Aguilar, Colorado, on October 3, 1983. *Philip Mason*

The last new units delivered in Burlington's attractive Chinese red, Colorado & Southern U30C's 891, 893 and a quartet of SD's (three of them in the classic black-and-gray scheme) work southbound #76 near Fountain, Colorado, on February 3, 1969. *Steve Patterson*

With their train wrapped around Crawford Curve, BN U30C 5908, Oakway SD60's 9068, 9004, 9033 and BN SD40-2 7236 struggle up Crawford Hill near Belmont, Nebraska, with a 14,000-ton coal train on October 20, 1988. The aging U30C was added to the head end of Extra OWY 9068 East after having a seized wheel set changed out on the mainline outside Crawford.
William D. Miller

U30CG

Horsepower	3000
Engine	FDL16
Production Dates	11/67-12/67
Total Built	6

Original Owner:

Santa Fe 6

Making like the PA's they replaced, Santa Fe U30CG's 401 and 404 exit Albuquerque, New Mexico, with #23, the *Grand Canyon,* in September 1968.   *Steve Patterson*

Before the Santa Fe U28CG's had even arrived on the property, purists decried the audacious decision to assign lowly hood units to a train as prestigious as the *Texas Chief.* Steam generators, high-speed gearing and warbonnet paint, they said, did not put the big C-C's in league with the legendary PA's and stainless steel-flanked F's they were built to replace.

As if to make amends, Santa Fe petitioned the builders for a semi-streamlined second-generation passenger diesel in 1967. EMD came up with the FP45, while GE produced the U30CG. Built on a standard U30C platform, with a 3000-h.p. FDL16, A.C./D.C. drive and stock machinery, the U30CG was essentially a U30C wrapped in a cowl carbody, geared for 95 m.p.h and equipped with a steam generator. Santa Fe

took delivery of U30CG's 400-405 in December 1967 and January 1968.

With its fluted, full-cowl carbody and pug nose, the esthetics of the semi-streamlined, 67-foot 3-inch, 400,000-pound U30CG did little to appease the purists. Santa Fe was equally unimpressed and the original half-dozen U30CG's were the only ones built.

ALL RED AT SOMERVILLE

Santa Fe Extra 8002 West, Somerville, Texas, May 12, 1973. *Steve Patterson*

The order boards are horizontal, the lineside signals are red and train orders are strung out for an eastbound as Extra 8002 West holds the siding at Somerville, Texas, in the early hours of May 12, 1973. Santa Fe's Gulf lines are deluged with traffic and Russian grain shipments have strained operations to the breaking point. Dispatchers and train crews working this ABS-signaled, train order-governed territory are being pushed to the limit. Somerville, where Galveston Subdivision trains set out cars for the Port of Beaumont, has been swamped with so much traffic that a yardmaster has been assigned to manage the nine-track yard at the small Texas junction.

On the train sheets and manifests, Extra 8002 West is just another train of Russian grain, but its extraordinary power is enough to persuade the night yardmaster at Somerville to take a well-deserved break on a pleasant spring night. In lieu of a tripod, Steve Patterson props his camera on a barrel to record a single time exposure of the westbound grain train, with a trio of U30CG's and a standard six-motor sister.

Patterson's brief recess had little impact on the fluidity of the small yard, but it served posterity well. Somerville remains a busy junction, but the depot, order boards and train order forks, the yardmaster's job and the big GE's are gone.

U33B

Horsepower	3300
Engine	FDL16
Production Dates	9/67-8/70
Total Built	137

Original Owners:

Rumbling over the former CGW Robert Street Bridge in St. Paul, Minnesota, RI U33B 290, ex-U25B slug 284 and road-weary U33B 299 cross the Mississippi River with a southbound transfer on April 22, 1978.   *Steve Glischinski*

GE took the lead in the four-motor horsepower race with the introduction of the U33B in the summer of 1967. Summoned home to Erie for modifications, U30B test beds 301-304 re-emerged in July wearing the same black paint, but with bright yellow noses and oversized radiators that jutted from the hood like stubby wings. Internally, they were little changed from their U30 configuration, but the larger radiators, made necessary by increased horsepower, heralded the arrival of the 3300-h.p. U33B.

Unlike previous new models, the U33 supplemented, rather than superseded, the U30 as GE widened its U-boat offerings and closed in on the competition. The first production U33B's were New York Central 2858 and 2859, outshopped from Erie in September 1967. Built and numbered among NYC U30B's 2830-2889, NYC 2858 and 2859 carried builder's plates reading U30B, but their distinctive oversized radiators readily identified them as high-horsepower U33B's.

In common with early U30's, the first U33's had a fairing that smoothed the transition from the engine hood to the wide radiators; GE 301-304, NYC 2858-2859 and Seaboard Coast Line 1719-1734 were the only U33B's built with

this feature. U33B production totaled only 137 units, with the lion's share acquired by Penn Central. Between September 1968 and June 1970, 81 U33B's joined ex-NYC 2858-2859 on the PC roster. Rock Island and Seaboard Coast Line were the only other railroads to purchase U33B's. Seaboard Coast Line's 29 units received rebuilt Blomberg trucks from EMD trade-ins, while all other U33B's rode on standard AAR-B trucks.

SHADES OF THE BULLET

Silver Springs, New York, 1550, February 25, 1982: Conrail TV-52, with U33B 2920, SD40-2 6418 and SD40 6311, overtakes D&H BM-2, led by a rare three-builder lashup consisting of M-K rebuilt RS3 502, U23B 2305 and ex-Reading GP39-2 7405. *Greg McDonnell*

There's a bone-chilling wind howling out of the northwest as D&H train BM-2 freezes to the rails in the siding at Silver Springs, New York. Exercising trackage rights over Conrail's ex-Erie Southern Tier line, the eastbound D&H symbol freight, headed by M-K rebuilt RS3 502, U23B 2305 and ex-Reading GP39-2 7405, is outranked by just about every CR train on the road. The circumstances that have forced BM-2 into the siding on this bitterly cold February 1982 afternoon are not yet evident, but the fact that the D&H train has been cooling its wheels at "GE" for nearly an hour underscores its less-than-preferred status with the Hornell dispatcher.

At 1550, the cause of BM-2's delay becomes apparent as the drone of distant diesels heralds the approach of a Conrail eastbound. Moments later, TV-52, led by U33B 2920 and a pair of SD's, swings through the curve approaching Silver Springs and slams past the lowly D&H drag with all the pomp of the old Erie *Bullet*, a hot Buffalo-New York merchandiser of the late thirties. Still able to command premier TV train assignments at age 13, the 2920 is king of the road.

A Penn Central veteran, the aging U33B has survived the blackest days of the PC bankruptcy. The days of lurching, rocking and rolling over deteriorating main lines and cautiously picking her way through decrepit trackage and decaying terminals are history. For the 2920, riding high on the wave of Conrail's recovery, these are the glory days.

Swirling steam envelops the consist of Amtrak's *Champion*, as SCL U33B 1742 and two GE companions overtake the New York-Florida streamliner with a southbound freight at Jacksonville, Florida, on January 23, 1974.   *Scott Hartley*

Trailing two carloads of U.S. Army tanks and short train of dimensional loads, Penn Central U33B 2907 ducks under the Seneca Street bridge in Buffalo, New York, with an eastbound extra at 1217, June 8, 1977.   *Greg McDonnell*

Standing among the pumpkins at Sidney, New York, B&M U33B 190 (ex-PC/CR 2916), MEC U25B 225 and D&H GP38-2 7319 wait in the siding with a D&H northbound on October 3, 1983.   *Philip Mason*

Very few U-boats found homes in the used locomotive market, but Pennsylvania anthracite haulers Reading & Northern and Blue Mountain & Reading have been among the notable exceptions. Freshly painted in Reading-inspired colors, RBM&N U33B's 3301 and 3304 pose with the Reading Technical & Historical Society's restored GP30 5513 at West Cressona, Pennsylvania, on February 9, 1991.   *Scott Hartley/Denis Connell*

U33C

Horsepower	3300
Engine	FDL16
Production Dates	1/68-1/75
Total Built	375

Original Owners:

Southern Pacific	212
Burlington Northern	39
Santa Fe	25
Penn Central	24
Great Northern	15
Delaware & Hudson	12
Erie Lackawanna	12
Illinois Central	10
Northern Pacific	10
Southern	10
Milwaukee	4
S.J. Groves & Sons	2

Wearing Great Northern's short-lived Big Sky blue, GN U33C 2543, F45 440 and SD45 422 head up #82 at Minneapolis, Minnesota, on January 31, 1970.   *Ed Kanak; Alan Miller Collection*

Although the distinctive wingspan radiators immediately distinguished the U33C from the U30C, the internal differences were far more subtle. In fact, the first U33C's, Milwaukee Road 8000-8004, were ordered as U30C's and upgraded to U33's while under construction. Citing the slight differences between the two models, many railroads willingly sacrificed 300 horsepower in favor of the lower price and cheaper operating costs of the U30C. As a result, sales of the 3300-h.p. C-C , although significant, were less impressive than those of its best-selling 3000-h.p. counterpart.

The U33C did break new ground for GE, selling to such unlikely customers as EMD/four-motor advocate Illinois Central and highway construction contractor S.J. Groves. For the most part, U33C sales were small one-time orders for a dozen units or less, with one exception: Southern Pacific. SP went for the U33C in a big way, purchasing 212 of the 375 units built. By comparison, the next largest fleet belonged to BN, whose 64 U33C's included 25 units inherited from Great Northern and Northern Pacific.

Produced between January 1968 and January 1975, the U33C underwent no significant carbody changes, with the exception of elimination of the radiator fairing on units built after July 1968.

CHANGING OF THE GUARD

Eastbound on the Cal-P SP U33C 8638 and F7A 6349 roll 117 cars over the Suisun Bay Bridge at Benicia, California, at 3:10 P.M., April 19, 1972.   *J.D. Schmid*

High above the murky waters of Suisun Bay, SP U33C 8638 and Black Widow F7A 6349 rumble across the impressive Suisun Bay Bridge between Martinez and Benicia, California, on April 19, 1972. Still fresh-looking in scarlet and gray, the 8638 is just a month away from her third birthday, while the 6349, the second-last surviving Southern Pacific F7 in Black Widow paint, has celebrated her last.

Once numbering 770 units, the ranks of SP's freight-service F's have been decimated by retirements and trade-ins on second generation diesels. More than a few have fallen victim to SP's growing fleet of GE U-boats. Indeed, a number of the 6349's sisters were traded to General Electric on the 15-unit U33C order that included the 8638.

The pairing of an SP U33C and F7A is a rare combination that will soon be impossible, for even as the 8638 and 6349 work eastward on the Cal-P, workers at Erie and La Grange are assembling U33C's and SD45T-2's that will seal the fate of the 6349 and put an end to the F-unit era in the Golden Empire.

Detouring over Burlington Northern trackage after a trestle fire closed their own line, Milwaukee Road U33C 5701 and U25B 5055 depart Tacoma, Washington, on June 12, 1977. Ordered as U30C's, Milwaukee Road 8000-8004 (later renumbered 5700-5704) were upgraded to 3300 h.p. during construction at Erie, becoming the first U33C's in the process. Illustrating the early carbody design with the sheet-metal fairing to smooth transition from the engine hood to the oversize radiators, Milwaukee 5701 (ex-MILW 8001) is the second U33C built.   *Keith E. Ardinger*

Snaking through a spectacular S-curve, Burlington Northern U33C 5734, SD45 6435, U33C 5749 and SD45 6548 drop downgrade with a southbound extra near Trinidad, Colorado, on April 1, 1976.   *Steve Patterson*

Westbound near Collier's, New York, D&H U33C's 758, 753 (ex-EL 3303) and a C628 meet D&H PA 18, leading an eastbound excursion dubbed "Susquehanna Valley Special" on September 29, 1973. *Brian Jennison*

In the warm glow of a late spring afternoon, Erie Lackawanna U33C 3304 and E8A 829 bring SC-99 into Hornell, New York, at 1815, May 23, 1974.   *Greg McDonnell*

Glistening in factory-fresh paint, Illinois Central U33C's 5052 and 5055 march a southbound symbol freight out of Homewood, Illinois, on June 17, 1968. Just over a year later, in September 1969, IC 5055 was destroyed in a rear-end collision with a coal train at Riverdale, Illinois.   *Dave Ingles*

Sunlight streams into the storied ex-GM&O Iselin Shop in Jackson, Tennessee, as IC U33C 5054 undergoes repairs on May 30, 1977.   *Dave Ingles*

Deep in the Mojave Desert, westbound Santa Fe U33C's 8513, 8511, C30-7 8019 and U36C 8716 labor up the famed Ash Hill grade on the Needles District at Klondike, California, on April 2, 1978.   *Dave Stanley*

The Tehachapis brood in the distance and wildflowers paint the desert floor a brilliant yellow as Southern Pacific U33C's 8630, 8610 and SD45 8994 depart Mojave, California, with a westbound drag at 1405, March 23, 1978.
Greg McDonnell

One of many Southern Pacific U33C's leased to NdeM, SP 8696 pilots NdeM RSD12 7432 and a mixed consist of boxcars, head-end equipment and heavyweight passenger cars on Nuevo Laredo-Mexico City #4 near Rinconada, Nuevo Leon, Mexico, in March 1980. *Matthew J. Herson, Jr*

Part of Northern Pacific's last GE order before the BN merger, NP U33C 3304 pauses at Pasco, Washington, with SD45 3604 and a U28C on September 8, 1969.   *Alan Miller*

Hired to help move a mountain, S.J. Groves and Sons U33C's 507 and 508 were purchased by the contractor building Interstate 280 between Roseland and West Orange, New Jersey. Along with ex-Minnesota Transfer RS3 200, (SJG 509), the big U-boats were put to work hauling rock on a construction railroad built down the middle of the I-280 right of way. Trailing a string of air-dumps, S.J. Groves 508 cruises I-280 through Roseland, New Jersey, on June 29, 1970. Upon completion of the project, SJG 507 and 508 became BN 5764 and 5765. *James C. Herold; Keith E. Ardinger Collection*

The sole survivor among 39 U33C's built for BN in 1971, Squaw Creek Coal 5752 (ex-BN 5752) teams up with ex-Santa Fe RSD15 9842 on a coal train leaving Booneville, Indiana, for the Ohio River transloaders at Yankeetown on November 6, 1987. Along with ex-Southern U33C 3809, the 5752 was purchased to replace the former Santa Fe "Alligators", which were subsequently sold to Indiana Hi-Rail. *Tom Lambrecht*

The four-cycle bark of FDL16's and Alco 251's drowns out the whine of a single EMD 645 as D&H U33C's 756, 762, a GP38-2, two C420's and a pair of rebuilt RS3's lift westbound tonnage out of Afton, New York, in August 1982.   *Stan J. Smaill*

Blasting out of Buffalo, New York, PC U33C 6542, freshly shopped Conrail U33C 6543 (ex-PC 6543) and PC U28C 6522 (ex-PRR 6522) approach Tower 47 with a westbound TV train at 1247, December 8, 1976. *Greg McDonnell*

Working upgrade along the Deerfield River, D&H U33C's 650, 662 and Southern SD45 3123 grind through Rices, Massachusetts, with westbound B&M train FIME on February 1, 1986. Dressed in Guilford paint, D&H 650 was built as Penn Central 6540 and acquired via Naporano Iron & Metal after its retirement in August 1985 as Conrail 6845. Lightning-striped 662 is a D&H original, built as the 762 in December 1970. *Scott Hartley*

Displaying green signals for the photographer, Southern Pacific U33C idles the night away on the service track at West Oakland, California, on January 25, 1982. *J.D. Schmid*

Fighting upgrade out of San Luis Obispo, SP U33C 8773, SD35 4701, U25B 6723 and GP20 4107 claw their way around the horseshoe curve west of Goldtree, California, at 4:20 P.M., June 3, 1977. Assisting the 88-car westbound on Margarita Hill, GP35's 6546, 6623 and 6658 are cut into the train 55 cars back.   *J.D. Schmid*

U23B

Horsepower	2250
Engine	FDL12
Production Dates	8/68-6/77
Total Built	481

Original Owners:

Resplendent in classic black-and-gold, brand-new Monon U23B 603 poses on the N&W interchange at Erie, Pennsylvania, on April 4, 1970.   *Bill Volkmer; Keith E. Ardinger Collection*

In the midst of the "more-is-better" high-horsepower buying sprees of the late sixties, a new motive power trend emerged as railroads began to express renewed interest in intermediate-size locomotives. To meet this demand, GE expanded its catalog to include the U23 series.

Packing a V12 FDL prime mover rated at 2250-h.p., the U23B appeared, at first glance, to be identical to the U30B. However, the U23B was 24" shorter and the 12-cylinder engine required only six extra-height hood doors to access power assemblies, compared to eight on the 16-cylinder U30B. Beyond this subtle difference, the U23B was externally identical to its 3000-h.p. contemporary.

Delivered in August and September 1968, Delaware & Hudson 301-316 were the first U23B's, and the only ones with radiator fairings. During the next nine years, the U23B would be produced with far more significant variations than the small sheet-metal fairings. Southern Railway kept up its long-standing tradition and ordered all 70 of its U23B's with high short hoods, while C&O and WP orders specified rebuilt Blomberg trucks from EMD trade-ins. Outshopped in January 1973, Louisville & Nashville 2708 debuted GE's new 4-axle floating-bolster truck and all 90 L&N U23B's rode on the optional FB2's. Milwaukee, MoPac, NdeM and Southern also ordered at least some of their U23B's on FB2 trucks.

Beneath the hood, there were more U23B variations. Early U23B's were equipped with the D.C. GT581 main generator dating back to Alco-GE FA2's, FB2's and RS3's, while most later units were built with A.C. GTA-11 main alternators.

Unlike most domestic models, the "U" in U23B truly meant universal. In addition to 10 FCP and 30 NdeM units sent to Mexico, 16 U23B's were exported to Peru, for use at Southern Peru Copper's Cuajone Mine and its railroad to the seaport of Ilo. In deference to steep grades and tunnels encountered in the downhill movement of ore, road engines 40-45 were outfitted with additional radiators made necessary by extended dynamic brake operation. Mine engines 50-59 were built with remote control.

Although overshadowed by GP38/GP38-2 sales exceeding 2600 units, the U23B was nevertheless successful. With production totaling 481 units, the U23B ranks as second-best seller among U-series locomotives. Outshopped from Erie in June 1977, Conrail U23B 2798 was the last domestic U-boat built.

THE HARD WAY

Santa Fe's westbound mainline local, with U23B 6315 and ailing GP20 3106, triples Edelstein Hill, west of Chillicothe, Illinois, at 1600, April 12, 1977.   *Greg McDonnell*

Just west of Chillicothe, Illinois, the Santa Fe mainline climbs out of the Illinois River valley on a twisting, 5-mile, 1.1 percent grade known as Edelstein Hill. A helper grade in the steam season, Edelstein has been tamed by generations of multiple-unit diesel consists and barely slows the progress of heavily powered intermodal trains. On April 12, 1977, though, the fabled hill has brought Santa Fe's westbound mainline local to its knees. Barely out of Chillicothe, alarm bells ring out in the cab of U23B 6315 as the trailing unit,

GP20 3106, packs it in. Despite heroic efforts of the hopelessly over-tonnaged 6315, the train—stretched out around Houlihan's curve—stalls at milepost 133. With westbound traffic piling up behind, and the ailing GP20 unable to load, the hapless local is forced to double the hill.

After some quick tonnage calculations and caustic comments from the caboose, the 6315 digs in and attacks the hill with the first half of the train. In an incredible, pulse-quickening, near-deafening performance, the diehard GE

slowly, painfully, inches westward, only to stall again, albeit three or four car-lengths closer to Edelstein.

Having suffered the ultimate indignity, Extra 6315 West reduces the cut to 15 cars, and as a westbound piggybacker, headed up by a GP38, U28CG and a U25B, cruises effortlessly upgrade on the south track, the humbled local takes on storied Edelstein the hard way—tripling the hill.

The first U23B built, D&H 2301 rests at Rouses Point, New York, along with sisters 2310, 2308 and Baldwin RF16 Sharks 1205 and 1216 on April 11, 1975. With the exception of the 315, wrecked in 1968, the D&H U23B's were transferred to Maine Central by Guilford in 1983. *Greg McDonnell*

With her once-proud Bicentennial colors showing through fading blue paint, bedraggled-looking D&H U23B 2312 and RS11 5006 rumble over the Conrail's Buffalo River drawbridge in Buffalo, New York, with transfer SK-1 at 1800, June 18, 1983. Prior to receiving the simplified blue-and-yellow scheme, 2312 celebrated the Bicentennial in red-white-and-blue paint as D&H 1776.
Greg McDonnell

Passing Maranacook Lake, Maine Central 280, 288 and 281, the road's last operable U23B's, work the WARI on the Back Road at Winthrop, Maine, on May 26, 1990. Disguised by Guilford paint, blocked-out nose lights and a new road number, MEC 280 is none other than D&H 2301, the first U23B built.   *Brian Jennison*

Detouring on SP during a Western Pacific tunnel-enlarging program, WP U23B's 2263, 2254, a GP40 and an SW1500 work the eastbound OWPX over Altamont Pass, east of Altamont, California, at 1:30 P.M., February 10, 1982. Upon completion of the tunnel work, WP trains will return to their own line over Altamont Pass and the Southern Pacific route will be abandoned.
J.D. Schmid

Western Pacific U23B 2261 blackens the sky as the hogger on the SN Detour widens out the throttle approaching Tracy, California, with coil steel empties on October 26, 1980. A regular WP assignment working between Stockton and Pittsburg, California, the SN Detour is detouring on SP's Brentwood Line after a washout closed its regular Santa Fe route. *Brian Jennison*

Dwarfed by the impressive Southern Railway James River trestle, Norfolk Southern U23B 3923, an NS SD40-2 and a pair of Conrail units work a northbound NS/CR runthrough near Lynchburg, Virginia, on June 8, 1990.   *David Patch*

Running long hood forward, Southern U23B 3950 and GP30's 2602, 2538 and 2580 race southbound hotshot #187 through Cumberland Falls, Kentucky, on September 21, 1985. *J.P. Baukus, Jr.*

Showing off her high short hood, a standard feature on all 70 Southern U23B's, SOU 3917 leads GP38 2819 on the eastbound D41-D at Bloomington, Illinois, on September 19, 1989. *Steve Smedley*

Crossing the Kinnickinnic draw, Milwaukee Road U23B's 5001, 5000 and a pair of rebuilt Geeps depart Milwaukee, Wisconsin, with an eastbound freight on Christmas Day 1977.   *J.P. Baukus, Jr.*

The brakeman on a Rock Island transfer powered by FP7's 410 and 406 trudges up to the tower as an eastbound C&O manifest, led by U23B 2301, U25B 8116, GP40 4075 and GP9 5929, cruises through Pullman Jct. in Chicago, Illinois, on October 7, 1971.   *Greg McDonnell*

Reflecting the Southern Railway background of newly appointed president William H. Moore, Penn Central U23B's 2750-2776 were delivered in 1973 with dual controls and long-hood-forward configuration. Operating as Moore intended, PC U23B 2753 leads U30B 2871 and U25B's 2532 and 2608 on a westbound drag passing Tifft Street in Buffalo, New York, at 1835, June 8, 1977.   *Greg McDonnell*

In 1973, the Missouri-Kansas-Texas Railroad became the 43rd road to order GE U-boats, taking delivery of U23B's 350-352 in May. Unfortunately, Katy's relationship with GE was short and not so sweet. Strangers on a road ruled by EMD's, the U23B's were short-lived and went to EMD as GP39-2 trade-ins after just ten years of service. Three years old and almost mid-way through her brief career, Katy U23B 350 leads a pair of GP40's in the hot midday sun at Parsons, Kansas, in June 1976.
Thomas Hoffman; Keith E.Ardinger Collection

One of six Missouri Pacific U23B's to receive EMD-style cabs during wreck repairs, Central Michigan 8902, ex-MP 4506, leads sister 4502 over the Saginaw River swing bridge at Saginaw, Michigan, at 1050, October 26, 1989. Central Michigan, operator of ex-GTW trackage north of Durand, Michigan, purchased six MP U23B's in 1989.
Greg McDonnell

Bracketing GP38 2040, MoPac U23B's 2255 and 2254 head a westbound freight stopped to change crews at Jefferson City, Missouri, on September 22, 1974. Renumbered 4505 and 4504 in 1980, the two GE's were among the half-dozen sold to Central Michigan in 1989.   *David R. Busse*

Holding the main at Worthville, Kentucky, L&N U23B 2752, a U30C and U25C 1519 set out a cut of coal loads for the transloaders at Carrollton on May 19, 1979.   *Jeff Mast*

Air horns blaring, throttle wide open, CSX U23B 3253, GP40 6563, BQ23-7 3008 and GP38DC 2085 scream through Wartrace, Tennessee, Chattanooga-bound with R539 at 1617, July 14, 1990.   *Greg McDonnell*

Racing ahead of an advancing storm, L&N U23B 2814, GP38-2 4060, GP30 1050 and U23B 2817 pass the elevators at Manchester, Indiana, with northbound #298 on May 3, 1980.   *J.P. Baukus, Jr.*

Flying green flags, FCP U23B 543, M420TR 530, RSD12 513 and RSD5 829 lead First 4 north of Santa Ana, Sonora, Mexico, on January 7, 1979.   *Matthew J. Herson, Jr.*

Shop foreman Alex Torres confers with two of his men as FCP U23B 542 undergoes a complete overhaul at the Pacific Region shops at Empalme, Sonora, Mexico, on February 15, 1993.   *Greg McDonnell*

Striking the time-honored pose, brakemen cling to the car sides as NdeM U23B 9103 and RSD12 7441 perform switching chores in a small town near Saltillo, Nuevo Leon, Mexico, in April 1975.   *Jim Reddington*

The hogger on an eastbound Lehigh Valley drag widens
out the throttle as U23B's 509, 507 and 505 pull through the
S-curve at Greens Landing, Pennsylvania, at 1515, September
10, 1975.   *Greg McDonnell*

Exercising trackage rights on Amtrak's ex-New Haven mainline, Providence & Worcester U23B 2203, B23-7 2201, U23B's 2204 and 2202 storm through Mill River Jct., in New Haven, Connecticut, with CT-2, the Danbury stone train, on May 27, 1993. While the 2201 was bought new by P&W, the trio of U23B's were acquired secondhand from Conrail. Leading the consist, P&W 2203 is ex-Conrail 2798, the last U-boat built. Retired by Conrail, all ten units from the final U-boat order have been resold. Reading & Northern purchased CR 2789 2791 and 2793, while the remaining seven were picked up by P&W. *David Patch*

The hammering exhaust of GE FDL16's competes with crashing thunder as Conrail U23B's 2792, 2740 and B23-7 1935 struggle up Clifton Hill in Niagara Falls, Ontario, with the BUCP-3 in the midst of a violent thunderstorm at 2140, June 13, 1984. *Greg McDonnell*

U23C

Horsepower	2250
Engine	FDL12
Production Dates	3/68-9/70
Total Built	223

Original Owners:

RRFSA (Brazil)	170
Santa Fe	20
Penn Central	19
Burlington	9
Lake Superior & Ishpeming	5

Working a traditional U23C haunt, Santa Fe 7510 and 7500 pause at Whitewater, New Mexico, with a mine run on September 23, 1972.   *Joe McMillan*

Lake Superior & Ishpeming 2300, the first U23C, rolled out of Erie in March 1968, five months before the first U23B. Despite its early start, the U23C achieved just a fraction of the sales racked up by its four-motor catalog companion. Only four U.S. railroads, Santa Fe, Burlington, LS&I and Penn Central, bought U23C's and domestic sales totaled a mere 53 units. However, export U23C sales more than tripled that figure.

Rede Ferroviaria Federal S.A. (Federal Railways of Brazil) purchased 170 U23C's between 1972 and 1976. RFFSA 3901-3920 were built at Erie without trucks and completed by GE do Brasil's Campinas, Sao Paulo, plant, using Brazilian truck castings and Erie-supplied traction motors. The remaining 150 RFFSA U23C's were assembled entirely by GE do Brasil.

WHILE THE ORE BOATS SLUMBER

Leased to CP Rail, LS&I U23C 2302 leads CP RS10 8468 on a southbound time freight at Bolton, Ontario, April 4, 1970. *James A. Brown*

Multi-million-mile, high-profile careers were never in the cards for the 53 domestic U23C's. For the most part, they spent their time relegated to low-speed drag service, terminals and secondary lines. Santa Fe's 7500's toiled in the New Mexico desert, moving trains of copper ore, while Burlington's nine U23C's were purchased to haul southern Illinois coal. Penn Central posted U23C's to hump duty, yard chores and transfer assignments, while LS&I 2300-2304 labored in the Marquette Range in Michigan's Upper Peninsula.

Built to lug iron ore from the Empire and Tilden mines to the ore docks at Marquette, Michigan, the LS&I 2300's rarely ventured more than 20 miles from home. However, when ice chokes Whitefish Bay and Great Lakes shipping shuts down for the winter, the ore-hauling railroad goes into hibernation. For years, LS&I diesels were leased out during this period and in the winters of their youth, the U23C's were cut loose to roam the continent until the shipping season reopened in spring. The U-boats were also rented out at other times and several of their number spent the summer of '72 in the mountains of B.C. on lease to the British Columbia Railway.

The ore boats are still laid up, but the shipping season is drawing near as LS&I U23C 2302 leads CP RS10 8468 past the station at Bolton, Ontario, on April 4, 1970. Only a few months old, the 2302 is spending her first winter on lease to CP Rail. Wheeling a southbound CPR time freight over the Mactier Subdivision at 50 miles per hour is a far cry from dragging an 11,000-ton ore train out of the Empire Mine, but while the ore boats slumber, the 2302 is getting at least a taste of the glory of big-time mainline railroading.

Coming off the Savanna line with a local freight, Burlington U23C 461 encounters sister 460 and SD9 449 on a mainline westbound at Galesburg, Illinois, on April 17, 1970. The last locomotives purchased by CB&Q, SD45's 516-530 and U23C's 460-468 were delivered in early 1969, wearing the pre-merger version of what was to have been the Burlington Northern paint scheme. *Dave Ingles*

Returning home to Enola Yard with a westbound transfer run, Conrail U23C's 6900 and 6904, ex-PC 6700 and 6704, cross the Susquehanna River on Pennsy's famed Rockville Bridge at Harrisburg, Pennsylvania, in October 1991. *Richard Steinheimer*

Slogging upgrade out of Marquette, Michigan, LS&I U23C's 2304, 2303 and U25C 2501 inch their way toward Eagle Mills with a Hill Extra, moving coal to the mine power plants at 1010, April 24, 1982.   *Greg McDonnell*

Deep in copper mining country, Santa Fe U23C's 7506 and 7512 labor upgrade at Star Shaft, New Mexico, returning ore empties to the mine at Santa Rita on May 10, 1974.   *Joe McMillan*

U36B

Horsepower	3600
Engine	FDL16
Production Dates	5/70-12/74
Total Built	125

Original Owners:

Seaboard Coast Line...............108
Auto-Train................................13
Conrail...4

Fresh out of Building 26, brand new Auto-Train U36B's 4002 and 4000 pose for their first photos at their Erie, Pennsylvania, birthplace on November 18, 1971.   *Bill Volkmer; Keith E. Ardinger Collection*

The U33B's reign as America's most powerful B-B diesel was remarkably brief, as GE test beds 301-304 reportedly began operating at 3600 h.p. as early as October 1967. However, the black-and-yellow U36B's traveled across the nation in their dual role as test beds and demonstrators for more than two years before the first production U36B emerged from Erie.

Riding reconditioned Blomberg trucks from an EMD trade-in, Seaboard Coast Line U36B 1748 was outshopped in May 1970. Seaboard accorded the new model no special status and began numbering its U36B's right after its last U33B. As far as Seaboard was concerned, the U36B was little more than a U33B boosted to 3600-h.p. The increased horsepower of the

U36B, accomplished with advanced fuel-rack settings and some beefed-up components, required no external changes and the new model was almost identical to its 3300-h.p. predecessor.

The U36B's standing as the most powerful four-axle diesel on the continent did little to boost its sales. In fact, only Seaboard Coast Line expressed interest in the model. SCL took delivery of 108 U36B's between May 1970 and March 1972. For its Lorton, Virginia-Sanford, Florida, (and later Louisville-Sanford) auto-carrying passenger service, Auto-Train ordered the only other U36B's built. Operating primarily on Seaboard Coast Line trackage, Auto-Train specified that its U36B's be built to SCL

standards, right down to the Blomberg trucks.

SCL and Auto-Train orders accounted for all 125 U36B's built, but A-T's bankruptcy added a third U36B buyer to the list. Because of Auto-Train's worsening financial state, A-T U36B's 4013-4016, built in December 1974, were completed but never delivered. Wearing full Auto-Train livery, the units languished in the back yard at Erie until they were sold to Conrail in 1976. Reconditioned and re-trucked with AAR-B's at the railroad's request, Conrail's first new locomotives and GE's last U36B's were outshopped as CR 2971-2974 in September 1976.

OUT OF THE FAST LANE

Hauling Tampa-bound dry rock, SCL U36B 1836 and MATE-4 3220 cross the north fork of the Alafia River at Nichols, Florida, in March 1979.   *Emery J. Gulash*

The U36B was railroading's answer to the muscle car, a turbo-charged, high-horsepower, high-performance machine built for speed. Seaboard Coast Line, owner of 108 of the 125 U36B's built, assigned multiples of the high-powered hoods to hot piggyback trains, time freights and the famed Tropicana "Juice Train." With their speedometers pegged at the legal 79 m.p.h limit for hour after hour, Auto-Train's SCL copies racked up tens of thousands of miles in Lorton-Sanford and Louisville-Sanford service, while in later years Conrail's

quartet raced nightly Buffalo-New York City RoadRailers over the Water Level Route like ghosts of the Steel Fleet.

Far from the fast lane, a number of SCL U36B's labor deep in the phosphate fields of Florida's Bone Valley, where speeds rarely top 40 m.p.h. and 10,000-ton trains are the order of the day. In the Bone Valley, tractive effort replaces speed as a requisite and the 3600-h.p. hoods are teamed with GE-built MATE road slugs constructed on U36B platforms.

Tampa-bound with a trainload of "dry rock"

(processed, kiln-dried phosphate), SCL U36B 1836 and MATE-4 3220 creep across the long wooden trestle spanning the north fork of the Alafia River at Nichols, Florida, in March 1979. Caked with phosphate dust and streaked with oil, the 1836 won't be flexing its 3600-horsepower muscle to break any speed records. Merely moving the heavy train requires every ounce of energy that can be squeezed from the FDL16 pounding beneath its dirty black hood...and in the Bone Valley, that's accomplishment enough.

Flying white flags, SCL U36B 1849, Mate 4 3224 and U36B 1846 cross the drawbridge at Drayton Hall, South Carolina, with a dimensional load special in May 1973.
Leroy Robl; Keith E. Ardinger Collection

Birmingham-bound, Seaboard System U36B 5769, U23B 3279, C30-7 7039, SD40-2 8241 and a U36B roll through the red clay and tall pines near Mobile, Alabama, with a hotshot out of New Orleans in April 1986.   *J. Parker Lamb*

Dressed in full Conrail paint and retrucked with AAR-B's, but still sporting their SCL-style nose lights, ex-Auto-Train U36B's 2972 and 2974 roll a westbound drag through South Fork, Pennsylvania, on September 13, 1981. Built for Auto-Train in December 1974, but never delivered, AT U36B's 4013-4016 were reconditioned and sold in September 1976 as Conrail 2971-2974.   *Thomas Seiler*

Demonstrating on Delaware & Hudson, GE U36B prototypes 304 and 303 cruise along the shore of Lake Champlain, leaving Port Henry, New York, with a D&H southbound in September 1968. After nearly five years of test-bed and demonstrator service as part of the 301-304 demo set, GE 303 and 304 were rebuilt to their original U30B configuration and sold as Western Pacific 770 and 771.   *Eric Clegg*

U36C

Horsepower	3600
Engine	FDL16
Production Dates	10/71-4/75
Total Built	218

Original Owners:

Santa Fe	100
Nacionales de Mexico	84
Erie Lackawanna	13
Ferrocarril del Pacifico	10
Clinchfield	7
Milwaukee	4

Facing the transfer-table pit, Clinchfield U36C 3605 and F3Au 801 rest at Erwin, Tennessee, on June 7, 1976.   *Keith E. Ardinger*

In October 1971, six years after EMD turned out its first SD45, workers at Erie put the finishing touches on GE's first 3600-h.p. C-C freighter. From its zebra-striped pilot to its massive wingspan radiators, Clinchfield 3600 looked no different than a U33C. Riveted to its frame, though, was a shiny builder's plate etched "MODEL U36C...HP 3600." Beneath the hood, increased fuel-rack settings and steel-capped pistons helped the U36C's FDL16 prime mover produce the same horsepower as the SD45's 20-cylinder 645 engine.

Unfortunately, the U36C was too late for the party. Interest in 3600-h.p. C-C's had peaked and most railroads were returning to more conservative power policies favoring locomotives in the 2000-3000-h.p. range. Catalogued concurrently with the U30 and U33C, the U36C was outsold by both models. Four of the six railroads that opted for the U36C placed small orders: Milwaukee purchased only 4 units and Clinchfield took 7, EL bought 13, while FCP's 10 were the last U36C's built. Santa Fe and NdeM, on the other hand, found favor with the big C-C's. "Uncle John" picked up an even hundred U36C's, while NdeM followed close behind with 84 units. Twenty steam generator-equipped U36CG's delivered in 1974 gave NdeM a combined total of 104 units and a slight edge over Santa Fe for title to the largest U36C fleet.

Santa Fe U36C 8721 was wrecked in 1981 and spent several years languishing in storage while the railroad considered its fate. In the spring of 1985, the 8721 was admitted to the Cleburne, Texas, shops, but Santa Fe had more than wreck repairs in mind for the battered U-boat. Sporting a Dash 8-style nose and dressed in the red-and-yellow "Kodachrome" paint scheme of the anticipated (but never consummated) SP-SF merger, the former 8721 was outshopped in May 1985 as AT & SF 9500. Downrated to 3000 h.p. and upgraded with Dash 8 motor thermal protection, Sentry wheel-slip control and Dash 7-series enhancements (notably the tilted oil cooler visible just ahead of the radiators), the 9500 was the pilot for an ambitious SF30C capital rebuild program planned for all 98 surviving Santa Fe U36C's. Although canceled after Cleburne completed just 70 SF30C's, the program stands as the only major railroad-initiated capital rebuild project involving U-boats.

TIME WARP

NdeM U36C 8900 and a sister, lead a westbound freight at Oriental, Veracruz, Mexico, February 28, 1974.
Keith E. Ardinger

Caught in a time warp, brand new NdeM U36C's 8900 and a sister pause in front of the old stone depot at Oriental with a westbound drag. The calendar reads February 28, 1974, but the factory-fresh U-boats find themselves in a land of old-order railroading, where friction-bearing freight cars, 40-foot boxcars and Form 31's are the order of the day. The fat-boilered Consols are gone, but narrow-gauge passenger trains destined for Teziutlan still polish the dual-gauge rails in front of the depot and Oriental has changed little since the days when drags from Veracruz rolled into town behind lanky HR-class NdeM 2-6-6-2's.

From its venerable stone depot, with ornate ironwork and telegraph lines running under the eaves, to the dual-gauge track and friction-bearing tank cars in the yard, Oriental is steeped in operating history and traditional railroading, but the new GE's parked in front of the depot are the face of the future. Class engine 8900 and her dusty sister are members of the first wave of a U-boat invasion that will help redieselize NdeM and establish Mexico as a GE stronghold for decades to come.

Following in the footsteps of 2-6-6-2's, NdeM U36C's 8934 and 8985 labor upgrade at Jilotepic, Veracruz, Mexico, on March 4, 1975. Built as part of the narrow-gauge Ferrocarril Interoceano, the line from Veracruz to Oriental was standard gauged in 1947 and dieselized in the mid-sixties. Diesels and standard gauging have failed to tame this rugged piece of railroad, though, and the eastbound train requires not only two U36C's on the head end, but two more cut in as mid-train helpers. *Keith E. Ardinger*

Minutes later, the struggling eastbound has gained only a few dozen feet of elevation as the head-end units pass above U36C helpers 8908 and 8927, spliced into a seemingly endless string of empty pipe gons.
Keith E. Ardinger

Just in from Marion, Erie Lackawanna U36C 3318 and U33C's 3307 and 3314 tie up at Dayton, Ohio, on September 15, 1974. *David P. Oroszi*

Neatly appointed in Conrail blue, CR U36C 6591, ex-EL 3320, leads U33C 6566, still in EL paint, on NY-6 near Lancaster, New York, at 0943, July 1, 1976. Built as EL 3303, the 6566 spent most of her career as D&H 753, one of three EL U33C's swapped for a trio of D&H SD45's. In anticipation of the Conrail merger, the six units were returned to their respective owners in December 1975. *Greg McDonnell*

Hard by Highway 66, westbound Santa Fe U36C 8701 and a pair of SD's slam past an eastbound hotshot in a high-speed meet on the Albuquerque Division double track near Hackberry, Arizona, on October 9, 1973.   *Steve Patterson*

The rising sun casts a golden glow on Santa Fe U36C 8785, F45 5917, C30-7's 8023, 8113 and a string of pigs and containers as a westbound intermodal train nears Summit, California, at 6:28 A.M., July 31, 1981.   *J.D. Schmid*

Splitting the semaphores east of Delhi, Colorado, Santa Fe SF30C 9522, Dash 8-40CW's 800, 811 and a pair of SF30C's race the westbound 1-448-21 over the Raton Subdivision on September 21, 1992. *Terry Chicwak*

Leading a "dog's breakfast" lashup of high-horsepower second generation units and more than a mile of piggybacks and auto racks, Santa Fe SF30C 9522 (ex-U36C 8710) glides downgrade at Yucca, Arizona, on March 2, 1987. On the horizon, the yellow face of a following westbound shimmers in the desert heat. *John C. Lucas*

U36CG

Horsepower	3430/3600
Engine	FDL16
Production Dates	4/74-5/74
Total Built	20

Original Owner:

Nacionales de Mexico..............20

Trailing a mixed bag of bought-new and hand-me-down passenger equipment, NdeM U36CG 8941 stands ready to depart Saltillo, Nuevo Leon, Mexico, in April 1975.   *Jim Reddington*

In spite of very limited interest, GE continued to advertise a passenger or dual-service version of almost every U-series model intended for mainline service. In fact, with the exception of the U50C's, every six-motor U-boat built had a steam generator compartment located behind the cab. Until 1974, Santa Fe, with ten U28CG's and six custom-built U30CG's, had been the only railroad to exercise this option. Six years after the Santa Fe U30CG's were built, GE dusted off the CG package to construct 20 U36CG's for NdeM. While the Santa Fe U30CG's had been built with custom-ordered cowl carbodies, the NdeM units were off-the-shelf machines with steam generator equipment neatly tucked away in the intended compartment behind the cab. Delivered in April and May 1974, NdeM 8938-8957 were the last steam generator-equipped U-boats built.

U34CH

Even though NdeM had steam generators installed in 20 of its U36C's, the big 3600-h.p. C-C could hardly be considered a passenger locomotive. Yet the very first U36C's were commissioned to haul passengers. The U34CH, designed for commuter-train service at the request of the New Jersey Department of Transportation, was essentially a U36C modified to divert a portion of its 3600 h.p. to drive an auxiliary alternator that provided hotel power to passenger equipment. Nominally rated at 3430 h.p., the U34CH's actual available horsepower was determined by the HEP demands of the train being hauled. With its HEP alternator conveniently occupying the steam generator compartment, the U34CH was externally identical to the U33 and U36C.

In October 1970, a full year before Clinchfield received the first U36C's, GE outshopped EL/NJDOT 3351, the first of 32 U34CH's to be built for commuter service on EL lines west of Hoboken, New Jersey. Dressed in a handsome blue-and-silver paint scheme and lettered for Erie Lackawanna and NJDOT, the big GE's and new all-electric Pullman-Standard coaches replaced tired EL RS3's and E8's, ex-Erie Stillwell coaches and former Lackawanna "Boonton" cars.

Eight years later, a 33rd U34CH was created using former C&NW U30C 934. Contracted to GE's Pittsburgh, Pennsylvania, facility, the construction of Metro-North U34CH 4183 was financed by New York State as part of its contribution toward NJDOT operations in New York on the Port Jervis line. Completed in October 1978, the 4183 was painted in NJDOT colors and assigned to the Hoboken U34CH pool.

Horsepower	3430/3600
Engine	FDL16
Production Dates	11/70-1/73
Total Built	32 (+1)*

Original Owners:

New Jersey DOT 32
Metro-North.............................1*

*Metro-North 4183 rebuilt from C&NW U30C 934.

Across the Hudson, the twin towers of the World Trade Center shimmer in the distance, while NJ Transit U34CH's 4176 and 4166 await departure time at Hoboken, New Jersey, on January 15, 1985. *Greg McDonnell*

Climbing through Black Rock Cut, east of Port Jervis, New York, NJT U34CH 4162 pushes hard on the rear of train #58, Hoboken-bound, on October 22, 1993. Still dressed in the faded blue-and-silver of her EL/NJDOT days, the veteran GE is nearing the end of her career. *Scott Hartley*

U50C

Horsepower	5000
Engine	FDL12 (two)
Production Dates	9/69-11/71
Total Built	40

Original Owner:

Union Pacific 40

Under a pall of exhaust, Union Pacific U50C 5021, SD40 3028 and GP20 496 work a westbound drag near Green River, Wyoming, on May 16, 1974. *James C. Herold*

In early 1968, as Union Pacific's 8500-h.p. gas-turbines neared retirement, UP motive-power czar David S. Neuhart returned to the builders seeking a new generation of double-engined diesels to replace the aging giants. Electro-Motive updated its DD series to produce the twin 16-645E3A-engined, 6600-h.p. DDA40X, while GE engineers took the U50 concept back to the drawing board and returned with the U50C. Between 1969 and 1971, UP purchased 47 DDA40X Centennials and 40 U50C's.

Geared for 80 m.p.h., the 417,000-pound, 79-foot-long U50C was built for speed, packing two 2500-h.p. 7FDL12's and riding on the six-axle trucks of turbine trade-ins. On the drawing board, the U50C was a sound concept; on the road, it was not. Aluminum wiring used in the big units was a disaster and electrical problems plagued the U50C's right from the start. In February 1970, four-month-old class engine 5000 was sidelined by a serious electrical fire and by 1974 fires had put four of the still-new U50C's out of action for good. To make matters worse, the massive weight of the big C-C's was causing stress cracks in their rebuilt turbine trucks.

GE worked in vain to remedy the numerous U50C maladies and Morrison-Knudsen was asked to quote on rewiring all 40 units with copper cable. The prohibitive cost of such a project, combined with other factors—not the least of which was their lack of versatility—ruled out rebuilding. By 1976, all 40 U50C's were out of service. After less than a half-dozen years in operation, UP 5000-5017 were retired in March 1977. The remaining units were written off in February 1978 and all 40 U50C's were eventually scrapped.

Unfortunate Son

Union Pacific U50 38 poses with U50C's 5005 and 5010 on the service tracks at North Platte, Nebraska, in August 1970. *Stan J. Smaill*

Standing at the back gate of GE's Erie, Pennsylvania, locomotive plant, brand-new Union Pacific U50C 5029 sparkles in the morning sun as she awaits delivery on August 1, 1971. Even sitting still, the 5029 is an impressive machine, from her silvered turbine trucks to her towering cab and wingspan radiators. On the road, with her twin 7FDL12's wide open and 80 m.p.h. gearing pushed to the limit, the 5029 should be even more impressive. However, there are unseen flaws in her design and defects beneath her shiny yellow hood that will doom the 5029 and her kind to a checkered career and premature retirement.

Out on the Overland Route, the 5029's sisters are already experiencing problems: fires, elec-trical faults and road failures. For the entire class, the writing is on the wall—and in dozens of U50C work orders, warranty claims and road failure reports. Before she even rolls out the gate, the 5029's fate has been sealed.

More than a thousand miles from Erie, two generations of twin-engined GE freighters pose side by side on the service tracks at North Platte, Nebraska. Aging and obsolete, but with tens of thousands of miles of revenue service behind her and thousands more to come, Union Pacific U50 38 wears the "Dependable Transportation" slogan on her cabside; appropriately, U50C 5005 does not.

Union Pacific U50C 5029, GE Erie, Pennsylvania, August 1, 1971. *Greg McDonnell*

U18B

Horsepower	1800
Engine	FDL18
Production Dates	3/73-10/76
Total Built	163

Original Owners:

Seaboard Coast Line	105
Nacionales de Mexico	45
Maine Central	10
Texas Utilities	2
Providence & Worchester	1

Working back to back on an eastbound local, SCL U18B's 378 and 373 cross the Little Manatee River at Ruskin, Florida, in May 1983.   *Emery J. Gulash*

While the four-motor, 1800-h.p. UD18 heralded the U-boat invasion, another 1800-h.p. B-B hood closed out the domestic U-boat line. Introduced in 1973, the U18B was the last domestic U-designation model added to the GE catalog before the U-boat line was superseded by the Dash 7 series in 1976. The smallest of all domestic U-series models, the 54-foot 8-inch U18B packed an eight-cylinder 7FDL8 engine under the hood and weighed in at as little as 111 tons in its lightweight version. Available with AAR-B or FB2 trucks, as well as trade-in EMD Blombergs, the U18B sold 163 units to five customers.

Some observers likened the U18B to half a U36B, a comparison apparently endorsed by Seaboard Coast Line. SCL, the only railroad to embrace the U36B, bought the first and the most U18B's. Standard-weight SCL U18B's 300-392 joined big brother U36B's in service in the Florida phosphate fields, bumped Baldwin switchers from heavy yard chores and replaced RS2's and RS3's on locals and in branchline service system-wide. In a break with tradition, SCL 300-324 were ordered with FB2 trucks, while sisters 325-392 rode on EMD Blombergs like most other SCL four-axle GE's. Riding FB2 trucks and sporting tiny 1200-gallon fuel

tanks, lightweight U18B's 250-261 replaced RSC2's and RSC3's on branchlines with frail bridges and light axle loadings.

Beyond SCL territory, the U18B found acceptance from Maine to Mexico, not to mention Texas and Rhode Island. Nacionales de Mexico imported 45 AAR-B-trucked U18B's, while Texas Utilities (TUGX) picked up a pair equipped for remote-control operation and Maine Central bought 10 Blomberg-trucked units built to SCL specifications. Riding FB2 trucks and delivered as a single-unit order in October 1976, Providence & Worcester U18B 1801 was one of the last U-boats built.

Don't Call 'Em Baby, Baby

Headed for the mountains, MEC U18B's 403, 407, 406 and 408 work eastbound tonnage along the Moose River near Concord, Vermont, on September 26, 1981.
Thomas L. Seiler

The first splashes of fall color are painting the forest as Maine Central 403 "General Peleg Wadsworth" leads a perfectly matched set of Independence Class U18B's along the Moose River at East St. Johnsbury, Vermont, on September 26, 1981. Almost six feet shorter than other B-B U-series models, with half as many cylinders and half the power of a U36B, the U18's were dubbed "baby boats" in some circles. However, what the U18B lacks in size,

it makes up for in sound. The authoritative bark of the U18's compact 7FDL8 engine gives the bantam U-boat the ability to out-shout—if not out-work—its larger siblings.

Displaying golden eagles emblazoned on their fronts and christened with names from the Revolutionary War, the Independence Class U18B's are braced for battle as they cruise along the Moose River. The legendary grades that gave the Mountain Subdivision its

name and reputation are waiting ahead. Within two hours, the White Mountains will echo the razor-sharp exhaust of laboring 7FDL8's and the stalwart GE's will take Crawford Notch with all the fury of triple-headed MEC Mikes. The sight and sound of a brace of U18B's battling upgrade is unforgettable, and as those who have witnessed their heroic and authoritive performance will readily testify, you just don't call 'em "baby."

Still in original SCL paint, SBD U18B 364 works with repainted MATE 4 3205 and U36B 1853, switching orange juice cars at the Tropicana Juice plant in Bradenton, Florida, on Christmas Eve 1984. *Scott Hartley*

Returning home with seven cars and a caboose, SBD U18B 1959 trundles through Laurel, Florida, working the northbound
Sarasota Switcher on March 19, 1987.   *Scott Hartley*

Treading slowly across the barren desert floor, NdeM U18B 9032 leads a 15-car mixed train near Esperanza, Jalisco, Mexico, on March 15, 1981.   *Matthew J. Herson, Jr.*

Just in from Mattawamkeag, MEC U18B 406 rests in the evening sun in Bangor, Maine, while C424 453 (originally EL 2406) works past on the westbound BKPO at 1725, September 13, 1993. *Greg McDonnell*

Still riding its original FB2 trucks, Providence & Worcester U18B 1801 patrols the backstreets of Willimantic, Connecticut, with interchange traffic for the Central Vermont in January 1979. The 1801 has since been retrucked with AAR-B's from RS3 1501 and the line into Willimantic has been taken out of service. *Thomas Carver*

P30CH

Horsepower	3000
Engine	FDL16
Production Dates	8/75-12/75
Total Built	25

Original Owner:

Amtrak 25

Preparing for departure, Amtrak P30CH's 717, 716, 705 and 706 stand on the head end of #53, the southbound *Auto Train*, at Lorton, Virginia, on October 4, 1989.   *Greg McDonnell*

Although the P30CH did not carry a U-series model designation, the husky-looking, 193-ton, 3000-h.p. passenger hauler was every bit a U-boat beneath its full-cowl carbody. Cousin to the U30CG, the P30CH was a U30C derivative, custom built for Amtrak in 1975. Designed for use with Amtrak's newly ordered Amfleet equipment, the P30CH was outfitted with two 12V715 Detroit Diesel engines that supplied 750-k.w. hotel power to the all-electric passenger cars. To accommodate the HEP equipment, located in the rear of the carbody, the P30CH was five feet longer than the U30C/U30CG.

Delivery of P30CH's 700-724 was complicated by controversial high-speed tracking problems with the C-C trucks they shared with Amtrak's GE-built E60C electrics. After minor modifications, the big GE's settled into assignments out of Chicago and New Orleans. Singlehandedly, the P30's often pulled medium-haul trains, such as the *Illini* and *Cardinal* from the Windy City, but in multiple they were preferred power on the Chicago-New Orleans *Panama Limited* and the New Orleans-Los Angeles *Sunset Limited*.

MIDNIGHT EXPRESS

Amtrak P30CH's 709, 721, 720 and 703 lead #53 through Doswell, Virginia, at 1751, October 3, 1989.
Greg McDonnell

As the late-afternoon shadows slowly creep across the platform, a quartet of Amtrak P30's idle impatiently in front of the terminal building at Lorton, Virginia. Flat-faced, cowl-bodied creatures, the big GE's are in their twilight years, but they've found their niche on Amtrak #53, the overnight *Auto Train* to Sanford, Florida. Scrawled on the dirty flanks of a tired P30CH, the hastily scribbled words "Midnight Express!" conjure visions of a late-night crew change and lanterns bobbing in the darkness, of muffled voices and air horns calling out in the night. In two words, an unknown railroader somewhere in the Carolina night has captured the essence of Amtrak's least glamorous, but most impressive, train.

Seventy miles south of Lorton, the sun is setting on RF&P's double-track speedway as the signal guarding the CSX diamond at Doswell, Virginia, winks to high green for Amtrak #53. A smudge of exhaust appears in the distance, a headlight pops into view and the call of hard-working FDL's grows ever louder as four P30's climb over the horizon with an incredible 42-car consist.

Racing headlong into the night, Amtrak 709, 721, 720 and 703 descend upon Doswell, air horns wailing, engines screaming. Up in the cab, the warm glow of the setting sun highlights the face of the engineer, a heroic figure in confident command of a passenger train like no other. In an explosion of sound

and a fury of blurred stainless steel and platinum mist, #53 rips through Doswell. Forty - two cars, a mismatched collection of Amfleet coaches, Heritage sleepers, diners and dome cars, followed by a string of 20 bi-level auto carriers, slice past. In a heartbeat, #53 is gone. A flashing red marker blinks in the distance and the hammering exhaust of wide-open FDL's fades as the "Midnight Express" dissolves into the gathering gloom of the approaching night.

SUPER 7...U·BOATS AT HEART

On one of its first shakedown runs, Super 7-
B23 demonstrator GECX 2000 leads GP40's
B&P 3119, R&S 106, R&S 105, GP9 211
and PNC (ex-SP) SD45 9128 on a Buffalo &
Pittsburgh southbound at East Salamanca,
New York, at 0715, April 24, 1989.
Greg McDonnell

In the late 1980's, as third-generation GE Dash 8's rolled off the assembly line, U-boat trade-ins gathered in the Erie, Pennsylvania, back yard of America's number one locomotive builder. In addition to traded-in Santa Fe, MoPac and WP U23B's, UP U30C's and Southern U33C's, GE sought out retired U-boats from other sources. Retrieved from scrap yards and storage lines throughout the country, U23B's, U33B's and U30, U33 and U36C's of Milwaukee, MoPac and SP, D&H, PC and Reading heritage were brought home to Erie. By 1988, GE's back lot held a rainbow-hued

collection of nearly 100 tired and rusting U-boats. The reasons behind this massive homecoming were not immediately apparent, but General Electric had big plans for the road-weary veterans.

Hauled off the scrapline in August 1988, Western Pacific U23B 2263 was selected as the prototype for GE's new Super 7 project, an ambitious program to breathe new life into old U-boats and provide low-cost, reliable power in the process. After several months and hundreds of man-hours, the former WP 2263 emerged from Erie in April 1989, reborn as GECX 2000,

a 2250-h.p., Super 7-B23. With a Dash 8 cab, carbody and dynamic brake system, micro-processor-managed motor thermal protection and Sentry adhesion control blended with late Dash 7 technology and components, GECX 2000 bore little physical or technological resemblance to a U23B. However, powered by a remanufactured 7FDL12 (upgraded with Dash 8 power assemblies, injectors and built on the platform of WP 2263, the Super 7 was indeed a U-boat at heart.

Utilizing the carcasses of WP U23B's 2251 and 2257, along with Southern U33C's 3811,

3812 and UP U30C 2956, Morrison-Knudsen was contracted to build Super 7-B23 demonstrators 2001-2002 and Super 7-C30's 3000-3002 at its Boise, Idaho, facility. Thirty years after GE rolled out the XP24 prototypes, the six reincarnated U-boats hit the road as Super 7 demonstrators.

Concurrent with the Super 7 program, General Electric acquired the former Bombardier/Montreal Locomotive Works plant in Montreal, Quebec. With Erie pumping out new Dash 8's at near capacity, the ex-MLW facility was selected to produce Super 7 rebuilds. By mid-1989, the same erecting bays that produced generations of steam locomotives and Alco-design diesels were turning WP U23B's into Monongahela Super 7-B23's. In addition to 10 Monongahela Super 7-B-23's, the Montreal plant outshopped FNM Super 7-C30's 14020-14022, GECX Super 7-C30's 3003-3010, and Roberval & Saguenay Super 7-B23's 50-52 before orders dried up.

Before closing in 1993, the old MLW plant also produced new U-boats for export, including U6B's and U15C's for the Philippines and U10B's for Mozambique. Although the U-series was dropped for North American models in 1977-78, GE continues to market the Universal series as a technologically improved export line.

While the Super 7 series drew little interest from American roads, the concept was well received south of the border. In addition to the three Montreal rebuilds, Nacionales de Mexico ordered 100 all-new Super 7N-C30's and began a program to rebuild its own six-motor U-boats into Super 7's in Mexican shops. By 1993, FNM shops at Aguascalientes, Concarril, Empalme and San Luis Potosi had outshopped nearly 100 FNM Super 7-C30's, rebuilt from NdeM and FCP U30C's, U36C's and U36CG's, as well as C30-7's. Appropriately, the U-boat has a future in the land that first accepted the heavy-duty GE U-series road diesel.

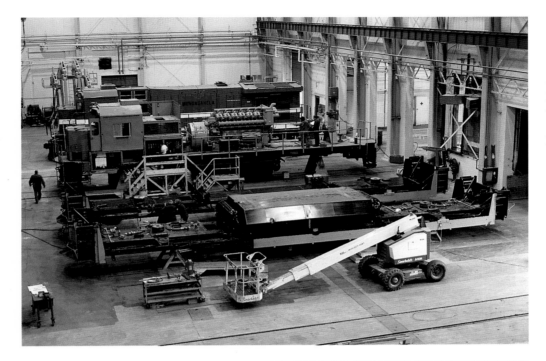

Monongahela Super 7-B23's 2300, 2301, 2302 and 2303, being built from WP U23B's 2254, 2255, 2252 and 2253 respectively, take shape on the erecting floor of the former Montreal Locomotive Works in Montreal, Quebec, on August 30, 1989. At the head of the line, MGA 2300 is fully painted and nearly complete, while the frames of 2302 and 2303 are still being prepared. *Robert Lambrecht*

The morning sun is still climbing over the Alleghenies as Monongahela Super 7-B23 2303, leased Conrail C30-7 6600 and Super 7 2307, with coal empties for the Federal No. 2 mine, wait to be recrewed at Tag, on the Waynesburg & Southern near White Cottage, Pennsylvania, on November 2, 1992. *Greg McDonnell*

Under the watchful eye of proud shop workers, FNM 14010, the first Super 7-C30 built by the FNM shop at San Luis Potosi, Mexico, is trucked on April 26, 1990. Soon to be painted in FNM's two-tone blue, the 14010 began life as NdeM U36C 8903, outshopped from Erie in July 1973.
Robert Lambrecht

Awaiting rebirth as a Super 7-C30, heavily cannibalized FNM U36C 411, ex-FCP 411, languishes behind the Empalme, Sonora, Mexico, shops with C30-7 420 and FCP U30C 402 on February 16, 1993. Just yards away, Empalme shop workers are building FNM Super 7-C30 14097 on the platform of ex-FCP U36C 415.   *Greg McDonnell*

Passengers and peddlers mix on the platform and M420 574 waits in the wings as northbound #3, led by FNM Super 7-C30 14007, makes its stop at Empalme, Sonora, Mexico, at 1515, February 19, 1993. The Aguascalientes-built Super 7 bears little resemblance to NdeM U36C 8984, upon whose frame the unit is built, but as #3 lifts out of town, the performance of FNM 14007 will confirm that she's a U-boat at heart.   *Greg McDonnell*

EPILOGUE

Leaving the Canada Southern for home rails, C&O U25B's 2519, 2503 and GP30 3023 pass the semaphores at BX Tower in St. Thomas, Ontario, with Detroit-bound DT-41 in May 1969.   *Greg McDonnell*

The operator at BX Tower in St. Thomas, Ontario, has his hands full as several trains converge on the old NYC interlocker on the former Canada Southern main line. The raspy voice of the St. Thomas dispatcher growls out of a speaker on the cluttered desk, while the interlocking plant governing the junction with C&O's ex-Pere Marquette Subdivision No. 1, as well as the L&PS diamond, lights up like a Christmas tree. "DT-41's comin' by the Ball," says the tower operator, as he wrestles with a series of armstrong levers to line the C&O westbound onto home rails.

Outside, interlocking rods rattle and clank, forcing reluctant switches to reverse alignment; semaphores lazily drop into position and a headlight shimmers in the distance. "U-boats!" two young boys shout excitedly as the dirty yellow-and-blue face of a C&O GE materializes in the haze. What might have been just another train becomes an unforgettable event as DT-41, led by U25B's 2519, 2503 and GP30 3023, lumbers past the sprawling MCRR shops and the landmark Canada Southern station and picks its way through the crossovers to regain home iron. The throaty call of the two U25's drowns out the turbocharged whine of the GP30 as the hogger notches out for the home stretch. As DT-41 rumbles past the eastward-facing sema-

phores, a 14-year-old photographer captures his first color photographs of a GE U-boat.

For an impressionable young train watcher troubled by the decimation of first generation diesel fleets, the gutsy GE's injected a new dimension of interest, excitement and diversity to the SD- and GP-dominated world of new-order railroading. U-boats, with their popping four-cycle bark, spartan styling and distinctive personality, were the bold new challengers of EMD's indomitable hold on dieseldom.

As Alco, Baldwin, Lima and Fairbanks-Morse bastions crumbled, a new generation of GE diesels helped to fill the esthetic and emotional void. Indeed, through better than three decades of railroading, the loud-talking, tough-looking U-boats have played leading roles in some of the most exciting, memorable and melancholy moments, from the thrill of boyhood encounters with New York Central U25B's on the Canada Southern, to the sadness of a late-night vigil in the cab of a dying SP U25B in Bakersfield.

Preparing this work has unleashed a wave of U-boat remembrances: a cab ride in just-delivered N&W U30B 8500 at Conneaut, Ohio, and sneaking through the back gate at Erie to spend quiet moments examining the derelict hulks of GE 751 and 752, not to mention brand

new brand-new Santa Fe U23B's and L&N FA trade-ins; hooping orders to detouring Extra C&O 8128 East on the CP at St. Thomas, Ontario, and watching shopmen carefully rebuilding FCP U23B 542 at Empalme, Sonora; pacing EL U25B's through the Canisteo Valley and finding Southern Pacific U50 9950 in L.A.; peering sleepily out the window of Room 103 of the Walking Horse Hotel to watch a brace of CSX U36B's scream through Wartrace, Tennessee, and notching out on the throttle of a battered Conrail U25B on an unforgettable night on the Water Level Route.

The images and words presented on these pages pay homage, not only to a class of locomotives that triggered a motive power revolution, but to the people who designed them, built them and worked them. This volume is a tribute to those who labored on the erecting floors at Erie; in shops and roundhouses from Argentine, Bakersfield and Colonie, to Waterville, Waycross and West Oakland, and to those who have endured long nights and hard miles in the rocking, rattling cabs of the 3,600 U-boats built.

This book is also a tribute to the extraordinary efforts and sensitive art of the photographers who have generously contributed their work. The stories behind many of the photographs rate a book of their own. One of the great pleasures of producing this volume has been the opportunity to work with friends. Special thanks are in order to all of them: to John Denison for making this book possible; to Chris McCorkindale and Sue Breen for their talented design work; to Gordon Turner for copy editing; to Bill Miller for hours spent poring over the roster, checking and re-checking for accuracy; and to Bob Lambrecht for helping to motivate this work and for following through with invaluable research. Above all, I am indebted to my family for their patience and understanding. As always, my wife and best friend Maureen has provided the inspiration, moral support and guidance necessary to make yet another dream a reality.

BC Rail M630 726, a GE trade-in leased to FNM, looks on as battered FNM U23B 540 (ex-FCP 540) switches at Mexicali, Baja California, Mexico, on January 20, 1994. Mexico is Valhalla, not only for Alcos, but for aging U-boats.   *Greg McDonnell*

U·BOAT ROLLCALL

The following roster includes a unit-by-unit listing of every domestic model U-boat built. Continuing the format of this book, U-series models are presented chronologically, according to the first date that each model series was produced. The production of each model is then listed alphabetically according to the original owners, with subsequent numberings, sales, etc., in adjacent columns. Railroads are identified by their reporting marks in each column and dispostions are abbreviated using the codes listed in the table below.

Every attempt has been made to ensure that this roster is as accurate as possible. However, the dispositions of a number of locomotives are uncertain or unknown. Corrections, additions and updates are welcome. The author can be contacted at Boston Mills Press, 132 Main Street, Erin, Ontario, Canada L0G 1T0. Those contributing significant information will receive a complete printout of all new information one year after the publication date of this volume.

Status Codes:

GE	At GE Erie, PA.
OS	Out of service.
P	Preserved.
PO	Preserved and operational.
R	Retired.
Rx	Retired and presumed scrapped.
NRE	National Railway Equipment, Dixmoor, IL.
NRS	National Railway, Silvis, IL.
TGE	Traded-in to GE.
TGX	Traded-in to GE and scrapped.
W	Wrecked.
WX	Wrecked and scrapped.
X	Scrapped.
XAIM	To American Iron & Metal, Pueblo, CO, for scrap.
XAZ	To Azcon Corp. for scrap.
XBN	Scrapped by BN at West Burlington, IA.
XCC	To Chrome Crankshaft for scrap.
XCCS	To Chrome Crankshaft, Silvis, IL, for scrap.
XCIM	Scrapped Chatham Iron & Metal, Savannah, GA.
XCL	To Chrome Locomotive, Silvis, IL for scrap.
XCRH/87	Scrapped by Conrail, Holidaysburg, PA 1985-1987.
XDES	To Diesel Electric Service, St. Paul, MN, and scrapped.
XDH	Scrapped D&H Colonie (NY) Shops.
XDU	To Durbano Metals, Ogden, UT, for scrap.
XEC	To Erman Corp for scrap.
XEH	To Erman-Howell for scrap.
XFIM	Scrapped Fairfield Iron & Metal, Andrews, SC/Albertville, AL.
XGMT	To General Metals, Tacoma, WA for scrap.
XGS	To Gray Supply, Little Rock, AR for scrap.
XHM	Scrapped Hyman Michaels, Chicago, IL.
XIBS	Scrapped IBS Inc., Peoria, IL.
XILS	Independent Locomotive Service, Bethel, MN for scrap.
XIS	To Illinois Scrap for scrap.
XJJ	To D.J. Joseph, Jewett, TX, for scrap.
XLM	To Levin Metals, Richmond, CA for scrap.
XLO	Scrapped Levin Metals, Oakland, CA.
XLS	To Levin Metals, Sacramento, CA, for scrap.
XLNS	Scrapped L&N South Louisville (KY) Shops.
XLS	Scrapped by Louisville Scrap.
XMC	To Miller Compressing, Milwaukee, WI, for scrap.
XMCB	Scrapped MEC Brewer shops.
XMEC	Scrapped MEC Waterville (ME) shops.
XM-K	Scrapped by Morrison-Knudsen, Boise, ID.
XMLW	Scrapped at GE Montreal, Quebec.
XNMP	To National Metals, Phoenix, AZ for scrap.
XMPI	To Metal Processing Industries for scrap.
XMPS	To Motive Power Services, Spokane, WA, for scrap.
XMRP	Scrapped by P&LE, McKees Rocks, PA.
XMSA	To Midwest Steel & Alloy, Hubbard, OH, for scrap.
XNLR	Scrapped by MP at North Little Rock, AR.
XNM	To National Metals, Terminal Island, CA, for scrap.
XPIT	Scrapped Pittsburgh, PA.
XPL	To Pielet Bros. McCook, IL, for scrap.
XPLJ	To Pielet Bros. Joliet, IL, for scrap.
XPNC	To PNC Mt. Vernon, IL, for parts and scrap.
XPRI	Pacific Rail Industries, Colton, CA, for scrap.
XPT	Scrapped Pacific Terminals, Long Beach, CA.
XRAC	To RailCar Corp., Colorado Springs, CO, for scrap.
XSL	To St. Louis Auto Shredders for scrap.
XSPC	To Steel Processing Corp. Alabama, for scrap.
XSS	To Simon & Sons, for scrap.
XSW	Scrapped Southwest Railroad Car Parts, Longview, TX.
XUP	Scrapped by Union Pacific.
XWC	To Waycross Scrap, Waycross, GA, for scrap.
XWI	To Wilson for scrap.

Note: Scrap dates are based on date delivered to scrapper. Many units remained intact for some time after this date.

UM20B

Union Pacific

UM20B-A	Serial	Built	Options/Notes
750A, 750D	32218, 32220	9/54	GE Test Beds

Original Road No.	UP	Status	Notes
ERIE 750A	UP 620	TGX/63	1
ERIE 750D	UP 621	TGX/63	1

Notes:
1) Built as A-B-B-A test beds for development of GE domestic road units. Leased to Erie until mid-1959. Returned to GE Erie, PA, and rebuilt for sale to UP 10/21/59. Retired by UP 10/63 and traded in on U50's. Scrapped at GE.

Union Pacific

UM20B-B	Serial	Built	Options/Notes
750B, 750C	32219, 32221	9/54	GE Test Beds

Original Road No.	UP	Status	Notes
ERIE 750B	UP 620B	TGX/63	1, 2
ERIE 750C	UP 621B	TGX/63	1

Notes:
1) Built as A-B-B-A test beds for development of GE domestic road units. Leased to Erie until mid-1959. Returned to GE Erie, PA, and rebuilt for sale to UP 10/21/59. Retired by UP 10/63 and traded in on U50's. Scrapped at GE.
2) UP 620B, minus trucks, used by GE Erie until early seventies.

UD18

General Electric

UD18	Serial	Built	Options/Notes
1800-1801	32475-32476	6/56	GE Demonstrators

Original Road No.	NdeM	Status	Notes
GE 1800	NdeM 8000	WX/61	1, 2
GE 1801	NdeM 8001	Rx	1

Notes:
1) GE 1800-1801 tested on Erie Railroad before demonstrating on NdeM. To NdeM 8000-8001 in 1956.
2) NdeM 8000 wrecked. Retired 2/7/61 and scrapped.

Nacionales de Mexico

UD18	Serial	Built	Options/Notes
8000-8001	32475-32476	6/56	GE Demonstrators
8002-8009	32477-32484	11/56	Steam generators

Original Road No.	NdeM	Status	Notes
GE 1800	NdeM 8000	WX/61	1, 2
GE 1801	NdeM 8001	Rx	
	NdeM 8002	Rx	
	NdeM 8003	Rx/74	
	NdeM 8004	Rx	
	NdeM 8005	Rx/74	
	NdeM 8006	Rx/74	
	NdeM 8007	Rx	
	NdeM 8008	Rx	
	NdeM 8009	Rx	

Notes:
1) GE 1800-1801 tested on Erie before demonstrating on NdeM. To NdeM 8000-8001.
2) NdeM 8000 wrecked. Retired 2/7/61 and scrapped.

U25B

Atchison, Topeka & Santa Fe

U25B	Serial	Built	Options/Notes
1600-1603	34246-34249	4/62	
1604-1607	34250-34253	5/62	
1608-1615	34277-34284	2/63	

Original Road No.	1969 Re#	Status	Notes
ATSF 1600	ATSF 6600	TGX/79	
ATSF 1601	ATSF 6601	TGX/79	
ATSF 1602	ATSF 6602	TGX/79	
ATSF 1603	ATSF 6603	TGX/79	
ATSF 1604	ATSF 6604	TGX/79	
ATSF 1605	ATSF 6605	TGX/79	
ATSF 1606	ATSF 6606	TGX/79	
ATSF 1607	ATSF 6607	TGX/79	
ATSF 1608	ATSF 6608	TGX/79	
ATSF 1609	ATSF 6609	TGX/79	
ATSF 1612	ATSF 6612	TGX/79	
ATSF 1611	ATSF 6611	TGX/79	
ATSF 1610	ATSF 6610	TGX/79	
ATSF 1613	ATSF 6613	TGX/79	
ATSF 1614	ATSF 6614	TGX/79	1
ATSF 1615	ATSF 6615	TGX/79	1

Notes:
1) ATSF 1614-1615 built without oil bath/air filter hump on rear gangways.

Chesapeake & Ohio

U25B	Serial	Built	Options/Notes
2500-2504	34566-34570	8/63	
2505-2507	34724-34726	8/63	
2508-2537	34731-34760	10/63-1/64	

Original Road No.	1970 Re#	NdeM	Status	Notes
C&O 2500	C&O 8100	NdeM 7600	OS	1
C&O 2501	C&O 8101		TGX/79	3
C&O 2502	C&O 8102		TGX/79	3
C&O 2503	C&O 8103	NdeM 7601	OS	1
C&O 2504	C&O 8104		TGX/79	3
C&O 2505	C&O 8105	NdeM 7602	OS	1
C&O 2506	C&O 8106	NdeM 7603	OS	1
C&O 2507	C&O 8107		TGX/79	3
C&O 2508	C&O 8108		TGX/78	2
C&O 2509	C&O 8109		TGX/79	3

Original Road No.	1970 Re#	NdeM	Status	Notes
C&O 2510	C&O 8110		TGX/78	2
C&O 2511	C&O 8111		TGX/79	3
C&O 2512	C&O 8112		TGX/78	2
C&O 2513	C&O 8113	NdeM 7604	OS	1
C&O 2514	C&O 8114		TGX/79	3
C&O 2515	C&O 8115		TGX/79	3
C&O 2516	C&O 8116	NdeM 7605	OS	1
C&O 2517	C&O 8117		TGX/79	3
C&O 2518	C&O 8118		TGX/78	2
C&O 2519	C&O 8119		TGX/78	2
C&O 2520	C&O 8120		TGX/79	3
C&O 2521	C&O 8121	NdeM 7606	OS	1
C&O 2522	C&O 8122	NdeM 7607	OS	1
C&O 2523	C&O 8123		TGX/78	2
C&O 2524	C&O 8124		TGX/78	2
C&O 2525	C&O 8125	NdeM 7608	OS	1
C&O 2526	C&O 8126		TGX/79	3
C&O 2527	C&O 8127	NdeM 7609	OS	1
C&O 2528	C&O 8128	NdeM 7610	OS	1
C&O 2529	C&O 8129	NdeM 7611	OS	1
C&O 2530	C&O 8130		TGX/79	3
C&O 2531	C&O 8131		TGX/78	2
C&O 2532	C&O 8132	NdeM 7612	OS	1
C&O 2533	C&O 8133	NdeM 7613	OS	1
C&O 2534	C&O 8134		WX/72	4
C&O 2535	C&O 8135		TGX/78	2
C&O 2536	C&O 8136		TGX/78	2
C&O 2537	C&O 8137	NdeM 7614	OS	1

Notes:
1) Sold to DSI for $75,000 each in 1980. Rebuilt and repainted for NdeM at GE-Hornell. NY., 1980. All out of service in Mexico by mid eighties.
2) Traded in to GE 10/78 on B30-7's 8245-8254.
3) Traded in to GE in 1979 on B30-7's 8265-8278.
4) C&O 8134 wrecked Alpine, VA, 12/72 and scrapped.

Chicago, Burlington & Quincy

U25B	Serial	Built	Options/Notes
100-105	35194-35199	9/64-10/64	

Original Road No.	BN	Status	Notes
CB&Q 100	BN 5424	XPNC/81	
CB&Q 101	BN 5425	XPNC/81	
CB&Q 102	BN 5426	XPNC/81	
CB&Q 103	BN 5427	XPNC/81	
CB&Q 104	BN 5428	XPNC/81	
CB&Q 105	BN 5429	XPNC/81	

Erie Lackawanna

U25B	Serial	Built	Options/Notes
2501-2512	35160-35171	9/64-10/64	
2513-2527	35652-35666	7/65-9/65	

Original Road No.	CR	Status	Notes
EL 2501	CR 2570	XPL/84	1
EL 2502	CR 2571	XNIM/86	1
EL 2503	CR 2572	XNIM/86	1
EL 2504	CR 2573	X	
EL 2505	CR 2574	XPL/84	1
EL 2506	CR 2575	XPL/84	1
EL 2507	CR 2576	X	
EL 2508	CR 2577	XPL/84	
EL 2509	CR 2578	TGX/83	1
EL 2510	CR 2579	XPL/84	
EL 2511	CR 2580	X	
EL 2512	CR 2581	TGX/83	1
EL 2513	CR 2582	XMSA/81	
EL 2514	CR 2583	TGX/83	1
EL 2515	CR 2584	XPL/84	
EL 2516	CR 2585	XPL/84	
EL 2517	CR 2586	TGX/83	1
EL 2518	CR 2587	TGX/83	1
EL 2519	CR 2588	TGX/83	1
EL 2520	CR 2589	XPL/84	
EL 2521	CR 2590	XPL/84	
EL 2522	CR 2591	X	
EL 2523	CR 2592	XMSA/81	
EL 2524	CR 2593	TGX/83	1
EL 2525	CR 2594	TGX/83	1
EL 2526	CR 2595	XPL/84	
EL 2527	CR 2596	XPL/84	

Notes:
1) Traded in to GE on CR B36-7's.

General Electric

U25B (XP24)	Serial	Built	Options/Notes
751-752	33505-33506	5/59-6/59	Test Beds/Demos

Original Road No.	Status	Notes
GE 751	XGE	1,2,3
GE 752	at GE	1,2,3

Notes:
1) GE 751-752 built as XP24 test bed/demonstrators.
2) Traction motors from 751 and 752 re-used in Wabash U25B's.
3) GE 751 derelict and heavily stripped at GE Erie as late as 1969. GE 752 still at GE Erie 3/94 in derelict condition on shop trucks. Carbody used to test various paints.

General Electric

U25B	Serial	Built	Options/Notes
753-756	34220-34223	1/61-2/61	High nose
2501-2504	34234/6/7/9	2/62	2502-04 High Nose
51-54	34561-2/64-5	12/62	All low nose

Original Road No.	Resale	Re#	Status/Notes		M-K Rebuild
GE 753	SLSF 804		TGX/77	1	
GE 754	SLSF 805		TGX/77	1	
GE 755	SLSF 806		TGX/77	1	
GE 756	SLSF 807		TGX/77	1	
GE 2501	UP 633		OC&E 7602	2,4	
GE 2502	UP 635		BM&LP 5301	2,5	M-K 5301
GE 2503	UP 634		Slug	2,6	SP 1600
GE 2504	UP 636		Slug	2,7	OC&E 7607
GE 51	SLSF 812	BN 5214	XPNC/81	3	
GE 52	SLSF 814	BN 5216	XPNC/81	3	
GE 53	SLSF 815	BN 5217	XPNC/81	3	
GE 54	SLSF 813	BN 5215	XPNC/81	3	

Notes:
1) GE 753-756 sold to Frisco 12/61. Traded in to GE in 1977 on SLSF B30-7's 863-870.
2) GE 2501-2504 sold to UP 7/62.
3) GE 51-54 sold to Frisco 7/63.
4) UP 633 rebuilt Morrison-Knudsen to TE53-1-4E, repowered with EMD 16-567 engines and outshopped 7/76 as Oregon, California & Eastern 7602.
5) UP 635 to TE53-4E by M-K. Cut down to frame, re-engined with EMD 16-567B engine from B&O F7 and D12 main generator. Completely new carbody. Outshopped 8/75 as M-K 5301. Used on work project on Black Mesa & Lake Powell and purchased by BM&LP 1/77.
6) UP 634 rebuilt M-K to S3-3B slug. Outshopped 5/80 as SP 1600.
7) UP 636 (ex-GE 2504) rebuilt by M-K to TS3-3B slug; outshopped 1/76 as OC&E 7607.

Great Northern

U25B	Serial	Built	Options/Notes
2500-2508	34962-34668 34984-34985	4/64	
2509-2523	35566-35580	4/65-5/65	

Original Road No.	BN	Status	Notes
GN 2500	BN 5400	XPNC/81	
GN 2501	BN 5401	XPNC/81	
GN 2502	BN 5402	XPNC/81	
GN 2503	BN 5403	XPNC/81	
GN 2504	BN 5404	XPNC/81	
GN 2505	BN 5405	XPNC/81	
GN 2506	BN 5406	XPNC/81	
GN 2507	BN 5407	XPNC/81	
GN 2508	BN 5408	XPNC/81	
GN 2509	BN 5409	XPNC/81	
GN 2510	BN 5410	XPNC/81	
GN 2511	BN 5411	XPNC/81	
GN 2512	BN 5412	XPNC/81	
GN 2513	BN 5413	XPNC/81	
GN 2514	BN 5414	XPNC/81	
GN 2515	BN 5415	XPNC/81	
GN 2516	BN 5416	XPNC/81	
GN 2517	BN 5417	XPNC/81	
GN 2518	BN 5418	XPNC/81	
GN 2519	BN 5419	XPNC/81	
GN 2520	BN 5420	XPNC/81	
GN 2521	BN 5421	XPNC/81	
GN 2522	BN 5422	XPNC/81	
GN 2523	BN 5423	XPNC/81	

Louisville & Nashville

U25B	Serial	Built	Options/Notes
1600-1604	34713-34717	6/63	
1605-1608	34727-34730	8/63	
1609-1612	34761-34764	11/63-12/63	
1613-1626	35130-35143	6/64-10/64	

Original Road No.	SBD	CSX	Status	Notes
L&N 1600	SBD 1600		R/85	
L&N 1601	SBD 1601		XLS/84	
L&N 1602	SBD 1602		XPL/85	2
L&N 1603	SBD 1603	CSX 3403	R/87	1
L&N 1604	SBD 1604		R/85	
L&N 1605	SBD 1605	CSX 3405	R/86	
L&N 1606	SBD 1606	CSX 3406	R/86	
L&N 1607	SBD 1607		R/85	
L&N 1608	SBD 1608	CSX 3408	R/86	1
L&N 1609	SBD 1609	CSX 3409	R	
L&N 1610	SBD 1610		R/85	1
L&N 1611	SBD 1611		XNIM/86	1
L&N 1612	SBD 1612	CSX 3412	R/86	
L&N 1613	SBD 1613		R/86	
L&N 1614	SBD 1614	CSX 3414	R/86	
L&N 1615	SBD 1615		R/85	
L&N 1616	SBD 1616	CSX 3416	P/90	3
L&N 1617	SBD 1617	CSX 3417	R 4/89	
L&N 1618	SBD 1618		R/85	
L&N 1619	SBD 1619		XPL/85	2
L&N 1620	SBD 1620	CSX 3420	R/88	
L&N 1621	SBD 1621		XFIM/86	
L&N 1622	SBD 1622		XCIM/87	
L&N 1623	SBD 1623	CSX 3423	R/86	
L&N 1624	SBD 1624		R/86	
L&N 1625	SBD 1625	CSX 3425	XWC/88	
L&N 1626	SBD 1626	CSX 3426	R	1

Notes:
1) L&N 1603, 1608, 1610, 1611, 1615 and 1626 equipped to operate with slugs in yard service 1979-1980.
2) Traded in to GE on SBD B36-7's.
3) CSX 3416 last active CSX U25B; stored Waycross, GA., 4/1/89. Donated to B&O Museum 1990. On loan to Tennessee Valley Railroad Museum, Chattanooga, Tennessee, for restoration and display in 1993.

Milwaukee Road

U25B	Serial	Built	Options/Notes
380-391	35632-35643	6/65-8/65	

Original Road No.	1968 Re#	1973 Re#	Status	Notes
MILW 380			WX/68	1
MILW 381	MILW 5000	MILW 5050	XMC/84	
MILW 382	MILW 5001	MILW 5051	XMC/84	
MILW 383	MILW 5002	MILW 5052	XEH/84	
MILW 384	MILW 5003	MILW 5053	XMC/84	
MILW 385	MILW 5004	MILW 5054	XEH/84	
MILW 386	MILW 5005	MILW 5055	XMC/84	
MILW 387	MILW 5006	MILW 5056	P	2
MILW 388	MILW 5007	MILW 5057	P/84	3
MILW 389	MILW 5008	MILW 5058	Rx	
MILW 390	MILW 5009	MILW 5059	XMC/84	
MILW 391	MILW 5010	MILW 5060	Rx	

Notes:
1) MILW 380 wrecked Whitman, MN, 1966. Traded to GE for wreck replacement U28B MILW 380.
2) MILW 5056 sold to Miller Compressing for scrap in 1984; acquired by Illinois Railway Museum, Union, IL.
3) MILW 5057 to Webster Technical College, Sidney, NE, in 1984; then to Feather River Rail Society, Portola, CA, for display.

New York Central

U25B	Serial	Built	Options/Notes
2500-2529	34986-35015	1/64-9/64	
2530-2559	35423-35452	11/64-2/65	
2560-2569	35700 35691-35699	7/65-9/65	

Original Road No.	PC	CR	Status	Notes
NYC 2500	PC 2500	CR 2500	P	1
NYC 2501	PC 2501	CR 2501	TGX/83	2
NYC 2502	PC 2502	CR 2502	XPL/84	
NYC 2503	PC 2503	CR 2503	TGX/83	2
NYC 2504	PC 2504	CR 2504	TGX/83	2
NYC 2505	PC 2505	CR 2505	XCRH/87	
NYC 2506	PC 2506	CR 2506	XNIM/81	
NYC 2507	PC 2507	CR 2507	Rx	
NYC 2508	PC 2508	CR 2508	TGX/83	2
NYC 2509	PC 2509	CR 2509	XNIM/81	
NYC 2510	PC 2510	CR 2510	P	3
NYC 2511	PC 2511	CR 2511	XPL/84	
NYC 2512	PC 2512	CR 2512	Rx	
NYC 2513	PC 2513	CR 2513	XPL/84	
NYC 2514	PC 2514	CR 2514	Rx	
NYC 2515	PC 2515	CR 2515	XPL/84	
NYC 2516	PC 2516	CR 2516	XPL/84	
NYC 2517	PC 2517	CR 2517	TGX/83	2
NYC 2518	PC 2518	CR 2518	TGX/83	2
NYC 2519	PC 2519	CR 2519	XPL/84	
NYC 2520	PC 2520	CR 2520	Rx	
NYC 2521	PC 2521	CR 2521	TGX/83	2
NYC 2522	PC 2522	CR 2522	XMSA/81	
NYC 2523	PC 2523	CR 2523	XPL/84	
NYC 2524	PC 2524	CR 2524	XPL/84	
NYC 2525	PC 2525	CR 2525	XMSA/81	
NYC 2526	PC 2526	CR 2526	TGX/83	2
NYC 2527	PC 2527	CR 2527	TGX/83	2
NYC 2528	PC 2528	CR 2528	TGX/83	2
NYC 2529	PC 2529	CR 2529	TGX/83	2
NYC 2530	PC 2530	CR 2530	XMSA/81	
NYC 2531	PC 2531	CR 2531	TGX/83	2
NYC 2532	PC 2532	CR 2532	Rx	
NYC 2533	PC 2533	CR 2533	XPL/84	
NYC 2534	PC 2534	CR 2534	TGX/83	2
NYC 2535	PC 2535	CR 2535	XPL/84	
NYC 2536	PC 2536	CR 2536	Rx	5
NYC 2537	PC 2537		WX/68	4
NYC 2538	PC 2538	CR 2538	XCRH/87	
NYC 2539	PC 2539	CR 2539	XPL/84	
NYC 2540	PC 2540	CR 2540	XCRH/87	
NYC 2541	PC 2541	CR 2541	XCRH/87	
NYC 2542	PC 2542	CR 2542	XMSA/81	
NYC 2543	PC 2543	CR 2543	XNIM/86	
NYC 2544	PC 2544	CR 2544	XNIM/86	
NYC 2545	PC 2545	CR 2545	TGX/83	2
NYC 2546	PC 2546	CR 2546	NIM/86	
NYC 2547	PC 2547	CR 2547	TGX/83	2
NYC 2548	PC 2548	CR 2548	XNIM/86	
NYC 2549	PC 2549	CR 2549	XNIM/86	
NYC 2550	PC 2550	CR 2550	XPL/84	
NYC 2551	PC 2551	CR 2551	XPL/84	
NYC 2552	PC 2552	CR 2552	Rx	
NYC 2553	PC 2553	CR 2553	TGX/83	2
NYC 2554	PC 2554	CR 2554	XPL/84	2
NYC 2555	PC 2555	CR 2555	Rx	5
NYC 2556	PC 2556	CR 2556	Rx	
NYC 2557	PC 2557	CR 2557	TGX/83	2, 6
NYC 2558	PC 2558	CR 2558	XPL/84	6
NYC 2559	PC 2559	CR 2559	TGX/83	2, 6
NYC 2560	PC 2560	CR 2560	XPL/84	
NYC 2561	PC 2561		WX/71	7
NYC 2562	PC 2562	CR 2562	XMSA/81	
NYC 2563	PC 2563	CR 2563	TGX/83	2
NYC 2564	PC 2564	CR 2564	XPL/84	
NYC 2565	PC 2565	CR 2565	XCRH/87	
NYC 2566	PC 2566	CR 2566	XMSA/81	
NYC 2567	PC 2567	CR 2567	XCRH/87	
NYC 2568	PC 2568	CR 2568	XNIM/86	
NYC 2569	PC 2569	CR 2569	TGX/83	2

Notes:
1) CR 2500 preserved North East, PA. Restored to NYC 2500 at GE Erie, PA., in 1993.
2) Traded in to GE in 1983 on CR B36-7's 5000-5059.
3) CR 2510 preserved by NRHS Mohawk & Hudson River Chapter, Glenmount, NY.
4) NYC 2537 wrecked Ashtabula, OH, 9/23/68 after coal train lost brakes south of Asthtabula and ran away. Train derailed at OD Tower; NYC 2537, B&M 1710, 1735, PC 7447 and 66 cars derailed. NYC 2537 scrapped on site.
5) NYC 2555 equipped as master unit for radio controlled, mid-train helper tests in 1968; NYC 2536 equipped as receiver.
6) NYC 2557-2559 rated at 2800 h.p.
7) PC 2561 wrecked 12/25/71 and scrapped.

New York, New Haven & Hartford

U25B	Serial	Built	Options/Notes
2500-2509	35394-35403	10/64	
2510-2525	35718-35733	10/65-11/65	

Original Road No.	PC	CR	Status	Notes
NH 2500	PC 2660	CR 2660	XMSA/81	
NH 2501	PC 2661	CR 2661	XCRH/87	
NH 2502	PC 2662	CR 2662	Rx	
NH 2503	PC 2663	CR 2663	XMSA/81	
NH 2504	PC 2664	CR 2664	XCRH/87	
NH 2505	PC 2665	CR 2665	XMSA/81	
NH 2506	PC 2666	CR 2666	XCRH/87	
NH 2507	PC 2667	CR 2667	XPL/84	
NH 2508	PC 2668	CR 2668	XNIM/81	
NH 2509	PC 2669	CR 2669	Rx	
NH 2510	PC 2670	CR 2670	XPL/84	
NH 2511	PC 2671	CR 2671	Rx	
NH 2512	PC 2672	CR 2672	TGX/83	2
NH 2513	PC 2673	CR 2673	XNIM/81	
NH 2514	PC 2674	CR 2674	TGX/83	2
NH 2515	PC 2675	CR 2675	XPL/84	
NH 2516	PC 2676	CR 2676	XPL/84	
NH 2517	PC 2677	CR 2677	XCRH/87	
NH 2518	PC 2678	CR 2678	XCRH/87	
NH 2519	PC 2679	CR 2679	XCRH/87	
NH 2520			WX/68	1
	PC 2680	CR 2680*	XMSA/81	1
NH 2521	PC 2681	CR 2681	XCRH/87	
NH 2522	PC 2682	CR 2682	XCRH/87	
NH 2523	PC 2683	CR 2683	Rx	
NH 2524	PC 2684	CR 2684	XCRH/87	
NH 2525	PC 2685	CR 2685	PO/85	3

Notes:
1) Detouring freight lead by NH 2520, 2508 and 2503 collided with NH RS3 526 working yard at Walpole, MA, 12/17/68. New frame supplied to build wreck replacement outshopped as PC 2680.
2) Traded in to GE in 1983 on CR B36-7's 5000-5059.
3) CR 2685 to Connecticut Valley Railway Museum, Essex, CT, in 1985. Restored to operating condition as NH 2525.

Norfolk & Western

U25B	Serial	Built	Options/Notes
3515	35581	2/65	

Original Road No.	1970 Re#	Status	Notes
N&W 3515	N&W 8138	X/75	1

Notes:
1) N&W 3515 built as wreck replacement for Wabash 512. Retired 2/19/75 and scrapped.

Pennsylvania

U25B	Serial	Built	Options/Notes
2500-2506	34528-34534	8/62	
2507-2528	34539-34560	9/62-10/62	
2529-2533	35124-35128	9/64	
2534-2548	35530-35544	2/65-3/65	
2649-2658	35773-35782	11/65-12/65	

Original Road No.	1966 Re#	PC	CR	Status	Notes
PRR 2500	PRR 2600	PC 2600	CR 2600	XNIM/81	1
PRR 2501	PRR 2601	PC 2601	CR 2601	XNIM/86	1
PRR 2502	PRR 2602	PC 2602	CR 2602	XPL/84	1
PRR 2503	PRR 2603	PC 2603		WX/72	1, 2
PRR 2504	PRR 2604	PC 2604	CR 2604	PACY/X	1, 3
PRR 2505	PRR 2605	PC 2605	CR 2605	PACY/X	1, 3
PRR 2506	PRR 2606	PC 2606	CR 2606	PACY/X	1, 3, 6
PRR 2507	PRR 2607	PC 2607	CR 2607	XMSA/81	
PRR 2508	PRR 2608	PC 2608	CR 2608	XPL/84	
PRR 2509	PRR 2609	PC 2609	CR 2609	XPL/84	
PRR 2510	PRR 2610	PC 2610	CR 2610	XPL/84	
PRR 2511	PRR 2611	PC 2611	CR 2611	XCRH/87	6
PRR 2512	PRR 2612	PC 2612	CR 2612	XNIM/86	
PRR 2513	PRR 2613	PC 2613	CR 2613	XMSA/81	
PRR 2514	PRR 2614	PC 2614	CR 2614	XPL/84	
PRR 2515	PRR 2615	PC 2615	CR 2615	XPL/84	
PRR 2516	PRR 2616	PC 2616	CR 2616	XPL/84	
PRR 2517	PRR 2617	PC 2617	CR 2617	TGX/83	4
PRR 2518	PRR 2618	PC 2618	CR 2618	TGX/83	4
PRR 2519	PRR 2619	PC 2619	CR 2619	XMSA/81	
PRR 2520	PRR 2620	PC 2620	CR 2620	XNIM/86	
PRR 2521	PRR 2621	PC 2621	CR 2621	TGX/83	4
PRR 2522	PRR 2622	PC 2622	CR 2622	XNIM/86	
PRR 2523	PRR 2623	PC 2623	CR 2623	XNIM/86	6
PRR 2524	PRR 2624	PC 2624	CR 2624	TGX/83	4
PRR 2525	PRR 2625	PC 2625	CR 2625	XPNC/81	
PRR 2526	PRR 2626	PC 2626	CR 2626	TGX/83	4
PRR 2527	PRR 2627	PC 2627	CR 2627	XNIM/86	
PRR 2528	PRR 2628	PC 2628	CR 2628	XNIM/86	
PRR 2529	PRR 2629	PC 2629	CR 2629	TGX/83	4
PRR 2530	PRR 2630	PC 2630	CR 2630	XNIM/86	
PRR 2531	PRR 2631	PC 2631	CR 2631	XCRH/87	
PRR 2532	PRR 2632	PC 2632	CR 2632	XCRH/87	
PRR 2533	PRR 2633	PC 2633	CR 2633	XPL/84	
PRR 2534	PRR 2634	PC 2634	CR 2634	Rx	
PRR 2535	PRR 2635	PC 2635	CR 2635	TGX/83	4
PRR 2536	PRR 2636	PC 2636	CR 2636	XMSA/81	
PRR 2537	PRR 2637	PC 2637	CR 2637	XCRH/87	
PRR 2538	PRR 2638	PC 2638	CR 2638	XMSA/81	
PRR 2539	PRR 2639	PC 2639	CR 2639	XMSA/81	
PRR 2540	PRR 2640	PC 2640	CR 2640	XMSA/81	
PRR 2541	PRR 2641	PC 2641	CR 2641	XPL/84	
PRR 2542	PRR 2642	PC 2642	CR 2642	XCRH/87	
PRR 2543	PRR 2643	PC 2643	CR 2643	XCRH/87	
PRR 2544	PRR 2644	PC 2644	CR 2644	XPL/84	
PRR 2545	PRR 2645	PC 2645	CR 2645	XMSA/81	
PRR 2546	PRR 2646	PC 2646	CR 2646	XMSA/81	
PRR 2547	PRR 2647	PC 2647	CR 2647	XPL/84	
PRR 2548	PRR 2648	PC 2648	CR 2648	TGX/83	4
PRR 2649		PC 2649	CR 2649	XPL/84	5
PRR 2650		PC 2650	CR 2650	XCRH/87	
PRR 2651		PC 2651	CR 2651	XPL/84	
PRR 2652		PC 2652	CR 2652	XNIM/86	
PRR 2653		PC 2653	CR 2653	Rx/78	
PRR 2654		PC 2654	CR 2654	XNIM/81	
PRR 2655		PC 2655	CR 2655	XCRH/87	
PRR 2656		PC 2656	CR 2656	XCRH/87	
PRR 2657		PC 2657	CR 2657	TGX/83	4
PRR 2658		PC 2658	CR 2658	XCRH/87	

Notes:
1) PRR 2500-2506 financed through PRR subsidiary Waynesburg & Washington.
2) PC 2603 wrecked at Herndon, PA, 3/12/72 and scrapped.
3) CR 2604-2606 leased and relettered Prairie Central (through Waynesburg & Washington) in 1981. Stored after PACY shut down May 1984. Units scrapped.
4) Traded in to GE 1983 on CR B36-7's 5000-5059.

Pennsylvania U25B Notes Cont.

5) PRR 2649 wrecked c.2/66 between Conemaugh and Johnstown, PA, in 40 mph collision with helpers on stock train (PRR RSD15 8611 trailing). PRR 2649 suffered bent frame, nose and front end damage. Sent to GE for repairs. (Wreck replacement built?)
6) PC 2606, 2611, 2623 upgraded to 2800 h.p. 11/68.

Rock Island

U25B	Serial	Built	Options/Notes
200-205	34707-34712	5/63	
206-211	34718-34723	9/63-10/63	
212-224	35111-35123	4/64-6/64	
225-238	35701-35714	9/65-10/65	

Original Road No.	MEC	Status	Notes	Slug Rebuild
RI 200		Rx/79		
RI 201		Slug	1	RI 54
RI 202		Rx/79		
RI 203			1	RI 50
RI 204		Rx/80	3	
RI 205		Rx/80	3	
RI 206		Rx/80	3	
RI 207		Rx/79		
RI 208		Rx/79		
RI 209		Rx/80	3	
RI 210		Slug	1	RI 55
RI 211		Rx/80	3	
RI 212		WX/66	2	
RI 213		Rx/80	3	
RI 214		Rx/80	3	
RI 215		Rx/80	3	
RI 216		Rx/80	3	
RI 217		Rx/80	3	
RI 218		XCCS/81		
RI 219		XCCS/81		
RI 220		XCCS/81		
RI 221		WX/66	2	
RI 222		Slug	4	RI 284
RI 223		Rx/80		
RI 224		Rx/80	3	
RI 225	MEC 225	XMSA/88	5	
RI 226	MEC 226	XMEC/91	5	
RI 227	[MEC 227]	X/MEC	6	
RI 228	MEC 228	XMSA/88	5	
RI 229	MEC 229	XMSA/88	5	
RI 230	MEC 230	XMEC/88	5	
RI 231	MEC 231	WX/87	5, 8	
RI 232	MEC 232	XMEC/88	5	
RI 233	[MEC 233]	XMEC	6	
RI 234	MEC 234	XMSA/88	5, 7	
RI 235	[MEC 235]	X/MEC	6	
RI 236	[MEC 236]	XMCB/83	6	
RI 237	[MEC 237]	XMCB/83	6	
RI 238	MEC 238	XMSA/88	5	

Notes:
1) Rebuilt to slug Silvis (IL) shops: 201 to RI 54 8/79; 203 to 50 7/79 (re# 53); 210 to 55 03/80. RI 55 completed at Silvis after RI shut down and sold to Sandersville RR. 08/81.
2) RI 212 and 221 wrecked Logan, NM, 3/9/66 and traded to GE for U28B's 254 and 261.
3) Retired with ROCK shut down 3/80; all presumed scrapped at Silvis.
4) RI 222 wrecked and rebuilt Silvis 2/8/77 to RI slug 284 "The Great American Energy Saver" to run with U33B's 297 and 298.
5) Sold to MEC 6/80.
6) Sold to MEC 6/80. Cannibalized for parts; never operated.
7) Only RI U25B painted in ROCK blue and white scheme. Operated as MEC 234 in same paint until repainted MEC orange late/82.
8) MEC 231 wrecked in three-train collision at Fitchburg, MA.,1/27/87 and scrapped.

St. Louis-San Francisco

U25B	Serial	Built	Options/Notes
800-803	34227/231 34232/229	11/61-12/61	High Nose
804-807	34220-34223	1/61-2/61	High Nose/ex GE
808-811	34573/71-72 34563	7/63	
812-815	34561-2/64-5	4/63	ex-GE Demos
816-823	35522-35529	3/65	
824-831	35761-35768	1/66-2/66	

Original Road No.	SL-SF	BN	Status	Notes
SL-SF 800			TGX/77	1
SL-SF 801			TGX/77	1
SL-SF 802			TGX/77	1,4
SL-SF 803			TGX/77	1
GE 753	SL-SF 804		TGX/77	1, 2
GE 754	SL-SF 805		TGX/77	1,2,4
GE 755	SL-SF 806		TGX/77	1,2,4
GE 756	SL-SF 807		TGX/77	1,2,4
SL-SF 808		BN 5210	XPNC/81	
SL-SF 809		BN 5211	XPNC/81	
SL-SF 810		BN 5212	XPNC/81	
SL-SF 811		BN 5213	XPNC/81	
GE 51	SL-SF 812	BN 5214	XPNC/81	3
GE 54	SL-SF 813	BN 5215	XPNC/81	3
GE 52	SL-SF 814	BN 5216	XPNC/81	3
GE 53	SL-SF 815	BN 5217	XPNC/81	3
SL-SF 816		BN 5218	XPNC/81	
SL-SF 817		BN 5219	XPNC/81	
SL-SF 818		BN 5220	XPNC/81	
SL-SF 819		BN 5221	XPNC/81	
SL-SF 820		BN 5222	XPNC/81	
SL-SF 821		BN 5223	XPNC/81	
SL-SF 822		BN 5224	XPNC/81	
SL-SF 823		BN 5225	XPNC/81	
SL-SF 824		BN 5226	XPNC/81	
SL-SF 825		BN 5227	XPNC/81	
SL-SF 826		BN 5228	XPNC/81	
SL-SF 827		BN 5229	XPNC/81	
SL-SF 828		BN 5230	XPNC/81	
SL-SF 829		BN 5231	XPNC/81	
SL-SF 830		BN 5232	XPNC/81	
SL-SF 831		BN 5233	XPNC/81	5

Notes:
1) Traded in to GE in 1977 on SL-SF B30-7's 863-870.
2) GE 753-756 sold to SL-SF 12/61.
3) GE 51-54 sold to SL-SF 7/63.
4) SL-SF 802, 805-807 leased to Conrail by GE in 1978, then scrapped.
5) SL-SF 831 last U25B built.

Southern Pacific

U25B	Serial	Built	Options/Notes
7500-7505	34240-34245	3/62-4/62	
7506-7514	34698-34706	3/63-4/63	
7515-7527	34685-34697	3/63	
7528-7564	34765-34801	1/64-3/64	

Original Road No.	1966 Re#	3rd No.	4th No.	Status & Notes		Slug Rebuild
SP 7500	SP 6700			XNM/85	10	
SP 7501	SP 6701			XNM/85	10	
SP 7502	SP 6702			XNM/85	10	
SP 7503	SP 6703			XNM/85	10	
SP 7504	SP 6704			XNM/85	10	
SP 7505	SP 6705			XNM/85	10	
SP 7506	SP 6706			XNM/85	10	
SP 7507	SP 6707			XNM/85	10	
SP 7508	SP 6708	SP 6800	SP 3100	PO/88	1	
SP 7509	SP 6709			WX/73	2	
SP 7510	SP 6710			XNM/85	10	
SP 7511	SP 6711			TEBU	3	SP 1608
SP 7512	SP 6712			TEBU	3	SP 1606
SP 7513	SP 6713			XCC/78		
SP 7514	SP 6714			WX/77	4	
SP 7515	SP 6715			XNM/85	10	
SP 7516	SP 6716			XNM/85	10	
SP 7517	SP 6717	SP 7031		XLM/87	5	
SP 7518	SP 6718			XNM/85	10	
SP 7519	SP 6719			XNM/85	10	
SP 7520	SP 6720			XNM/85	10	
SP 7521	SP 6721			XNM/85	10	
SP 7522	SP 6722			XNM/85	10	
SP 7523	SP 6723			XNM/85	10	
SP 7524	SP 6724	SP 6801	SP 3101	XLM/87	6	
SP 7525	SP 6725			XNM/85	10	
SP 7526	SP 6726			XNM/85	10	
SP 7527	SP 6727			XNM/85	10	
SP 7528	SP 6728			XNM/85	10	
SP 7529	SP 6729			XNM/85	10	
SP 7530	SP 6730			XNM/85	10	
SP 7531	SP 6731			XNM/85	10	
SP 7532	SP 6732			XNM/85	10	
SP 7533	SP 6733	SP 7032		XLM/87	5	
SP 7534	SP 6734			XNM/85	10	
SP 7535	SP 6735			XNM/85	10	
SP 7536	SP 6736			TEBU	3	SP 1603
SP 7537	SP 6737			XNM/85	10	
SP 7538	SP 6738			XNM/85	10	
SP 7539	SP 6739			WX/73	7	
SP 7540	SP 6740			XNM/85	10	
SP 7541	SP 6741			TEBU	3	SP 1607
SP 7542	SP 6742			WX/77	8	
SP 7543	SP 6743			XNM/85	10	
SP 7544	SP 6744			TEBU	3	SP 1604
SP 7545	SP 6745	SP 7030		XLM/87	5	
SP 7546	SP 6746			XNM/85	10	
SP 7547	SP 6747			TEBU	3	SP 1605
SP 7548	SP 6748			XCC/78		
SP 7549	SP 6749			XNM/85	10	
SP 7550	SP 6750			XNM/85	10	
SP 7551	SP 6751			TEBU	3	SP 1610
SP 7552	SP 6752	SP 7033		XLM/87	5	
SP 7553	SP 6753			XCC/78		
SP 7554	SP 6754			TEBU	3	SP 1611
SP 7555	SP 6755			XSW/87	9	
SP 7556	SP 6756			XNM/85	10	
SP 7557	SP 6757			XNM/85	10	
SP 7558	SP 6758			TEBU	3	SP 1612
SP 7559	SP 6759			XNM/85	10	
SP 7560	SP 6760			XNM/85	10	
SP 7561	SP 6761			TEBU	3	SP 1601
SP 7562	SP 6762			XNM/85	10	
SP 7563	SP 6763			XNM/85	10	
SP 7564	SP 6764			XNM/85	10	
SP 7565	SP 6765			TEBU	3	SP 1602
SP 7566	SP 6766			TEBU	3	SP 1613
SP 7567	SP 6767			XNM/85	10	

Notes:
1) SP 6708 rebuilt to "U25BE" 6800 at Sacramento (CA) shops 9/75. Repainted red-white-and-blue "Spirit of 1776" for Bicentennial. Restored to standard SP colors; renumbered 3100 6/79. Retired 12/84 and sold to Levin Metals for scrap 10/87. Acquired by Orange Empire Railway Museum Perris, CA., 2/88.
2) SP 6709 wrecked in 1973. Cannibalized at Houston, TX., and scrapped Intercontinental Steel, Houston, TX, 1974.
3) Rebuilt to TEBU Tractive Effort Booster Unit (road slug) at Sacramento (CA) Shops in 1981.
4) SP 6714 wrecked 1977 and scrapped 1978 at Proler Steel.
5) SP 6717, 6733, 6745 and 6752 to Morrison-Knudsen Boise, ID. 3-4/77. Rebuilt at M-K to Sulzer-powered TE70-4S's SP 7030-7033 outshopped 2/24/78. First units to wear short-lived experimental "Daylight" paint scheme. Retired after lengthy storage and sold for scrap in 1987.
6) SP 6724 rebuilt to "U25BE" 6801 at Sacramento (CA) shops 10/76. Renumbered to 3101 6/79.
7) SP 6739 wrecked El Monte, CA, 4/2/73. Sold to Chrome Crankshaft for scrap.
8) SP 6742 wrecked in 1977 and sold to Chrome Crankshaft for scrap in 1978.
9) SP 6755 last U25B on SP property. Stored Aurant Yd, Los Angeles, CA in 1986; to Southwest RR Car parts for scrap 10/87.
10) Sold to Chrome Locomotive and stripped of reusable parts. Moved to National Metals, Terminal Island, and loaded intact aboard Japanese ships for shipment to Far East as scrap.

Union Pacific

U25B	Serial	Built	Options/Notes
625-628	34224-34226 34228	8/61	High nose
629-632	34238/33/30/35	5/62	High nose
633-636	34239, 34234 34236-34237	2/62	ex-GE demos 634-636 High nose
637-640	34535-34538	8/62-9/62	

Original Road No.	2nd No.	M-K Rebuild	Status & Notes		Slug Rebuild
UP 625			XM-K/81	1	
UP 626			XM-K/81	1	
UP 627			WTGX/70	2	
UP 628			OC&E 7604	1,4,11	
UP 629			Slug	1,5,11	OC&E 7606
UP 630			M-K 5303	1,6	
UP 631			M-K 5302	1,6	
UP 632			Slug	9	RI 283; RI 51
GE 2501	UP 633	OC&E 7602		1,3,4,11	
GE 2503	UP 634			1,3,8	SP 1600
GE 2502	UP 635	M-K 5301	BMLP	1,3,6	
GE 2504	UP 636		Slug 3	5,11	OC&E 7607
UP 637			Weyh 310	1,7	Rx/86
UP 638			OC&E 7605	1,4,10,11	
UP 639			OC&E 7601	1,4,11	
UP 640			OC&E 7603	1,4,11	

Notes:
1) UP 625-626, 628-631, 633-640 retired 9/72 and sold to Morrison-Knudsen, Boise, ID, 6/74. Painted solid black and lettered M-K 1-14 (not in order) for movement to Boise.
2) UP 627, 632 and RS27 677 wrecked in collision at Aikins, KS 11/23/68. UP 627 retired 8/70 and traded in to GE 9/71 on U50C.
3) GE 2501-2504 sold to UP 7/62. 2502-2504 (634-636) high nose.
4) UP 639, 633, 640 and 628 rebuilt Morrison-Knudsen to TE53-1-4E's, repowered with EMD 16-567 engines. Outshopped 6/76-9/76 as Oregon, California & Eastern 7601-7605. OC&E shut down 5/90; units to Texas-based Econorail in 1991.
5) UP 629 and 636 rebuilt M-K to S3-3B model slugs. Outshopped 6/76 and 7/76 as OC&E 7606-7607 to operate with OC&E 7601-7605. UP 628 one of only two U-boats ever chop-nosed. Squaw Creek (ex-SOU) U33C 3809 only other U-boat chopped. OC&E shut down 5/90; units to Texas-based Econorail in 1991.
6) UP 635, 631, 630 rebuilt to TE53-4E's by M-K. Cut down to frame, re-engined with EMD 16-567B engines from B&O F7's and D12 main generators. completely new carbodies built and units outshopped 8/75-9/75 as M-K 5301-5303. Used on work project on Black Mesa & Lake Powell. M-K 5301 purchased by BM&LP 1/77.
7) UP 637 rebuilt M-K to TE53-1-4E, repowered with EMD 16-567 and outshopped 12/75 as Weyerhauser Timber 310 for use on Headquarters, WA line. 8) UP 634 rebuilt M-K to S3-3B slug. Outshopped 5/80 as SP 1600.
9) UP 632 re-engined with 2500 h.p. 12-7FDL 4/69 as test bed for U50C development. Engine removed c.9/72 and hulk sold to Rock Island for parts. RI Silvis shops rebuilt 632 to slug outshopped 4/78 as RI 283. Renumbered RI 51 in 1979.
10) UP 638—stripped of engine and other components—repainted 7/73 to "We Can Handle It" scheme and briefly displayed with caboose, then returned to deadline.
11) Oregon, California & Eastern shut down 5/90; units to Texas-based Econorail in 1991.

Wabash

U25B	Serial	Built	Options/Notes
500	34254	5/62	A,B
501	34522	8/62	
502-505	34256-34259	5/62	
506-511	34519-21 34524/23/25	8/62	
512-513	34526-34527	8/62	
514	34255	5/62	

Original Road No.	N&W	1970 Re#	Status	Notes
WAB 500	N&W 3529	N&W 8152	XNIM/75	
WAB 501	N&W 3522	N&W 8145	XNIM/75	
WAB 502	N&W 3520	N&W 8143	XNIM/75	
WAB 503	N&W 3518	N&W 8141	XNIM/75	
WAB 504	N&W 3517	N&W 8140	XNIM/75	
WAB 505	N&W 3524	N&W 8147	XNIM/75	
WAB 506	N&W 3526	N&W 8149	XNIM/75	
WAB 507	N&W 3523	N&W 8146	XNIM/75	3
WAB 508	N&W 3521	N&W 8144	XNIM/75	
WAB 509	N&W 3516	N&W 8139	XNIM/75	
WAB 510	N&W 3525	N&W 8148	XNIM/75	
WAB 511	N&W 3528	N&W 8151	XNIM/75	
WAB 512			WX/64	1
WAB 513	N&W 3519	N&W 8142	XNIM/75	
WAB 514	N&W 3527	N&W 8150	WX/73	2

Notes:
A) Traction motors from GE 751-752 re-used in Wabash U25B order.
B) All overhauled by GE 1965-66; renumbered 3516-3529 (not in order).
1) Wabash 512 and C424 B902 wrecked 10/4/64 at Hannibal, MO. Wrecked 512 traded in to GE on N&W U25B 3515 purchased as replacement.
2) N&W 1920 and 8150 wrecked at Kansas City on ATSF in 1973. 8150 retired 12/27/73 and sold to United Iron & Metal, Roanoke, VA, for scrap 5/74.
3) Frame and trucks from one unit—possibly 8146—sold 1977 to Southeast Specialties, Jacksonville, FL and rebuilt 6/80 to slug: Georgetown RR S-1.

U25C

Atlantic Coast Line

U25C	Serial	Built	Options/Notes
3000-3003	34969-34972	12/63	
3004-3010	35064-35070	11/64	
3011-3013	35609-35611	10/65	
3014-3020	35612-35618	10/65-11/65	

Original Road No.	SBD	NdeM	Status	Notes
ACL 3000	SCL 2100	NdeM 7700	OS	2
ACL 3001	SCL 2101	NdeM 7701	OS	2
ACL 3002	SCL 2102	NdeM 7702	OS	2
ACL 3003	SCL 2103	NdeM 7703	OS	2
ACL 3004	SCL 2104	NdeM 7704	OS	2
ACL 3005	SCL 2105	NdeM 7705	OS	2
ACL 3006	SCL 2106	NdeM 7706	OS	2
ACL 3007	SCL 2107	NdeM 7707	OS	2
ACL 3008	SCL 2108	NdeM 7708	OS	2
ACL 3009	SCL 2109		XGEH/80	3
ACL 3010	SCL 2110	NdeM 7710	OS	2
ACL 3011	SCL 2111	NdeM 7800	OS	1,2
ACL 3012	SCL 2112	NdeM 7801	OS	1,2
ACL 3013	SCL 2113	NdeM 7802	OS	1,2
ACL 3014	SCL 2114	NdeM 7711	OS	2
ACL 3015	SCL 2115	NdeM 7712	WX	2
ACL 3016	SCL 2116	NdeM 7713	OS	2
ACL 3017	SCL 2117	NdeM 7714	OS	2
ACL 3018	SCL 2118	NdeM 7715	OS	2
ACL 3019	SCL 2119	NdeM 7716	OS	2
ACL 3020	SCL 2120		XGEH/80	3

Notes:
1) ACL 3011-3013 rated at 2800 h.p.
2) To NdeM 1980. Overhauled and repainted NdeM 7700-7716 at GE Hornell, NY. All out of service in Mexico by mid eighties.
3) SCL 2109 and 2120 scrapped by GE Hornell, NY, in 1980.

Chicago, Burlington & Quincy

U25C	Serial	Built	Options/Notes
550-561	35597-35608	8/65-9/65	

Original Road No.	BN	Status	Notes
CB&Q 550	BN 5630	XNIM/80	
CB&Q 551	BN 5631	WX/78	1
CB&Q 552	BN 5632	XNIM/80	
CB&Q 553	BN 5633	XNIM/80	
CB&Q 554	BN 5634	XNIM/80	
CB&Q 555	BN 5635	XNIM/80	
CB&Q 556	BN 5636	XNIM/80	
CB&Q 557	BN 5637	XNIM/80	
CB&Q 558	BN 5638	XNIM/80	
CB&Q 559	BN 5639	XNIM/80	
CB&Q 560	BN 5640	XNIM/80	
CB&Q 561	BN 5641	XNIM/80	

Notes:
1) BN 5631 wrecked 12/78 and scrapped 3/80.
2) BN 5630, 5632-5641 retired 8/80 and returned to lessor. To Naporano Iron & Metal 9/80 for scrap.

Lake Superior & Ishpeming

U25C	Serial	Built	Options/Notes
2500-2501	35062-35063	5/64-7/64	

Original Road No.	Status	Notes
LS&I 2500	X/90	1
LS&I 2501	P/92	2

Notes:
1) LS&I 2500 stored unserviceable 12/84; retired 10/89. Scrapped at Eagle Mills in 1990.
2) LS&I 2501 last U25C in operation anywhere. Out of service with engine and fire damage from at least 1982 until overhauled in 1986. Retired 10/89; prime mover installed in LS&I 3051. On display with caboose at Presque Isle Park, Marquette, MI.

Louisville & Nashville

U25C	Serial	Built	Options/Notes
1500-1517	35545-35546 35548-35557 35547 35558-35562	5/65-10/65	

Original Road No.	Status	Notes
L&N 1500	X	
L&N 1501	X	
L&N 1502	X	
L&N 1503	X	
L&N 1504	X	
L&N 1505	X	
L&N 1506	X	
L&N 1507	X	
L&N 1508	X	
L&N 1509	X	
L&N 1510	X	
L&N 1511	X	
L&N 1512	XNIM/86	
L&N 1513	X	
L&N 1514	XNIM/86	
L&N 1515	X	
L&N 1516	Rx/85	
L&N 1517	Rx/85	

Northern Pacific

U25C	Serial	Built	Options/Notes
2500-2514	35035-35049	5/64-6/64	
2515-2529	35582-35596	5/65-7/65	

Original Road No.	BN	Status	Notes
NP 2500	BN 5600	XHM/81	
NP 2501	BN 5601	XNIM/81	
NP 2502	BN 5602	XNIM/81	
NP 2503	BN 5603	XNIM/81	
NP 2504	BN 5604	XNIM/81	
NP 2505	BN 5605	XNIM/81	
NP 2506	BN 5606	XNIM/81	
NP 2507	BN 5607	XNIM/81	
NP 2508	BN 5608	XNIM/81	
NP 2509	BN 5609	XNIM/81	
NP 2510	BN 5610	XNIM/81	
NP 2511	BN 5611	XNIM/81	
NP 2512	BN 5612	XNIM/81	
NP 2513	BN 5613	XNIM/81	
NP 2514	BN 5614	XNIM/81	
NP 2515	BN 5615	XNIM/81	
NP 2516	BN 5616	XNIM/81	
NP 2517	BN 5617	XNIM/81	
NP 2518	BN 5618	XNIM/81	
NP 2519	BN 5619	XNIM/81	
NP 2520	BN 5620	XNIM/81	
NP 2521	BN 5621	XNIM/81	
NP 2522	BN 5622	XSS/81	
NP 2523	BN 5623	XNIM/81	
NP 2524	BN 5624	XNIM/81	
NP 2525	BN 5625	XNIM/81	
NP 2526	BN 5626	XSS/81	
NP 2527	BN 5627	XNIM/81	
NP 2528	BN 5628	XSS/81	
NP 2529	BN 5629	XSS/81	

Oro Dam Constructors

U25C	Serial	Built	Options/Notes
8010-8013	34815-34818	9/63	
8014-8016	34819-34821	3/64	
8017-8019	35563-35564 35629	12/65	

Original Road No.	2nd ORO	L&N	Status	Notes
ORO 8010			WX/65	1
ORO 8011	ORO 8020	L&N 1520	XNIM/86	1, 2, 3
ORO 8012		L&N 1518	XNIM/86	2, 3
ORO 8013		L&N 1519	XNIM/86	2, 3
ORO 8014		L&N 1521	XNIM/86	2, 3
ORO 8015		L&N 1522	XNIM/86	2, 3
ORO 8016			WX/65	1
ORO 8017		L&N 1523	XNIM/86	2, 3
ORO 8018		L&N 1524	XNIM/86	2, 3
ORO 8019		L&N 1525	XNIM/86	2, 3

Notes:
1) ORO Dam 8010 first U25C built. ORO 8010, 8011 on westbound empties collided head-on with 8016, 8014 on eastbound loads 10/7/65. ORO 8010 and 8016 scrapped at Zephyr, CA 12/65. ORO 8011 rebuilt at WP Sacramento (CA) shops and outshopped 6/66 as ORO 8020. ORO 8014 repaired and returned to service. ORO 8017-8019 purchased as wreck replacements. ORO 8019 last U25C built.
2) Sold to L&N at completion of project 10/67.
3) Retired 5/28/85 and traded-in to GE. Scrapped by NI&M.

Pennsylvania

U25C	Serial	Built	Options/Notes
6500-6509	35050-35059	4/65	Serials not sequential
6510-6519	35619-35628	11/65-12/65	

Original Road No.	PC	CR	1978 Re#	Status	Notes
PRR 6500	PC 6500	CR 6500	CR 6800	TGX/83	1,3
PRR 6501	PC 6501	CR 6501	CR 6801	TGX/83	1,3
PRR 6502	PC 6502	CR 6502	CR 6802	XPL/84	1,3
PRR 6503	PC 6503	CR 6503	CR 6803	TGX/83	1,3
PRR 6504	PC 6504	CR 6504	CR 6804	TGX/83	1,3
PRR 6505	PC 6505	CR 6505	CR 6805	TGX/83	1,3
PRR 6506	PC 6506	CR 6506	CR 6806	TGX/83	1,3
PRR 6507	PC 6507	CR 6507	CR 6807	TGX/83	1,3
PRR 6508	PC 6508	CR 6508	CR 6808	TGX/83	1,3
PRR 6509	PC 6509	CR 6509	CR 6809	TGX/83	1,3
PRR 6510	PC 6510	CR 6510	CR 6810	XPL/84	3
PRR 6511	PC 6511	CR 6511	CR 6811	TGX/83	3
PRR 6512	PC 6512	CR 6512	CR 6812	TGX/83	3
PRR 6513	PC 6513	CR 6513	CR 6813	XMSA/81	
PRR 6514	PC 6514	CR 6514	CR 6814	TGX/83	3
PRR 6515	PC 6515	CR 6515	CR 6815	TGX/83	3
PRR 6516	PC 6516	CR 6516	CR 6816	TGX/83	3
PRR 6517	PC 6517	CR 6517	CR 6817	XMSA/81	
PRR 6518	PC 6518	CR 6518	CR 6818	TGX/83	3
PRR 6519	PC 6519	CR 6519	CR 6819	TGX/83	3

Notes:
1) Serial sequence: 35050-35059 PRR 6504/05/06-09/6503/6500-6502.
2) Renumbered in 1978 to accommodate CR SD40-2's 6483-6524.
3) Traded in to GE 1983 on CR B36-7's 5000-5059.

U50

Southern Pacific

U50	Serial	Built	Options/Notes
8500-8502	34945-34947	5/64-6/64	A

Original Road No.	1965 Re#	1969 Re#	Status	Notes
SP 8500	SP 9550	SP 9950	XPT/78	
SP 8501	SP 9551	SP 9951	XPT/79	
SP 8502	SP 9552	SP 9952	XPT/79	

Notes:
A) SP 8500-8502 built using span bolster frames from traded-in UP turbines.

Union Pacific

U50	Serial	Built	Options/Notes
31-33	34891-34893	10/63	A
34-45	35094-35105	7/64-9/64	A
46-53	35644-35651	5/65-8/65	A

Original Road No.	Status	Notes
UP 31	TGX/74	
UP 32	TGX/74	
UP 33	TGX/73	
UP 34	TGX/74	
UP 35	TGX/73	
UP 36	TGX/74	
UP 37	TGX/74	
UP 38	TGX/73	
UP 39	TGX/74	
UP 40	TGX/74	
UP 41	TGX/74	
UP 42	TGX/74	
UP 43	TGX/74	
UP 44	TGX/74	
UP 45	XEC/77	
UP 46	TGX/73	
UP 47	TGX/74	
UP 48	TGX/74	
UP 49	TGX/74	
UP 50	TGX/74	
UP 51	XEC/77	
UP 52	TGX/73	1
UP 53	XEC/77	

Notes:
A) Built using reconditioned span-bolstered trucks from gas turbines in 51-75 series.
1) UP 52 built with experimental Cummins PT fuel system and rated at 5600 h.p. Standard equipment installed c.10/66 and unit derated to 5000 h.p.

U28B

Chicago, Burlington & Quincy

U28B	Serial	Built	Options/Notes
106-110	36101-36105	10/66	
111-115	36116-36120	12/66-1/67	
140-149	36106-36115	10/66-11/66	

Original Road No.	BN	Resale	Status	Notes
CB&Q 106	BN 5450	TTI 255		2
CB&Q 107	BN 5451	TTI 256		2
CB&Q 108	BN 5452		TGX/82	
CB&Q 109	BN 5453	TTI 257		2
CB&Q 110	BN 5454		XSL/87	
CB&Q 111	BN 5455	TTI 258		2
CB&Q 112	BN 5456	TTI 259		2
CB&Q 113	BN 5457		XPL/87	
CB&Q 114	BN 5458	TTI 260		2
CB&Q 115	BN 5459		XSL/87	
CB&Q 140	BN 5470		WX/84	1,3
CB&Q 141	BN 5471		XSL/87	1
CB&Q 142	BN 5472		XCL/87	1
CB&Q 143	BN 5473		XSL/87	1
CB&Q 144	BN 5474		XSW/87	1
CB&Q 145	BN 5475		XSL/87	1
CB&Q 146	BN 5476		XSL/87	1
CB&Q 147	BN 5477		XSS/85	1
CB&Q 148	BN 5478			1
CB&Q 149	BN 5479		XSL/87	1

Notes:
1) CB&Q 140-149 upgraded to U30B specs by GE in 1968.
2) To Transkentucky Transportation Inc. 5/87 via St. Louis Auto Shredders.
3) BN 5470 wrecked and sold to Phil Smith Salvage Co., Laurel, MT, 3/84 for scrap.

Great Northern

U28B	Serial	Built	Options/Notes
2524-2529	35987-35992	6/66	

Original Road No.	BN	Status	Notes
GN 2524	BN 5460	XPNC/81	
GN 2525	BN 5461	XPNC/81	
GN 2526	BN 5462	XPNC/81	
GN 2527	BN 5463	XPNC/81	
GN 2528	BN 5464	XPNC/81	
GN 2529	BN 5465	XPNC/81	

Louisville & Nashville

U28B	Serial	Built	Options/Notes
2500-2504	36079-36083	10/66-11/66	

Original Road No.	SBD	CSX	Serial	Built	Status	Notes
L&N 2500	SBD 5536	CSX 5319	36079	10/66	XCIM/87	
L&N 2501	SBD 5537	CSX 5320	36080	11/66	GC 1004	1
L&N 2502	SBD 5538	CSX 5321	36081	11/66		
L&N 2503	SBD 5539		36082	11/66	XLS/86	
L&N 2504	SBD 5540	CSX 5323	36083	11/66	WTNN 5323	2

Notes:
1) CSX 5320 to Georgia Central 1004.
2) CSX 5323 to Nashville & Eastern 5323, then to West Tennessee Railroad 5323.

Milwaukee Road

U28B	Serial	Built	Options/Notes
393-398	35745-35750	1/66	U25B carbody
130-135	36035-36040	7/66	
136-140	36136-36139	11/66-12/66	
380	36155	12/66	

Original Road No.	1968 Re#	1973 Re#	Status	Notes
MILW 393	MILW 5500		Rx	
MILW 394	MILW 5501		Rx	
MILW 395	MILW 5502		XMC/84	
MILW 396	MILW 5503		XMC/84	
MILW 397	MILW 5504		XMC/84	
MILW 398	MILW 5505		XMC/84	
MILW 130	MILW 5506		XMC/84	
MILW 131	MILW 5507		XMC/84	
MILW 132	MILW 5508		XMC/84	
MILW 133	MILW 5509		XMC/84	
MILW 134	MILW 5510		XMC/84	
MILW 135	MILW 5511		XMC/84	
MILW 137	MILW 6000	MILW 5600	XEH/84	1, 2
MILW 138	MILW 6001	MILW 5601	XEH/84	1, 2
MILW 139	MILW 6002	MILW 5602	XMC/84	1, 2
MILW 140	MILW 6003	MILW 5603	XMC/84	1, 2
MILW 380	MILW 6004	MILW 5604	XEH/84	3

Notes:
1) Upgraded to U30B specs.
2) MILW 5600-5604 equipped to operate with ex-RS3 slug SG-1 and ex-F7B slug SG-2.
3) MILW 380 wreck replacement for U25B 380.

New York Central

U28B	Serial	Built	Options/Notes
2822-2823	35878-35879	5/66	

Original Road No.	PC	Conrail	Status	Notes
NYC 2822	PC 2822	CR 2822	X	1
NYC 2823	PC 2823	CR 2823	X	1

Notes:
1) NYC 2822-2823 first U28B's in new carbody.

Norfolk & Western

U28B	Serial	Built	Options/Notes
1900-1929	35957-35986	7/66-9/66	High nose

Original Road No.	NdeM	Status	Notes
N&W 1900		TGX/78	1
N&W 1901		TGX/78	1
N&W 1902		Rx/78	
N&W 1903		TGX	
N&W 1904	NdeM 6900	OS	3
N&W 1905	NdeM 6901	OS	3
N&W 1906	NdeM 6902	OS	3
N&W 1907		TGX/78	1
N&W 1908		X	
N&W 1909	NdeM 6903	OS	3
N&W 1910		TGX/78	1
N&W 1911		X	
N&W 1912		X	
N&W 1913		Rx/78	
N&W 1914		TGX/78	1
N&W 1915		Rx/78	
N&W 1916		TGX/78	1
N&W 1917		TGX/78	1
N&W 1918		TGX/78	1
N&W 1919		TGX/78	1
N&W 1920		WX/73	2
N&W 1921		TGX/78	1
N&W 1922		X	
N&W 1923	NdeM 6904	OS	3
N&W 1924	NdeM 6905	OS	3
N&W 1925		TGX/78	1
N&W 1926	NdeM 6906	OS	3
N&W 1927		TGX/78	1
N&W 1928		TGX/78	1
N&W 1929		X	

Notes:
1) Retired 1978 and traded-in to GE on N&W C30-7's 8038-8082. Scrapped at Erie.
2) N&W 1920 and 8150 wrecked at Kansas City on ATSF in 1973. Both units retired and scrapped.
3) To NdeM 6900-6906 via DSI 2/79. Not all renumbered or repainted; most retired by 1987. All now out of service.

Pittsburgh & Lake Erie

U28B	Serial	Built	Options/Notes
2800-2821	35856-35877	2/66-3/66	U25B carbody

Original Road No.	Resale	Status	Notes
P&LE 2800		X/84	3
P&LE 2801		XNIM/89	
P&LE 2802	TTI 251		4
P&LE 2803		XNIM/89	
P&LE 2804		XNIM/89	
P&LE 2805		XNIM/89	
P&LE 2806		XMRP/84	3
P&LE 2807		XNIM/89	
P&LE 2808	TTI 245		4
P&LE 2809	TTI 247		2, 4
P&LE 2810	TTI 249	OS/88	2, 4, 6
P&LE 2811	TTI 252		2, 5
P&LE 2812	TTI 253		5

Pittsburgh & Lake Erie U28B Cont.

Original Road No.	Resale	Status	Notes
P&LE 2813		X	
P&LE 2814		XNIM/89	3
P&LE 2815		XNIM/89	
P&LE 2816		WX/81	6
P&LE 2817		XNIM/89	
P&LE 2818		XNIM/89	
P&LE 2819		XNIM/89	
P&LE 2820	TTI 250		4
P&LE 2821		XMRP/85	3

Notes:
1) P&LE 2800-2821 delivered in full New York Central paint and sublettered P&LE.
2) P&LE 2809-2811 leased to PC 1969-1971; 2809 and 2811 repainted full Penn Central paint, 2810 given PC nose crest only. All repainted P&LE upon return 1/72.
3) Froze up 2/84; retired 10/84 and scrapped.
4) To Transkentucky Transportation Inc. 6/85.
5) To Transkentucky Transportation Inc. 10/86.
6) Damaged while on lease to Beech Grove Coal, Lake City, TN, c./88.

Rock Island

U28B	Serial	Built	Options/Notes
240-249	35906-35915	3/66	U25B carbody
250-253	36003-36006	5/66	U25B carbody
254	36078	10/66	U25B carbody
255-261	36007-36013	6/66-8/66	
262-281	36156-36175	10/66-12/66	

Original Road No.	Resale/ Return	Status	Notes
RI 240		XCCS/81	
RI 241		XCCS/81	
RI 242	TTI 242		1
RI 243		XCCS	
RI 244	TTI 244		1
RI 245		XCCS	
RI 246	TTI 246		1
RI 247		XCCS/81	
RI 248	TTI 248	OS/88	1, 7
RI 249		XCCS/81	
RI 250		Rx	5
RI 251		Rx	5
RI 252	TTI 243		2
RI 253		Rx	5
RI 254	TTI 254		1, 3
RI 255		XCCS	
RI 256		XCCS/81	
RI 257		XCCS	
RI 258		XCCS	
RI 259		XCCS	
RI 260		XCCS	
RI 261	TTI 261		2, 4
RI 262	[UP 500]	XSS/82	6
RI 263	[UP 501]	XEH/81	6
RI 264	UP 502	XSS/82	6
RI 265	UP 503	XSS/82	6
RI 266	[UP 504]	XNIM/81	6
RI 267	[UP 505]	XSS/82	6
RI 268	UP 506	XSS/82	6
RI 269	UP 507	XSS/82	6
RI 270	UP 508	XPNC/81	6
RI 271	[UP 509]	XUP/81	6
RI 272	UP 510	XSS/82	6
RI 273	[UP 511]	XSS/82	6
RI 274	UP 512	XSS/82	6
RI 275	[UP 513]	XEH/81	6
RI 276	UP 514	XSS/82	6
RI 277	UP 515	XSS/82	6
RI 278	UP 516	XSS/82	6
RI 279	UP 517	XSS/82	6
RI 280	UP 518	XSS/82	6
RI 281	UP 519	XSS/82	6

Notes:
1) To Transkentucky Transportation Inc. 10/81 via Chrome Crankshaft.
2) To Transkentucky Transportation Inc. 1984 via Chrome Crankshaft.
3) RI 254 wreck replacement for RI U25B 212. Last U28B built with U25B carbody.
4) RI 261 wreck replacement for RI U25B 221.
5) Presumed scrapped by Chrome Crankshaft at ex-RI shops Silvis, IL.
6) RI 262-281 UP-owned. Returned to UP in April 1980 after Rock Island ceased operations. All but seven repainted UP, renumbered and operated in Omaha-North Platte, NE., service until mid-1982.
7) Damaged while on lease to Beech Grove Coal, Lake City, TN., c./88.

Southern Pacific

U28B	Serial	Built	Options/Notes
7025-7028	35852-35855	1/66	U25B carbody, A

Original Road No.	Status	Notes
SP 7025	TGX/84	1
SP 7026	XPL/85	1
SP 7027	TGX/84	1
SP 7028	P/88	1, 2

Notes:
A) SP 7025-7028 built as GE demonstrators, but diverted to SP.
1) Retired 3/79 and traded in to GE 12/84.
2) SP 7028 to Orange Empire Railway Museum, Perris,CA, in 1988.

U28C

Chicago, Burlington & Quincy

U28C	Serial	Built	Options/Notes
562-571	35751-35760	2/66-3/66	U25C carbody
572-577	35815-35820	4/66	U25C carbody

Original Road No.	BN	Status	Notes
CB&Q 562	BN 5650	XSS/81	
CB&Q 563	BN 5651	XSS/81	
CB&Q 564	BN 5652	XSS/81	
CB&Q 565	BN 5653	XSS/81	
CB&Q 566	BN 5654	XSS/81	
CB&Q 567	BN 5655	XGMT/81	
CB&Q 568	BN 5656	XSS/81	
CB&Q 569	BN 5657	XSS/81	
CB&Q 570	BN 5658	XPNC/81	
CB&Q 571	BN 5659	XGMT/81	
CB&Q 572	BN 5660	XPNC/81	
CB&Q 573	BN 5661	XNIM/81	
CB&Q 574	BN 5662	XNIM/81	
CB&Q 575	BN 5663	XPNC/81	
CB&Q 576	BN 5664	XNIM/81	
CB&Q 577	BN 5665	XNIM/81	

Louisville & Nashville

U28C	Serial	Built	Options/Notes
1525-1532	35892-35899	5/66-6/66	

Original Road No.	1967 Re#	SBD	CSX	Status/Notes	
L&N 1525	L&N 1533			WX/82	1
L&N 1526				WX/69	2
L&N 1527		SBD 1527	CSX 3526	Rx/89	3
L&N 1528				XPNC/79	
L&N 1529				XLNS/79	
L&N 1530				XCIM/87	
L&N 1531				X	
L&N 1532				XFIM/86	

Notes:
1) L&N 1525 (1st) renumbered L&N 1533 12/67 when ORO Dam U25C's acquired.
2) Southbound L&N coal train with 1542, 1215, 1428, 1411 collided head-on with northbound empties lead by 1407 and 1526 at Amhurst, TN, 5/12/69. All units scrapped.
3) CSX 3526 last active U28C. Stored Waycross, GA, 7/2/89.

Northern Pacific

U28C	Serial	Built	Options/Notes
2800-2801	35630-35631	4/66	U25C carbody
2802-2811	35882-35891	4/66-5/66	U25C carbody

Original Road No.	BN	Status	Notes
NP 2800	BN 5666	WX/80	1
NP 2801	BN 5667	XSS/81	
NP 2802	BN 5668	XNIM/81	
NP 2803	BN 5669	WX/74	2
NP 2804	BN 5670	XPNC/81	
NP 2805	BN 5671	XPNC/81	
NP 2806	BN 5672	XNIM/81	
NP 2807	BN 5673	XSS/81	
NP 2808	BN 5674	XNIM/81	3
NP 2809	BN 5675	XNIM/81	
NP 2810	BN 5676	XNIM/81	
NP 2811	BN 5677	XNIM/81	

Notes:
1) BN 5666 wrecked and scrapped 12/80.
2) BN 5913, 5907, 5669 and 5320 working as mid-train remotes wrecked and burned Wiggins, CO, 3/27/74. All but 5320 scrapped.
3) BN 5674 leased to DOT Pueblo Test Facility (painted DOT colors) 5/71 until arrival of DOT U30C 001.

Pennsylvania

U28C	Serial	Built	Options/Notes
6520-6525	36019-36024	9/66	
6526-6527	36026-36027	9/66	
6528	36025	9/66	
6529-6534	36028-36033	9/66-10/66	

Original Road No.	PC	CR	1978 Re#	Status & Notes
PRR 6520	PC 6520	CR 6520	CR 6820	XCRH/87
PRR 6521	PC 6521	CR 6521	CR 6821	XCRH/87
PRR 6522	PC 6522	CR 6522	CR 6822	XCRH/87
PRR 6523	PC 6523	CR 6523	CR 6823	XNIM/85
PRR 6524	PC 6524	CR 6524	CR 6824	XCRH/87
PRR 6525	PC 6525	CR 6525	CR 6825	XPIT/85
PRR 6526	PC 6526	CR 6526	CR 6826	XCRH/87
PRR 6527	PC 6527	CR 6527	CR 6827	XCRH/87
PRR 6528	PC 6528	CR 6528	CR 6828	XCRH/87
PRR 6529	PC 6529	CR 6529	CR 6829	XCRH/87
PRR 6530	PC 6530	CR 6530	CR 6830	XCRH/87
PRR 6531	PC 6531	CR 6531	CR 6831	XCRH/87
PRR 6532	PC 6532	CR 6532	CR 6832	XCRH/87
PRR 6533	PC 6533	CR 6533	CR 6833	XCRH/87
PRR 6534	PC 6534	CR 6534	CR 6834	XCRH/87

Notes:
1) Renumbered in 1978 to accommodate CR SD40-2's 6483-6524.

Southern Pacific

U28C	Serial	Built	Options/Notes
7150-7159	36068-36077	10/66-11/66	

Original Road No.	Status	Notes
SP 7150	TGX/84	1
SP 7151	TGX/84	1
SP 7152	TGX/84	1
SP 7153	XCC/84	1
SP 7154	TGX/84	1
SP 7155	XCC/84	1
SP 7156	TGX/84	1
SP 7157	XPL/85	1
SP 7158	TGX/84	1
SP 7159	TGX/84	1

Notes:
1) SP 7150-7159 retired 3/79. Traded in to GE 12/84; at least 7153 and 7155 scrapped at Chrome Crankshaft, San Bernardino, CA. Most others scrapped at Pielet Bros., McCook, IL.

Union Pacific

U28C	Serial	Built	Options/Notes
2800-2804	36014-36018	6/66	
2805-2809	36063-36067	8/66-9/66	

Original Road No.	Status	Notes
UP 2800	XSS/80	
UP 2801	XEC/82	
UP 2802	XPNC/80	
UP 2803	XPNC/80	
UP 2804	SLC	1
UP 2805	XRAC/79	
UP 2806	XEC/81	
UP 2807	XHM/79	
UP 2808	Rx	
UP 2809	XDES/80	

Notes:
1) UP 2804 retired and assigned to Salt Lake City, UT, diesel shop as training locomotive.

U28CG

Atchison, Topeka & Santa Fe

U28CG	Serial	Built	Options/Notes
350-359	35993-36002	7/66-8/66	Steam generator

Original Road No.	1969 re#	Status	Notes
ATSF 350	ATSF 7900	TGX/80	1
ATSF 351	ATSF 7901	TGX/80	1
ATSF 352	ATSF 7902	TGX/80	1
ATSF 353	ATSF 7903	TGX/80	1
ATSF 354	ATSF 7904	TGX/80	1
ATSF 355	ATSF 7905	TGX/80	1
ATSF 356	ATSF 7906	TGX/80	1
ATSF 357	ATSF 7907	TGX/80	1
ATSF 358	ATSF 7908	TGX/80	1
ATSF 359	ATSF 7909	TGX/80	1

Notes:
1) ATSF 350-359 retired 9/80 and traded-in to GE on B36-7's.

U30B

Atlantic Coast Line

U30B	Serial	Built	Options/Notes
975-978	36144-36147	2/67	

Original Road No.	SCL	SBD	2nd SBD	CSX	Status	Notes
ACL 975	SCL 1700	SBD 5517	5300	CSX 5300	XWC/88	
ACL 976	SCL 1701	SBD 5518	5301	CSX 5301	XSPC/88	
ACL 977	SCL 1702	SBD 5519	5302	CSX 5302	Rx	
ACL 978	SCL 1703	SBD 5520			XWC/88	

Chesapeake & Ohio

U30B	Serial	Built	Options/Notes
8200-8209	38218-38227	12/71-1/72	
8210-8222	38475-38487	11/72-12/72	
8223-8224	35881, 35880	5/66	ex GE Demos
8225-8234	40068-40077	12/74	FB2 trucks

Original Road No.	2nd Road No.	CSX	Resale	Status	Notes
C&O 8200		CSX 5328	NERR 5328		1
C&O 8201		CSX 5329		Rx	
C&O 8202		CSX 5330		Rx	
C&O 8203		CSX 5331		XWC/89	
C&O 8204		CSX 5332	GC 1006		2
C&O 8205		CSX 5333		Rx	
C&O 8206		CSX 5334		Rx	
C&O 8207		CSX 5335		Rx	
C&O 8208		CSX 5336		Rx	
C&O 8209		CSX 5337		WX/88	3
C&O 8210		CSX 5338	NERR 5338		1
C&O 8211		CSX 5339	NERR 5339		1
C&O 8212		CSX 5340	NERR 5340		1
C&O 8213		CSX 5341	GC 1010		2
C&O 8214		CSX 5342			
C&O 8215		CSX 5343	NERR 5343		1
C&O 8216		CSX 5344	NERR 5344		1
C&O 8217		CSX 5345	NERR 5345		1
C&O 8218		CSX 5346		Rx	
C&O 8219		CSX 5347	GC 1011		2
C&O 8220		CSX 5348		Rx	
C&O 8221		CSX 5349	GC 1002		2
C&O 8222		CSX 5350	GC 1003		2
GE 302	C&O 8223	CSX 5351	GC 1005	GC	2, 4
GE 301	C&O 8224	CSX 5352		Rx	4
C&O 8225		CSX 5353		Rx	
C&O 8226		CSX 5354		Rx	
C&O 8227		CSX 5355		Rx	
C&O 8228		CSX 5356		Rx	
C&O 8229		CSX 5357		Rx	
C&O 8230		CSX 5358	GC 1007		2
C&O 8231		CSX 5359		Rx	
C&O 8232		CSX 5360	GC 1008		2
C&O 8233		CSX 5361		Rx	
C&O 8234		CSX 5362		Rx	

Notes:
1) Sold to Nashville & Eastern
2) Sold to Georgia Central in 1990.
3) CSX 5337 wrecked Atlanta, GA, 1/88 and scrapped.
4) Built as U30B demonstrator/test beds. Rebuilt to U33B's 7/67. Upgraded to U36B specs in 1968 and operated until 12/70. Rebuilt to U30B standards and sold to C&O in 1972.

Chicago, Burlington & Quincy

U30B	Serial	Built	Options/Notes
150-154	36520-36524	1/68	

Original Road No.	BN	Status	Notes
CB&Q 150	BN 5480	R/86	
CB&Q 151	BN 5481	XGMT/84	
CB&Q 152	BN 5482	TGX/82	1
CB&Q 153	BN 5483	X	
CB&Q 154	BN 5484	X	

Notes:
1) BN 5482 traded in to GE 6/82 on B30-7A.

General Electric

U30B	Serial	Built	Options/Notes
301-302	35880-35881	5/66	
303-304	35935-35936	6/66	

Original Road No.	Resale	Re#	Status	Notes
GE 301	C&O 8224	CSX 5352	Rx	1,2,3
GE 302	C&O 8223	CSX 5351	GC 1005	1,3,5
GE 303	WP 770	WP 3070	XLM/90	1,4
GE 304	WP 771	WP 3071	XLM/90	1,4

General Electric U30B Notes:

1) Built as U30B demonstrator/test beds. Rebuilt to U33B's 7/67. Upgraded to U36B specs 10/30/67 and operated until 12/70.
2) GE 301 equipped with prototype FB2 truck in 1969.
3) GE 301-302 rebuilt to U30B standards and sold to C&O in 1972.
4) GE 303-304 rebuilt to U30B standards, retrucked with EMD Blombergs and sold to WP 5/71 for $199,228 ea. Both retired in 1980.
5) CSX 5351 sold to Georgia Central 1005 1990.

Illinois Central

U30B	Serial	Built	Options/Notes
5000-5005	36200-36205	2/67-3/67	

Original Road No.	IOWA	Status	Notes
IC 5000	IRRC 20	X	2
IC 5001	IRRC 21	X	2
IC 5002	IRRC 22	X	2
IC 5003		WX/79	1
IC 5004	IRRC 23	X	2
IC 5005	IRRC 24	WX/82	2,3

Notes:

1) IC 5003 wrecked 2/79 Bluford, IA, and scrapped 1980.
2) IC 5000-5002, 5004-5005 sold to Iowa Railroad 5/82. IRRC operation of RI main taken over by Iowa Interstate in 1984. Units scrapped.
3) Iowa 24 wrecked 10/20/82 and scrapped.

Louisville & Nashville

U30B	Serial	Built	Options/Notes
2505-2509	36443-36447	11/67	

Original Road No.	SBD	CSX	Status	Notes
L&N 2505			WX/78	1
L&N 2506	SBD 5541	CSX 5324	GC 1009	2
L&N 2507	SBD 5542		XCIM/85	
L&N 2508	SBD 5543	CSX 5326	Rx	
L&N 2509	SBD 5544	CSX 5327	XWC/88	

Notes:

1) L&N 3008, 2505, 2818 wrecked in collision with standing cars at Franklin, TN, 8/6/78. L&N 2505 scrapped South Louisville (KY) shops 12/79.
2) CSX 5324 sold to Georgia Central 1009.

Milwaukee Road

U30B	Serial	Built	Options/Notes
6005-6009	36500-36503 36499	1/68	

Original Road No.	1973 Re#	Status	Notes
MILW 6005	MILW 5605	XCCS/81	
MILW 6006	MILW 5606	XCCS/81	
MILW 6007	MILW 5607	XCCS/81	
MILW 6008	MILW 5608	XCCS/81	
MILW 6009	MILW 5609	XCCS/81	1

Notes:

1) MILW 6009 delivered as 6004 in error, renumbered 6009.
2) All MILW U30B's retired by 1980. Sold to Chrome Crankshaft, Silvis, IL., 1981 for scrap.

New York Central

U30B	Serial	Built	Options/Notes
2830-2839	36246-36255	11/66-2/67	
2840-2857	36379-36396	7/67-9/67	
2860-2889	36411-36440	9/67-12/67	

Original Road No.	PC	CR	Resale	Resale	Resale	Status & Notes	
NYC 2830	PC 2830	CR 2830				Rx	
NYC 2831	PC 2831	CR 2831				Rx	
NYC 2832	PC 2832	CR 2832				Rx	
NYC 2833	PC 2833	CR 2833				Rx	
NYC 2834	PC 2834	CR 2834				XNIM/86	
NYC 2835	PC 2835	CR 2835				XCRH/87	
NYC 2836	PC 2836	CR 2836				Rx	
NYC 2837	PC 2837	CR 2837				XCRH/87	
NYC 2838	PC 2838	CR 2838				XCRH/87	
NYC 2839	PC 2839	CR 2839				Rx/78	
NYC 2840	PC 2840	CR 2840				Rx	
NYC 2841	PC 2841	CR 2841				XCRH/87	
NYC 2842	PC 2842	CR 2842				XNIM/86	
NYC 2843	PC 2843	CR 2843				XCRH/87	
NYC 2844	PC 2844	CR 2844				XCRH/87	
NYC 2845	PC 2845	CR 2845				XCRH/87	
NYC 2846	PC 2846	CR 2846				Rx	
NYC 2847	PC 2847	CR 2847				XCRH/87	
NYC 2848	PC 2848	CR 2848				XCRH/87	
NYC 2849	PC 2849	CR 2849				XCRH/87	
NYC 2850	PC 2850	CR 2850				XNIM/86	
NYC 2851	PC 2851	CR 2851				XNIM/86	
NYC 2852	PC 2852	CR 2852				Rx	
NYC 2853	PC 2853	CR 2853				XNIM/86	
NYC 2854	PC 2854	CR 2854				XNIM/86	
NYC 2855	PC 2855	CR 2855				XNIM/86	
NYC 2856	PC 2856	CR 2856				XNIM/86	
NYC 2857	PC 2857	CR 2857				XNIM/86	
NYC 2860	PC 2860	CR 2860				XNIM/86	
NYC 2861	PC 2861	CR 2861				XNIM/86	
NYC 2862	PC 2862	CR 2862				XNIM/86	
NYC 2863	PC 2863	CR 2863				XNIM/86	
NYC 2864	PC 2864	CR 2864				XNIM/86	
NYC 2865	PC 2865	CR 2865				XNIM/86	
NYC 2866	PC 2866	CR 2866				XNIM/86	
NYC 2867	PC 2867	CR 2867				XNIM/86	
NYC 2868	PC 2868	CR 2868				XNIM/86	
NYC 2869	PC 2869	CR 2869				XNIM/86	
NYC 2870	PC 2870	CR 2870				XNIM/86	
NYC 2871	PC 2871	CR 2871				XNIM/86	
NYC 2872	PC 2872	CR 2872				XNIM/86	
NYC 2873	PC 2873	CR 2873				XNIM/86	
NYC 2874	PC 2874	CR 2874				XNIM/86	
NYC 2875	PC 2875	CR 2875	SFLR 2875	SRNJ 2875		X/93	2
NYC 2876	PC 2876	CR 2876	SFLR 2876	SRNJ 2876		CR/94	6
NYC 2877	PC 2877	CR 2877					
NYC 2878	PC 2878	CR 2878					
NYC 2879	PC 2879	CR 2879					
NYC 2880	PC 2880	CR 2880	NHI 401	OCTR 401			5
NYC 2881	PC 2881	CR 2881					
NYC 2882	PC 2882	CR 2882	PV 2882	GETY 28	SCTR 9016		2
NYC 2883	PC 2883	CR 2883					
NYC 2884	PC 2884	CR 2884	SFLR 2884	SRNJ 2884			2
NYC 2885	PC 2885	CR 2885					
NYC 2886	PC 2886	CR 2886					
NYC 2887	PC 2887	CR 2887	NHI 402	OCTR 402			5
NYC 2888	PC 2888	CR 2888	LVAL 901				4
NYC 2889	PC 2889	CR 2889				XNIM	

Notes:

1) CR 2850-2854, 2856-2862, 2864-2866, 2868-2874 returned to owner/lessor North American Car 1983 and stored Sayre, PA. All CR U30B's retired by 6/86.
2) CR 2875, 2876, 2884 to Shore Fast Line 5/83; to Southern Railroad of New Jersey 1992. SRRNJ 2875 scrapped at Winslow Jct., NJ in spring of 1993.
3) CR 2882 to Panther Valley 2882, then Gettysburg 2882; then to South Central Florida 9016 c./90.
4) CR 2888 to Lackawanna Valley 901 in 1985; repainted to O&W colors by Morristown & Erie.
5) CR 2880 and 2887 to New Hope & Ivyland 401-402 c./83. To McHugh Bros. Tyburn R.R. 401-402 1989. To Octoraro 401-402 1/93.
6) Sold to Conrail for trade-in credit in 1993.

Norfolk & Western

U30B	Serial	Built	Options/Notes
1930-1944	36256-36270	3/67-5/67	High nose
1945-1956	36326-36337	6/67	High nose
1957-1964	36338-36345	6/67-7/67	High nose; Dates and serials not in order (Note A)
8465-8514	37441-37490	8/70-1/71	High nose
8515-8539	37747-37771	5/71-11/71	High nose

Original Road No.	NdeM	Status	Notes	Road Slug
N&W 1930		TGX/79		
N&W 1931	NdeM 9700	OS	2	
N&W 1932		TGX/79		
N&W 1933	NdeM 9701	OS	2	
N&W 1934		TGX/78	1	
N&W 1935		TGX/78	1	
N&W 1936		TGX/78	1	
N&W 1937		TGX/78	1	
N&W 1938		TGX/78	1	
N&W 1939		TGX/78	1	
N&W 1940	NdeM 9702	OS	2	
N&W 1941	NdeM 9703	OS	2	
N&W 1942		TGX/78	1	
N&W 1943		TGX/78	1	
N&W 1944	NdeM 9704	OS	2	
N&W 1945		TGX/78 1		
N&W 1946		TGX/78 1		
N&W 1947		TGX/78 1		
N&W 1948		TGX/78 1		
N&W 1949		Rx/86	3,4	N&W 9700
N&W 1950		TGX/78 1		
N&W 1951		Rx		
N&W 1952		TGX/86	3,4	N&W 9701
N&W 1953	NdeM 9705	OS	2	
N&W 1954		TGX/78	1	
N&W 1955		Rx		
N&W 1956	NdeM 9706	OS	2	
N&W 1957	NdeM 9707	OS	2	
N&W 1958		TGX/78	1	
N&W 1959		R 10/86	3,4	N&W 9702
N&W 1960		TGX/78	1	
N&W 1961		TGX/79		
N&W 1962		TGX/79		
N&W 1963		TGX/78	1	
N&W 1964		TGX/78	1	
N&W 8465		TGX/78	1	
N&W 8466	NdeM 9708	OS	3	
N&W 8467		TGX/78	1	
N&W 8468				
N&W 8469	NdeM 9740	OS	3	
N&W 8470	NdeM 9709	OS	3	
N&W 8471	NdeM 9710	OS	3	
N&W 8472	NdeM 9711	OS	3	
N&W 8473		TGX/86	5, 6	
N&W 8474		Rx/86		
N&W 8475		XPL/86	7	
N&W 8476		XPL/86	7	
N&W 8477		Rx		
N&W 8478	NdeM 9712	OS	3	
N&W 8479	NdeM 9713	OS	3	
N&W 8480		TGX/78	1	
N&W 8481		Rx		
N&W 8482	NdeM 9714	OS	3	
N&W 8483		TGX/78	1	
N&W 8484		Rx		
N&W 8485		TGX/78	1	
N&W 8486		Rx		
N&W 8487		Rx/78		
N&W 8488		TGX/78	1	
N&W 8489	NdeM 9715	OS	3	
N&W 8490		Rx		
N&W 8491	NdeM 9716	OS	3	
N&W 8492	NdeM 9717	OS	3	
N&W 8493		TGX/78	1	
N&W 8494	NdeM 9741	OS	3	
N&W 8495	NdeM 9718	OS	3	
N&W 8496	NdeM 9719	OS	3	
N&W 8497	NdeM 9720	OS	3	
N&W 8498	NdeM 9721	OS	3	
N&W 8499		Rx		
N&W 8500	NdeM 9742	OS	3	
N&W 8501	NdeM 9722	OS	3	
N&W 8502	NdeM 9723	OS	3	
N&W 8503	NdeM 9743	OS	3	
N&W 8504	NdeM 9724	W/80	3	
N&W 8505		Rx		
N&W 8506		Rx		
N&W 8507	NdeM 9725	OS	3	
N&W 8508		TGX/78	1	
N&W 8509		Rx		
N&W 8510		Rx		
N&W 8511	NdeM 9726	OS	3	
N&W 8512		TGX/78	1	
N&W 8513	NdeM 9727	OS	3	
N&W 8514		Rx/78		
N&W 8515	NdeM 9728	OS	3	
N&W 8516		Rx/78		
N&W 8517	NdeM 9729	OS	3	
N&W 8518	NdeM 9730	OS	3	
N&W 8519		Rx		
N&W 8520		TGX/78	1	
N&W 8521	NdeM 9744	OS	3	
N&W 8522	NdeM 9731	OS	3	
N&W 8523	NdeM 9732	OS	3	
N&W 8524	NdeM 9733	OS	3	
N&W 8525	NdeM 9734	OS	3	
N&W 8526		TGX/78	1	
N&W 8527		Rx		
N&W 8528		TGX/78	1	
N&W 8529	NdeM 9735	OS	3	
N&W 8530		Rx/78		
N&W 8531	NdeM 9736	OS	3	
N&W 8532		Rx		
N&W 8533	NdeM 9737	OS	3	
N&W 8534		Rx		
N&W 8535		Rx		
N&W 8536		TGX/78	3	
N&W 8537	NdeM 9738	OS	3	
N&W 8538	NdeM 9739	OS	3	
N&W 8539		TGX/78	1	

Notes:

A) 1957-1964 serials out of sequence: 36343-36345; 36341-36342; 36338-36340.
1) Retired 1978 and traded in to GE on C30-7's 8038-8082.
2) To NdeM 9700-9739 2/79. Not all units renumbered or repainted. All out of service by 1987.
3) To NdeM 12/79 via GE Hornell. Not all units renumbered or repainted. All out of service.
4) N&W 1949, 1952, 1959 rebuilt Roanoke 11/77 to road slugs N&W 9700-9702. All retired by 10/86.
5) N&W 8473-8476 equipped to operate with ex-U30B slugs 9700-9702.
6) 8473 retired 10/1/86; last active N&W U30B.
7) Traded in to GE in 1986; to Pielet for scrap.

Seaboard Air Line

U30B	Serial	Built	Options/Notes
800-814	36121-36135	12/66-1/67	Blomberg trucks, A

Original Road No.	SCL	SBD	2nd SBD	CSX	Status	Notes
SAL 800	SCL 1704	SBD 5521			X R/86	
SAL 801	SCL 1705	SBD 5522	5305	CSX 5305	GC 1001	1
SAL 802	SCL 1706	SBD 5523	5306	CSX 5306	XWC/88	
SAL 803	SCL 1707	SBD 5524	5307	CSX 5307	Rx	
SAL 804	SCL 1708	SBD 5525	5308		XCIM/87	
SAL 805	SCL 1709	SBD 5526	5309	CSX 5309	XCIM/87	
SAL 806	SCL 1710	SBD 5527			XCIM/87	
SAL 807	SCL 1711	SBD 5528	5311	CSX 5311	Rx	
SAL 808	SCL 1712	SBD 5529	5312	CSX 5312	Rx	
SAL 809	SCL 1713	SBD 5530	5313		Rx/86	
SAL 810	SCL 1714	SBD 5531	5314		XWC/88	
SAL 811	SCL 1715	SBD 5532	5315		XWC/88	
SAL 812	SCL 1716	SBD 5533	5316		XCIM/87	
SAL 813	SCL 1717	SBD 5534	5317	CSX 5317	Rx	
SAL 814	SCL 1718	SBD 5535			XWC/88	

Notes:

A) First GE's built with trade-in EMD Blomberg trucks.
1) CSX 5305 to Georgia Central 1001.

St. Louis-San Francisco

U30B	Serial	Built	Options/Notes
832-835	36850-36853	10/68-11/68	
836-843	37164-37171	8/69-9/69	
844-853	39928-39937	5/73	
854-857	39901-39904	8/74-9/74	
858-862	40257-40261	3/75	

Original Road No.	BN	Resale	Status	Notes
SL-SF 832	BN 5770		XSW/87	
SL-SF 833	BN 5771		R/86	
SL-SF 834	BN 5772		R/86	
SL-SF 835	BN 5773		R/86	
SL-SF 836	BN 5774		R/86	
SL-SF 837	BN 5775		R/86	
SL-SF 838	BN 5776		R/86	
SL-SF 839	BN 5777		R/86	
SL-SF 840	BN 5778		R/86	
SL-SF 841	BN 5779		R/86	
SL-SF 842	BN 5780		XSW/87	
SL-SF 843	BN 5781		XGMT/85	
SL-SF 844	BN 5782		XPL/92	
SL-SF 845	BN 5783		XPL/92	
SL-SF 846	BN 5784		R/86	1
SL-SF 847	BN 5785		XPL/92	
SL-SF 848	BN 5786		R/87	
SL-SF 849	BN 5787		XPL/92	
SL-SF 850	BN 5788		XPL/92	
SL-SF 851	BN 5789		R/86	
SL-SF 852	BN 5790		XPL/92	
SL-SF 853	BN 5791		R/90	
SL-SF 854	BN 5792			
SL-SF 855	BN 5793		R/86	
SL-SF 856			WX/74	2
SL-SF 857	BN 5794	KYLE 5794		4
SL-SF 858	BN 5795	KYLE 5795		4
SL-SF 859	BN 5796	KYLE 5796		4
SL-SF 860	BN 5797			3
SL-SF 861	BN 5798		XSW/90	
SL-SF 862	BN 5799	KYLE 5799		4

Notes:

1) SL-SF 846 GE's 2500th domestic U-series locomotive.
2) SL-SF 856 wrecked and scrapped.
3) 5797 last BN U30B in service.
4) BN 5794, 5795, 5796, 5799 to KYLE 5/91 via Pielet Bros.

Western Pacific

U30B	Serial	Built	Options/Notes
751-755	36451-36455	9/67	Blomberg trucks
756-759	36833-36836	9/68	Blomberg trucks
760-769	36998-37007	4/69-5/69	Blomberg trucks
770-771	35935-35936	6/66	Blomberg trucks ex-GE demos

Original Road No.	1972 Re#	Re#	Status	Notes
WP 751	WP 3051		P/84	2
WP 752	WP 3052		XDU/84	
WP 753	WP 3053		XSL/88	
WP 754	WP 3054		XSL/88	
WP 755	WP 3055		XDU/84	
WP 756	WP 3056		XSL/85	
WP 757	WP 3057		XJJ/84	
WP 758	WP 3058		XDU/84	
WP 759	WP 3059		XDU/84	3
WP 760	WP 3060		XDU/84	
WP 761	WP 3061		XSL/88	
WP 762	WP 3062		XDU/84	4
WP 763	WP 3063		XDU/84	
WP 764	WP 3064		XSL/84	
WP 765			WX/72	3
WP 766	WP 3066		XDU/84	
WP 767	WP 3067		XDU/84	
WP 768	WP 3068		XSL/88	
WP 769	WP 3069		XSL/88	4

Western Pacific U30B Cont.

Original Road No.	WP	1972 Re#	Status	Notes
GE 303	WP 770	WP 3070	XLM/90	5
GE 304	WP 771	WP 3071	XLM/90	5

Notes:
1) WP 3051-3059, 3061-3064, 3066-3069 retired 10/83.
2) WP 3051 donated by UP to Feather River Rail Society, Portola, CA, in 1984.
3) WP 759, 762 and 765 wrecked on BN at Woodland, WA, 7/22/71. WP 759 repaired and renumbered 3059 by Morrison-Knudsen, Boisie, ID. WP 762 repaired GE Chicago, IL, and renumbered 3062. WP 765 sold to Schnitzer, Oakland, CA for scrap 6/72.
4) Cab and body parts of retired WP 3069 used to repair UP C30-7 2412 in 1987. Rest of unit to GE for Super 7 program in 1988. Unit moved to GE Montreal for rebuilding.
5) WP 3070 and 3071 built as GE U30B demonstrator/test beds. Rebuilt to U33B's 7/67. Upgraded to U36B specs 10/67 and operated until 12/70. Rebuilt to U30B standards, retrucked with EMD Blombergs and sold to WP 5/71 for $199,228 ea. Both retired in 1980. Sold for scrap 1990.

U30C

Atlantic Coast Line

U30C	Serial	Built	Options/Notes
3021-3024	36140-36143	11/66-12/66	A

Original Road No.	SCL	CSX	Status	Notes
ACL 3021	SCL 2121	CSX 7277	R	
ACL 3022	SCL 2122	CSX 7278	R	
ACL 3023	SCL 2123	CSX 7279	XNIM/91	
ACL 3024	SCL 2124	CSX 7280	R/92	

Notes:
A) First U30C's built; builder's plates read U28C.

Burlington Northern

U30C	Serial	Built	Options/Notes
5300-5305:1	38241-38246	1/72	
5306-5319	38247-38260	1/72-2/72	
5320-5334	38350-38364	3/72-5/72	
5335-5352	38556-38573	11/72-12/72	
5353-5364:1	38574-38585	12/72	
5365-5394	39924-39953	8/74-11/74	
5300-5305:2	40390-40395	5/75	
5353-5364:2	40378-40389	5/75	
5806-5813	39289-39296	7/73	
5814-5823	39419-39428	11/73-12/73	
5824-5833	39713-39731*	4/74-5/74	*Serials odd only
5834-5835	40396, 40398	6/75	
5836-5839	40600-40606*	6/75	*Serials even only
5912-5918	39282-39288	7/73	
5919-5928	39429-39438	11/73-12/73	
5929-5938	39714-39732*	4/74-5/74	*Serials even only
5939-5944	40397-40607*	6/75	*Serials odd only

Original Road No.	2nd No.	3rd No.	Status	Notes
BN 5300:1	BN 5800		XPL/90	1
BN 5301:1	BN 5801		XAZ/90	1
BN 5302:1	BN 5802		P/88	1, 13
BN 5303:1	BN 5803		XPL/90	1
BN 5304:1	BN 5804		XEH/89	1
BN 5305:1	BN 5805		XPL/89	1
BN 5306			XAZ/90	
BN 5307			XSL/87	2
BN 5308			XPNC/87	2
BN 5309			XEH/87	2
BN 5310			XSL/87	2
BN 5311			XPNC/87	2
BN 5312			XSL/87	2
BN 5313			XSL/87	2
BN 5314			XSL/87	2
BN 5315			XSL/87	2
BN 5316			XSL/87	2
BN 5317			XSL/87	2
BN 5318			XPL/90	
BN 5319			XSL/87	2
BN 5320			XPL/90	6
BN 5321	KYLE 5321			3
BN 5322	KYLE 5322			3
BN 5323			XPNC/87	2
BN 5324			XSL/87	2
BN 5325	BN 1776	BN 5325	XPL/90	4
BN 5326			XBN/89	
BN 5327			XBN/88	
BN 5328			XPNC/87	
BN 5329			XSL/89	
BN 5330			XPL/90	
BN 5331	KYLE 5331		KYLE/91	14
BN 5332	KYLE 5332		KYLE/91	14
BN 5333			XAZ/90	
BN 5334			XAZ/90	
BN 5335			XSW/89	
BN 5336	BN 800B	BN 4500	XPNC/87	5
BN 5337			WX 5/80	
BN 5338			XSW/89	
BN 5339			XMPS/90	
BN 5340			XSW/89	
BN 5341			XMPS/90	
BN 5342			XMPS/90	
BN 5343			XMPS/90	
BN 5344			XMPS/90	
BN 5345			XMPS/90	
BN 5346			XSW/89	
BN 5347			XSW/89	
BN 5348			XMPS/90	
BN 5349			XMPS/90	
BN 5350			XMPS/90	
BN 5351			XMPS/90	
BN 5352			XSW/89	
BN 5353:1	BN 5900		XMPS/90	1
BN 5354:1	BN 5901		XMPS/90	1
BN 5355:1	BN 5902		XMPS/90	1
BN 5356:1	BN 5903		XMPS/90	1
BN 5357:1	BN 5904		XMPS/90	1
BN 5358:1	BN 5905		XMPS/90	1
BN 5359:1	BN 5906		WX/80	1
BN 5360:1	BN 5907		WX 3/74	1, 6
BN 5361:1	BN 5908		XMPS/90	1
BN 5362:1	BN 5909		XMPS/90	1
BN 5363:1	BN 5910		XMPS/90	1,7
BN 5364:1	BN 5911		XMPS/90	1
BN 5365				
BN 5366			R/87	
BN 5367				
BN 5368			XAZ/90	
BN 5369				
BN 5370			XAZ/90	
BN 5371			R/93	
BN 5372			R/93	
BN 5373			R/93	
BN 5374				
BN 5375				
BN 5376			R/93	
BN 5377			R/93	
BN 5378				
BN 5379				
BN 5380				
BN 5381			XBN/93	
BN 5382				
BN 5383				
BN 5384				
BN 5385			XPL/92	
BN 5386				
BN 5387				
BN 5388			R/93	
BN 5389			R 2/87	
BN 5390				
BN 5391			R/93	
BN 5392			R/93	
BN 5393			R 3/87	
BN 5394				
BN 5806			XPL/90	
BN 5807			XAZ/90	
BN 5808	KYLE 5808			3
BN 5809			XAZ/90	
BN 5810	KYLE 5810			3
BN 5811			XPL/90	
BN 5812			XPL/89	
BN 5813			XAZ/90	
BN 5814			WX/85	8
BN 5815			NRE/91	9
BN 5816			NRE/91	9
BN 5817			NRE/91	9
BN 5818			NRE/91	9
BN 5819	KYLE 5819			3
BN 5820	KYLE 5820			3
BN 5821	KYLE 5821			3
BN 5822			XPL/90	
BN 5823			XPL/90	
BN 5824			XILS/89	
BN 5825	LS&I 3004			14
BN 5826			XILS/89	
BN 5827	LS&I 3050			14
BN 5828	LS&I 3001			14
BN 5829			XILS/89	GE 4/94
BN 5830	LS&I 3002			14
BN 5831			XILS/89	
BN 5832	LS&I 3008			14
BN 5833			XILS/89	GE 4/94
BN 5834			NRE/90	10
BN 5835			NRE/90	10
BN 5836			NRE/90	10
BN 5837			NRE/90	10
BN 5838			R/90	
BN 5839			NRE/90	10
BN 5912			XAZ/90	
BN 5913			WX/74	6
BN 5914			WX/84	11
BN 5915			XBN/89	
BN 5916			XAZ/90	
BN 5917			XPL/90	
BN 5918	KYLE 5918			3
BN 5919			NRE/91	9
BN 5920			NRE/91	9
BN 5921			NRE/91	9
BN 5922			NRE/91	9
BN 5923			NRE/91	9
BN 5924			XPL/90	
BN 5925	KYLE 5925			3
BN 5926			XAZ/90	
BN 5927			XPL/90	
BN 5928	KYLE 5928			3
BN 5929	LS&I 3005			14
BN 5930	LS&I 3051			14
BN 5931	LS&I 3000			14
BN 5932	LS&I 3006			14
BN 5933			XILS/89	
BN 5934	LS&I 3007			14
BN 5935			XILS/89	
BN 5936	LS&I 3052			14
BN 5937	LS&I 3003			14
BN 5938	LS&I 3053			14
BN 5939			XCR/91	10, 12
BN 5940			NRS/90	10
BN 5941			NRS/90	10
BN 5942			NRS/90	10
BN 5943			NRS/90	10
BN 5944			NRS/90	10
BN 5300:2			NRS/90	1
BN 5301:2			XCR/91	1, 12
BN 5302:2			NRS/90	1
BN 5303:2			R/90	1
BN 5304:2			NRS/90	1
BN 5305:2			R/90	1
BN 5353:2			XAZ/90	1
BN 5354:2			XAZ/90	1
BN 5355:2			XAZ/90	1
BN 5356:2			XAZ/90	1
BN 5357:2			XAZ/90	1
BN 5358:2			XAZ/90	1
BN 5359:2			XAZ/90	1
BN 5360:2			XAZ/90	1
BN 5361:2			XAZ/90	1
BN 5362:2			XAZ/90	1
BN 5363:2			NRE/90	1
BN 5364:2			NRE/90	1

Notes:
1) BN 5300:1-5305:1 renumbered 5800-5805 1973; BN 5300:2-5305:2 built 5/75. BN 5353:1-5364:1 renumbered 5900-5911 1973; BN 5353:2-5364:2 built 5/75.
2) Retired 3/87 and returned to lessor.
3) Retired 10/90; to Kyle via Pielet Bros 12/90-1/91.
4) BN 5325 repainted in red-white-and-blue bicentennial paint scheme 4/10/75. Restored to BN 5325 in standard colors. Retired 10/90 and scrapped by Pielet Bros.
5) BN 5336 wrecked and rebuilt as cabless B-unit 800B. Renumbered 4500. Retired 2/86 and sold to PNC for scrap.
6) BN 5913, 5907, 5669 and 5320 working as mid-train remotes wrecked and burned Wiggins, CO, 3/27/74. All but 5320 scrapped.
7) BN 5910 wrecked 8/2/79 on Crawford Hill, NE.
8) BN 5814 wrecked and sold to Simon & Sons 6/85 for scrap.
9) Retired 1/91 and returned to lessor.
10) Retired 1990 and returned to lessor. Sold to National Railway Equipment 12/90.
11) BN 5914 wrecked in head-on collision Wiggins, CO, 4/13/84 and scrapped.
12) BN 5939 and 5301:2 retired 12/90 and sold to NRS. To Conrail Juniata shops for parts; trucks to GE ex-ATSF C30-7 8046 and 8087 being rebuilt under contract. Both units scrapped, however, engine, generator and radiator section of BN 5301 (minus trucks) moved to Nelson's Alternative Disposal Systems, south of Erie, PA, for use as power generator.
13) BN 5802 (ex-5302) preserved 3/88 for display in Gillette, WY.
14) Returned to lessor 04/89 and sold to LS&I.

Chicago & North Western

U30C	Serial	Built	Options/Notes
930-936	36650-36656	1/68-2/68	

Original Road No.	NdeM	Rebuild	Status	Notes
C&NW 930	NdeM 930		OS	1
C&NW 931	NdeM 931		OS	1
C&NW 932	NdeM 932		OS	1
C&NW 933	NdeM 933		OS	1
C&NW 934		MNCR 4183		2
C&NW 935	NdeM 935		OS	1
C&NW 936	NdeM 936		OS	1

Notes:

1) C&NW 930-933, 935-936 to NdeM 930-933, 935-936 9/78. Only 932 left active by 1988; all out of service by 1990.
2) C&NW 934 rebuilt GE Pittsburg 8-10/78 to Metro-North Commuter Railroad U34CH 4183. Joined NJDOT U34CH fleet in service out of Hoboken as MNCR's contribution to Hoboken, New Jersey-Port Jervis, New York, "West of Hudson" commuter service.

Chesapeake & Ohio

U30C	Serial	Built	Options/Notes
3300-3303	36300-36303	6/67	
3304-3312	36767-36775	5/68-7/68	

Original Road No.	Status	Notes
C&O 3300	XPLJ/85	1
C&O 3301	XPLJ/85	1
C&O 3302	XPLJ/85	1
C&O 3303	XPLJ/85	1
C&O 3304	XNIM/84	2
C&O 3305	XNIM/84	2
C&O 3306	XNIM/84	2
C&O 3307	XNIM/84	2
C&O 3308	XNIM/84	2
C&O 3309	XNIM/84	2
C&O 3310	XNIM/84	2
C&O 3311	XNIM/84	2
C&O 3312	XNIM/84	2

Notes:
1) C&O 3300-3303 traded-in to GE 8/85; to Pielet Bros. Joliet, IL, for scrap.
2) C&O 3304-3312 retired 8/83, scrapped NI&M 1984.

Colorado & Southern

U30C	Serial	Built	Options/Notes
890-893	36791-36794	6/68-7/68	

Original Road No.	1979 Re#	BN	Status	Notes
C&S 890	C&S 5396	BN 5396	XSL/87	
C&S 891	C&S 5397	BN 5397	XSL/87	
C&S 892	C&S 5398	BN 5398		
C&S 893	C&S 5399	BN 5399		

Delaware & Hudson

U30C	Serial	Built	Options/Notes
701-706	36232-36237	2/67-3/67	
707-712	36493-36498	12/67	

Original Road No.	NdeM	Status	Notes
D&H 701	DH 701	OS	1, 2
D&H 702	DH 702	OS	1, 3
D&H 703	DH 703	OS	1
D&H 704	DH 704	OS	1, 3
D&H 705	DH 705	OS	1
D&H 706	DH 706	OS	1, 2
D&H 707	DH 707	OS	1
D&H 708	DH 708	OS	1
D&H 709	DH 709	OS	1
D&H 710	DH 710	OS	1
D&H 711	DH 711	OS	1, 3
D&H 712	DH 712	OS	1

Notes:
1) D&H 701-712 to NdeM as DH 701-712 10/78-1/79. All out of service by mid-1980's.
2) D&H 701, 706 shopped Auto Train Sanford, FL, prior to shipment to Mexico 1/79.
3) D&H 702, 704 and 711 shopped GE-Hornell, NY, prior to shipment to Mexico 1/79.

Department of Transportation Pueblo, CO, Test Track

U30C	Serial	Built	Options/Notes
001	38090	6/71	

Original Road No.	Status	Notes
DOT 001		1

Notes:
1) DOT 001 built for use at DOT Test Center Pueblo, CO. Unit replaced BN U28C 5674 leased by DOT.

Detroit Edison

U30C	Serial	Built	Options/Notes
007-012	38235-38240	2/72-3/72	Serials not sequential, A
018-022	40737-40741	7/75	

Original Road No.	Resale	Re#	Status	Notes
DE 007				
DE 008				
DE 009				
DE 010				
DE 011				
DE 012	B&M 640	B&M 663		1
DE 018				
DE 019				
DE 020				
DE 021				
DE 022				

Detroit Edison U30C Notes:

A) DE 007-012 are serial nos. 38237/39/38/40/35/36.
1) DE 012 to B&M 640 (later B&M 663) via Helm 2/86.

Ferrocarril del Pacifico

U30C	Serial	Built	Options/Notes
401-404	37369-37372	11/69-12/69	
405-408	37695-37698	3/71	

Original Road No.	Status	Notes	Super 7 Rebuild	Super 7 Rebuild
FCP 401	X/87			
FCP 402	For SS7	1	EMP/93	
FCP 403		2	FNM 14067	EMP/92
FCP 404		2	FNM 14084	EMP/92
FCP 405				
FCP 406		2	FNM 14066	EMP/92
FCP 407	X/87	2	FNM 14065	EMP/92
FCP 408				

Notes:
1) FCP 402 stripped to frame at FNM Empalme shops 2/93 for Super 7 rebuild.
2) Rebuilt to Super 7-C30 by FNM shops Empalme, Sonora.

Kaiser Steel

U30C	Serial	Built	Options/Notes
1030-1034	36762-36766	3/68	

Original Road No.	Status	Notes
Kaiser 1030	Stored	
Kaiser 1031	Stored	
Kaiser 1032	Stored	
Kaiser 1033	Stored	
Kaiser 1034	Stored	

Notes:
1) Kaiser 1030-1034 built to SP specifications, but ballasted to 432,000 pounds—heaviest single-engined U-boats built.
2) Kaiser shut down 3/86; units still stored Fontana, CA 1/94.

Louisville & Nashville

U30C	Serial	Built	Options/Notes
1470-1499	38415-38444	6/72-8/72	
1534-1547	37008-37021	3/69-4/69	
1548-1562	37258-37272	10/69-3/70	
1563-1582	37952-37971	5/71-8/71	

Original Road No.	SBD	CSX	Status	Notes
L&N 1470	SBD 7200	CSX 7200	R	
L&N 1471	SBD 7201	CSX 7201	R/91	
L&N 1472	SBD 7202	CSX 7202	XSPC/93	
L&N 1473	SBD 7203	CSX 7203	XPL/92	
L&N 1474	SBD 7204	CSX 7204	R	
L&N 1475	SBD 7205	CSX 7205	R	
L&N 1476	SBD 7206	CSX 7206	XPL/91	
L&N 1477	SBD 7207	CSX 7207	R	
L&N 1478	SBD 7208	CSX 7208	XPL/91	
L&N 1479	SBD 7209	CSX 7209	R	
L&N 1480	SBD 7210	CSX 7210	XPL/92	
L&N 1481	SBD 7211	CSX 7211	R/91	
L&N 1482	SBD 7212	CSX 7212	R/92	
L&N 1483	SBD 7213	CSX 7213	R	
L&N 1484	SBD 7214	CSX 7214	R	
L&N 1485	SBD 7215	CSX 7215	R	
L&N 1486	SBD 7216	CSX 7216	XPL/92	
L&N 1487	SBD 7217	CSX 7217	XPL/92	
L&N 1488	SBD 7218	CSX 7218	R	
L&N 1489	SBD 7219	CSX 7219	R/91	
L&N 1490	SBD 7220	CSX 7220	R/91	
L&N 1491	SBD 7221	CSX 7221	R	
L&N 1492	SBD 7222	CSX 7222	R/91	
L&N 1493	SBD 7223	CSX 7223	R	
L&N 1494	SBD 7224	CSX 7224	R/91	
L&N 1495	SBD 7225	CSX 7225	XNIM/91	
L&N 1496	SBD 7226	CSX 7226	R	
L&N 1497	SBD 7227	CSX 7227	R	
L&N 1498	SBD 7228	CSX 7228	XPL/92	
L&N 1499			WX/77	1
L&N 1534	SBD 7229	CSX 7229	XLS/93	
L&N 1535	SBD 7230	CSX 7230	R	
L&N 1536	SBD 7231	CSX 7231	R	
L&N 1537	SBD 7232	CSX 7232	R	
L&N 1538	SBD 7233	CSX 7233	XPL/92	
L&N 1539	SBD 7234	CSX 7234	R	
L&N 1540	SBD 7235	CSX 7235	R	
L&N 1541	SBD 7236	CSX 7236	R/92	
L&N 1542			WX/69	2
L&N 1543	SBD 7237	CSX 7237	R	
L&N 1544	SBD 7238	CSX 7238	R	
L&N 1545	SBD 7239	CSX 7239	R	
L&N 1546	SBD 7240	CSX 7240	XPLJ/91	
L&N 1547	SBD 7241	CSX 7241	R	
L&N 1548	SBD 7242	CSX 7242	XSPC/93	
L&N 1549	SBD 7243	CSX 7243	R	
L&N 1550	SBD 7244	CSX 7244	R	
L&N 1551	SBD 7245	CSX 7245	R/91	
L&N 1552	SBD 7246	CSX 7246	XSPC/93	
L&N 1553	SBD 7247	CSX 7247	XNIM/91	
L&N 1554	SBD 7248	CSX 7248	XPL/92	
L&N 1555	SBD 7249	CSX 7249	R/91	
L&N 1556	SBD 7250	CSX 7250	R	
L&N 1557	SBD 7251	CSX 7251	R/91	
L&N 1558	SBD 7252	CSX 7252	XPL/92	
L&N 1559	SBD 7253	CSX 7253	XSPC/93	
L&N 1560	SBD 7254	CSX 7254	XSPC/93	
L&N 1561	SBD 7255	CSX 7255	XPL/92	
L&N 1562	SBD 7256	CSX 7256	XSPC/93	
L&N 1563	SBD 7257	CSX 7257	R	
L&N 1564	SBD 7258	CSX 7258	R/93	3
L&N 1565	SBD 7259	CSX 7259	R	
L&N 1566	SBD 7260	CSX 7260	R/92	
L&N 1567	SBD 7261	CSX 7261	R	
L&N 1568	SBD 7262	CSX 7262	R	
L&N 1569	SBD 7263	CSX 7263	R	
L&N 1570	SBD 7264	CSX 7264	R	
L&N 1571	SBD 7265	CSX 7265	R/91	
L&N 1572	SBD 7266	CSX 7266	R	
L&N 1573	SBD 7267	CSX 7267	R	
L&N 1574	SBD 7268	CSX 7268	XPL/92	
L&N 1575	SBD 7269	CSX 7269	R/92	
L&N 1576	SBD 7270	CSX 7270	XNIM/91	
L&N 1577	SBD 7271	CSX 7271	R	
L&N 1578	SBD 7272	CSX 7272	R	
L&N 1579	SBD 7273	CSX 7273	R	
L&N 1580	SBD 7274	CSX 7274	XPL/92	
L&N 1581	SBD 7275	CSX 7275	R/91	
L&N 1582	SBD 7276	CSX 7276	R/91	

Notes:
1) L&N 1499 delivered in special black-white-and-gold "XR Series" paint scheme. Repainted standard L&N colors 8/76. Wrecked N. Corbin, KY, 1/5/77 and scrapped.
2) Southbound L&N coal train with 1542, 1215, 1428, 1411 and northbound empties lead by 1407 and 1526 in head-on collision at Amhurst, TN, 5/12/69. All units scrapped.
3) CSXT 7258 last U30C in service on CSX; used as load test unit at Huntingdon, WV, shops until replaced by SD45-2 8969 in 1993.

Milwaukee Road

U30C	Serial	Built	Options/Notes
5651-5658	39916-39923	8/74	

Original Road No.	Super 7 Rebuild	Super 7 Shop/date	Status	Notes
MILW 5651	GECX 3006	MTL 7/90		1,2
MILW 5652	GECX 3005	MTL 7/90		1,2
MILW 5653	GECX 3003	MTL 6/90		1,2
MILW 5654	GECX 3008	MTL 9/90		1,2
MILW 5655	GECX 3004	MTL 6/90		1,2
MILW 5656	GECX 3010	MTL 10/90		1,2
MILW 5657	GECX 3007	MTL 8/90		1,2
MILW 5658			XMLW	1,2

Notes:
1) Built to BN specifications for use on runthrough coal trains.
2) All retired by 1980; to GE for Super 7 program 9/88. All moved to GE-Montreal (MLW) for rebuilding as Super 7-C30's GECX 3003- 3010; MILW 5658 scrapped at GE Montreal c./91.

Missouri Pacific

U30C	Serial	Built	Options/Notes
960-965	36700-36705	3/68-4/68	
966-969	37022-37025	5/69	
970-973	37559-37562	6/70-7/70	
974-978	38011-38015	8/71-9/71	
979-983	38261-38265	2/72	
25-29	39210-39214	6/73	
3329-3334	39500-39504	1/74-2/74	

Original Road No.	1973 Re#	1974 Re#	1979 Re#	Status & Notes	
MP 960	MP 1	MP 3300	MP 2965	TGE	1
MP 961	MP 2	MP 3301	MP 2966	TGE	1
MP 962	MP 3	MP 3302	MP 2967	TGE	1
MP 963	MP 4	MP 3303	MP 2968	TGE	1
MP 964	MP 5	MP 3304	MP 2969	TGE	1
MP 965	MP 6	MP 3305	MP 2970	ECCO	1,6
MP 966	MP 7	MP 3306	MP 2971	Rx	
MP 967	MP 8	MP 3307	MP 2972	XNLR/85	
MP 968	MP 9	MP 3308	MP 2973	XAIM/85	
MP 969	MP 10	MP 3309	MP 2974	XAIM/85	
TP 970	TP 11	TP 3310	MP 2975	TGE	1
TP 971	TP 12	TP 3311	MP 2976	TGE	1,2
TP 972	TP 13	TP 3312	MP 2977	TGE	1
TP 973	TP 14	TP 3313	MP 2978	TGE	1
MP 974	MP 15	MP 3314	MP 2979	XPL/87	3
MP 975	MP 16	MP 3315	MP 2980	XPL/87	3
MP 976	MP 17	MP 3316	MP 2981	XPL/87	3
MP 977	MP 18	MP 3317	MP 2982	XPL/87	3
MP 978	MP 19	MP 3318	MP 2983	XPL/87	3
MP 979	MP 20	MP 3319	MP 2984	TGE/88	4,5
MP 980	MP 21	MP 3320	MP 2985	TGE/88	5
MP 981	MP 22	MP 3321	MP 2986	XSW/89	
MP 982	MP 23	MP 3322	MP 2987	XSW/89	
MP 983	MP 24	MP 3323	MP 2988	TGE/88	5
MP 25		MP 3324	MP 2989	XSW/89	
MP 26		MP 3325	MP 2990	XSW/89	
MP 27		MP 3326	MP 2991	XSW/89	
MP 28		MP 3327	MP 2992	XSW/89	
MP 29		MP 3328	MP 2993	GE	5
TP 3329			TP 2994	XPL/87	3
TP 3330			TP 2995	XPL/87	3
TP 3331			TP 2996	XPL/87	3
TP 3332			TP 2997	XPL/87	3
TP 3333			TP 2998	XPL/87	3
TP 3334			TP 2999	XPL/87	3

Notes:
1) MP 2965-2970, 2975-2978 retired 5/85 and traded in to GE on MP C36-7's.
2) MP 3311 wrecked Meeker, LA, rebuilt at North Little Rock, AR, shops with EMD cab.
3) Traded in to GE in 1987 on UP Dash 8 40-C's; to Pielet Bros. for scrap.
4) MP 3319 wrecked 1974. Repaired without cab and nose and operated as B-unit for at least 10 months until new cab and nose applied.
5) To GE for Super 7 program.
6) Traded in to GE 05/85, to Enterprise Coal Co., Robinson Creek, KY, in 1987.

Norfolk & Western

U30C	Serial	Built	Options/Notes
8000-8002	39841-39843	3/74	

Original Road No.	Status	Notes
N&W 8000	XLS/93	
N&W 8001	XLS/93	
N&W 8002	XLS/93	

Notes:
1) N&W 8000-8002 built with low noses; all retired 12/91 and scrapped at Roanoke, VA, in 1993 by Louisville Scrap.

Pennsylvania

U30C	Serial	Built	Options/Notes
6535-6539	39096-36100	1/67	

Original Road No.	PC	CR	1979 re#	Status	Notes
PRR 6535	PC 6535	CR 6535	CR 6835	XCRH/87	
PRR 6536	PC 6536	CR 6536	CR 6836	XCRH/87	
PRR 6537	PC 6537	CR 6537	CR 6837	XCRH/87	
PRR 6538	PC 6538	CR 6538	CR 6838	Rx	
PRR 6539	PC 6539	CR 6539	CR 6839	XCRH/87	

Notes:
1) PRR 6535-6539 ordered as U28C's.

Reading

U30C	Serial	Built	Options/Notes
6300-6304	36318-36322	6/67-7/67	

Original Road No.	1st CR Road No.	2nd CR Road No.	Status	Notes
RDG 6300	CR 6579	CR 6840	P	1,2
RDG 6301	CR 6580	CR 6841	GE	1
RDG 6302	CR 6581	CR 6842	GE	1
RDG 6303	CR 6582	CR 6843	GE	1
RDG 6304	CR 6583	CR 6844	GE	1

Notes:
1) CR 6840-6844 retired 1983 and sold to C&NW for parts. Resold to GE c.1988 for Super 7 program. Not used.
2) CR 6840 to Reading Co. Technical & Historical Society 8/91 for preservation.

Rock Island

U30C	Serial	Built	Options/Notes
4582-4599	39479-39496	10/73-12/73	A

Original Road No.	Status	Notes
RI 4582	X	
RI 4583	X	
RI 4584	X	
RI 4585	X	
RI 4586	X	
RI 4587	X	
RI 4588	X	
RI 4589	X	
RI 4590	X	
RI 4591	X	
RI 4592	X	
RI 4593	X	
RI 4594	X	
RI 4595	X	
RI 4596	X	
RI 4597	X	
RI 4598	X	
RI 4599	X	

Notes:
A) RI 4582-4599 delivered with GE "XR Series" stencilling on frame.
1) All returned to lessor North American Car after RI ceased operations; stored at Silvis. Still on hand 10/88. Presumed scrapped by Chrome Locomotive at ex-RI shops, Silvis, IL.

SOO Line

U30C	Serial	Built	Options/Notes
800-809	36715-36724	4/68-6/68	

Original Road No.	Status	Notes
SOO 800	XPL/83	1
SOO 801	XPL/84	2
SOO 802	XPL/84	2
SOO 803	XPL/84	2
SOO 804	XPL/84	2
SOO 805	XPL/83	1
SOO 806	XPL/83	1
SOO 807	XPL/84	2
SOO 808	XPL/84	2
SOO 809	XPL/84	2

Notes:
1) Traded in to EMD 1/83 and scrapped Pielet Bros.
2) Traded in to EMD 1984 and scrapped Pielet Bros.

Southern

U30C	Serial	Built	Options/Notes
3100-3104	36483-36487	12/67	

Original Road No.	1969 Re#	Status	Notes
SOU 3100	SOU 3800	Rx/82	1
SOU 3101	SOU 3801		2
SOU 3102	SOU 3802	Rx/82	
SOU 3103	SOU 3803	Rx/82	
SOU 3104	SOU 3804	Rx	

Notes:
1) SOU 3800 and 3805 severely damaged in wreck at Atlanta, GA., 7/73; both repaired GE-Chamblee, GA.
2) SOU 3801 Assigned to McDonough, GA, training center 1982. Last SOU U30C. Replaced in 1992 by B36-7 3819.

Southern Pacific

U30C	Serial	Built	Options/Notes
7900-7929	36620-36649	2/68-7/68	
7930-7936	37172-37178	10/69	L-shaped windshield

Original Road No.	Status	Notes
SP 7900	TGX/84	1
SP 7901	TGX/84	1
SP 7902	TGX/84	1
SP 7903	TGX/84	1
SP 7904	TGX/84	1
SP 7905	TGX/84	1
SP 7906	TGX/84	1
SP 7907	TGX/84	1
SP 7908	TGX/84	1
SP 7909	TGX/84	1
SP 7910	XPL/85	1
SP 7911	TGX/84	1
SP 7912	TGX/84	1
SP 7913	TGX/84	1
SP 7914	TGX/84	1
SP 7915	TGX/84	1
SP 7916	TGX/84	1
SP 7917	TGX/84	1
SP 7918	TGX/84	1
SP 7919	TGX/84	1
SP 7920	TGX/84	1
SP 7921	TGX/84	1
SP 7922	TGX/84	1
SP 7923	TGX/84	1
SP 7924	TGX/84	1
SP 7925	TGX/84	1
SP 7926	TGX/84	1
SP 7927	TGX/84	1
SP 7928	Rx	
SP 7929	TGX/84	1
SP 7930	TGX/84	1
SP 7931	TGX/84	1

Southern Pacific U30C Cont.

Original Road No.	Status	Notes
SP 7932	TGX/84	1
SP 7933	TGX/84	1
SP 7934	TGX/84	1
SP 7935	TGX/84	1
SP 7936	TGX/84	1

Notes:
1) SP 7900-7927, 7929-7936 retired 6/84; traded-in to GE 12/84 on B36-7's; many (all?) scrapped at Pielet Bros. 1985.

Union Pacific

U30C	Serial	Built	Options/Notes
2810-2829	38300-38319	4/72-6/72	
2830-2859	38795-38824	2/73-5/73	
2860-2869	39200-39209	6/73	
2870-2899	39591-39620	3/74-7/74	
2900-2904	39847-39851	7/74	
2905-2919	40044-40058	4/75-2/76	
2920-2959	40925-40964	7/76-10/76	

Original Road No.	Status	Notes	Super 7 Rebuild	Super 7 Shop/Date
UP 2810	XPL/86			
UP 2811	XSL/85			
UP 2812	XSL/85			
UP 2813	XPL/87	1		
UP 2814	XSL/85			
UP 2815	XPL/87	1		
UP 2816	XEH/85			
UP 2817	XSL/85			
UP 2818	XEH/85			
UP 2819	XDU/85			
UP 2820	WX/80	2		
UP 2821	XSL/85			
UP 2822	XPL/87	1		
UP 2823	XPL/87	1		
UP 2824	XPL/86			
UP 2825	XEH/85			
UP 2826	XSL/85			
UP 2827	XPL/86			
UP 2828	XPL/87	1		
UP 2829	XPL/92	11		
UP 2830	XSL/85	3		
UP 2831	XPL/86			
UP 2832	XPL/92	11		
UP 2833	XPL/87	1		
UP 2834	XPL/86	4		
UP 2835	XPL/86			
UP 2836	XPL/87	1		
UP 2837	XPL/86			
UP 2838	XPL/86			
UP 2839	XPL/86			
UP 2840	XAZ/91			
UP 2841	XEH/85			
UP 2842	XEH/86			
UP 2843	XEH/85			
UP 2844	XPL/86			
UP 2845	XEH/85			
UP 2846	XSL/85			
UP 2847	XEH/85			
UP 2848	XPL/86			
UP 2849	XPL/87	1		
UP 2850	XPL/86			
UP 2851	XPL/86			
UP 2852	XPL/86			
UP 2853	XPL/86			
UP 2854	XPL/86			
UP 2855	XPL/86			
UP 2856	XSL/86			
UP 2857	XPL/86			
UP 2858	XPL/87	1		
UP 2859	XIS/86			
UP 2860	XWI/88			
UP 2861	XPL/86			
UP 2862	XIS/86			
UP 2863	XPL/86			
UP 2864	XWI/88			
UP 2865	XPL/88			
UP 2866	XEH/85			
UP 2867	XSW/87			
UP 2868	XSL/86			
UP 2869	XPL/86			
UP 2870	WX/79	5		
UP 2871	WX/86	6		
UP 2872	XPL/87	1		
UP 2873	XPL/87	1		
UP 2874	XPL/86			
UP 2875	XSW/88			
UP 2876	XSW/87			
UP 2877	WX/84	7		
UP 2878	TGE/88	11		
UP 2879	XPL/87	1		
UP 2880	XPL/86			
UP 2881	XPL/87	1		
UP 2882	XPL/87	1		
UP 2883	TGE/88	11		
UP 2884	XPL/86			
UP 2885	XPL/87	1		
UP 2886	XPL/87	1		
UP 2887	XPL/87	1		
UP 2888	XPL/87	1		
UP 2889	XPL/88	8		
UP 2890	XPL/87	1		
UP 2891	XPL/88			
UP 2892	XWI/88			
UP 2893	XPL/87	1		
UP 2894	TGE/89			
UP 2895	XPL/89			
UP 2896	XPL/87	1		
UP 2897	TGE/89			
UP 2898	TGE/88	11		
UP 2899	XPL/86			
UP 2900	XPL/88	8		
UP 2901	XPL/87	1		
UP 2902	XSW/89			
UP 2903	XPL/86			
UP 2904	TGE/89			
UP 2905	XSW/89			
UP 2906	XPL/87	1		
UP 2907	XPL/89			
UP 2908	XPL/89			
UP 2909	XSW/89			
UP 2910	XPL/90			
UP 2911	XSW/89	12		
UP 2912	XSL/88			
UP 2913	XPL/88			
UP 2914	XPL/87	1		
UP 2915	XPL/87	1		
UP 2916	XSW/89			
UP 2917	XPL/89			
UP 2918	XWI/88			
UP 2919	XPL/87	1		
UP 2920	XPL/87	1		
UP 2921	XPL/87	1		
UP 2922	XPL/90			
UP 2923	XPL/87	1		
UP 2924	XPL/88			
UP 2925	XSW/89			
UP 2926	XPL/87	1		
UP 2927	XWI/88			
UP 2928	XPL/87	1		
UP 2929	XPL/88	8		
UP 2930	XSW/88			
UP 2931	XPL/87	1		
UP 2932	XPL/88	8		
UP 2933	XSW/89			
UP 2934	XPL/89			
UP 2935	XPL/87	1		
UP 2936	XPL/87	1		
UP 2937	XPL/87	1		
UP 2938	XPL/87	1		
UP 2939	XSW/89			
UP 2940	XSW/89			
UP 2941	XPL/87	1, 3		
UP 2942	XPL/87	1		
UP 2943	XPL/89			
UP 2944	GE/90			
UP 2945	XSW/89			
UP 2946	TGE/88	11		
UP 2947	XPL/88	8		
UP 2948	WX/82	9		
UP 2949	XPL/88	8		
UP 2950	XSW/89			
UP 2951	GE/90			
UP 2952	XSW/87			
UP 2953	XPL/88	8		
UP 2954	XGS/89			
UP 2955	XPL/92	11		
UP 2956		10	GECX 3002	MK 6/89
UP 2957	XSW/90			
UP 2958	XPL/87	1		
UP 2959	XPL/88	8		

Notes:
1) Traded in to GE in 1987 on UP Dash 8-40's 9100-9174; to Pielet Bros. for scrap.
2) UP 2820 wrecked Hayward, CA, 4/9/80 while on WP. Scrapped.
3) UP 2830 and 2941 wrecked near Delphi, IN, 4/77 while on N&W. Repaired ICG Paducah.
4) UP 2834 hit rock slide at Cotter, AR, 12/28/84. To Pielet Bros. for scrap 8/86.
5) UP 2870 wrecked on MP at Hitchita, OK, 12/20/79 and scrapped.
6) UP 2871 wrecked on C&NW c./86; purchased by C&NW in settlement.
7) UP 2877 wrecked on runaway ore train Silver Bow, MT, 11/24/84 and scrapped by UP at Pocatello, ID.
8) Traded in to GE 1988; held for Super 7 program; to Pielet Bros. for scrap 8/88.
9) UP 2948 wrecked on MP near Glaise Jct., AR, 10/4/82 and scrapped.
10) UP 2956 traded in to GE 4/88. Rebuilt Morrison-Knudsen, Boise, ID, 6/89 to Super 7-C30 GECX 3002.
11) To GE for Super 7 program.
12) Traded in to GE 1988; to Southwest RR Car Parts for scrap.
13) UP U30C, number unknown, cut down to frame at GE Erie for rebuilding as Alco-powered Super 7. Work never completed.

U30CG

Atchison, Topeka & Santa Fe

U30CG	Serial	Built	Options/Notes
400-405	36346-36351	11/67-12/67	

Original Road No.	1969 Re#	Status	Notes
ATSF 400	ATSF 8000	TGX/80	
ATSF 401	ATSF 8001	TGX/80	
ATSF 402	ATSF 8002	TGX/80	
ATSF 403	ATSF 8003	TGX/80	
ATSF 404	ATSF 8004	TGX/80	
ATSF 405	ATSF 8005	TGX/80	

Notes
1) ATSF 400-405 retired 9/80 and traded-in to GE on B36-7's.

U33B

New York Central

U33B	Serial	Built	Options/Notes
2858-2859	36397-36398	9/67	A

Original Road No.	PC Road No.	CR Road No.	Status	Notes
NYC 2858	PC 2858	CR 2858	XNIM/86	
NYC 2859	PC 2859	CR 2859	XNIM/86	

Notes:
A) NYC 2858-2859 first U33B's built. Builders plates read U30B.

Penn Central

U33B	Serial	Built	Options/Notes
2890-2915	36868-36893	9/68-11/68	
2916-2925	36939-36948	11/68-12/68	
2926-2935	36929-36938	11/68	
2936-2955	36949-36968	12/68	
2956-2970	37396-37410	5/70-6/70	Cancelled RI order

Original Road No.	CR Road No.	1st Resale	2nd Resale	Status & Notes	
PC 2890	CR 2890			XCCS/84	2
PC 2891	CR 2891				
PC 2892	CR 2892			XCCS/84	2
PC 2893	CR 2893	IARR 2893		XPL/86	8
PC 2894	CR 2894			XCCS/84	2
PC 2895	CR 2895	MOXV 2895	RBMR 3300		6
PC 2896	CR 2896	PVR/MOXV 2896	RBMR 3301		7
PC 2897	CR 2897			XPL/86	2
PC 2898	CR 2898			XCCS/84	2
PC 2899	CR 2899			Rx	
PC 2900	CR 2900			Rx	
PC 2901	CR 2901			XCCS/84	2
PC 2902	CR 2902			XCCS/84	2
PC 2903	CR 2903			XCCS/84	2
PC 2904	CR 2904			XPL/86	2
PC 2905	CR 2905			XCCS/84	2
PC 2906	CR 2906			XCCS/84	2
PC 2907	CR 2907			XPL/86	2
PC 2908	CR 2908			XCCS/84	2
PC 2909	CR 2909			XPL/86	
PC 2910	CR 2910			XPL/86	2
PC 2911	CR 2911			XCCS/84	2
PC 2912	CR 2912			XCCS/84	2
PC 2913	CR 2913			XPL/86	2
PC 2914	CR 2914	KKRR 29	RBMR 3302		10
PC 2915	CR 2915			XCCS/84	2
PC 2916	CR 2916	B&M 190		XPL/91	4
PC 2917	CR 2917	D&H 2917		XNIM/86	5
PC 2918	CR 2918	D&H 2918		XNIM/86	5
PC 2919	CR 2919	B&M 191		XPL/91	4
PC 2920	CR 2920	D&H 2920		XNIM/86	5
PC 2921	CR 2921			XCRH/87	
PC 2922	CR 2922	D&H 2922		XNIM/86	5
PC 2923	CR 2923			XNIM/86	5
PC 2924	CR 2924	D&H 2924		XNIM/86	5
PC 2925	CR 2925	B&M 192 LVAL 903	RBMR 3303		4
PC 2926	CR 2926			Rx	
PC 2927	CR 2927			Rx	
PC 2928	CR 2928			Rx	
PC 2929	CR 2929			Rx	
PC 2930	CR 2930	RBMR 3304			9
PC 2931	CR 2931			XPL/84	
PC 2932	CR 2932			CCS/84	
PC 2933	CR 2933			CCS/84	
PC 2934	CR 2934			CCS/84	
PC 2935	CR 2935			Rx/78	
PC 2936	CR 2936			Rx	
PC 2937	CR 2937			Rx	
PC 2938	CR 2938			XNIM/84	3
PC 2939	CR 2939			Rx	
PC 2940	CR 2940			Rx	
PC 2941	CR 2941			Rx	
PC 2942	CR 2942			WX/72	
PC 2943	CR 2943			XNIM/84	3
PC 2944	CR 2944			XNIM/84	3
PC 2945	CR 2945			Rx	
PC 2946	CR 2946			Rx	
PC 2947	CR 2947			XNIM/84	3
PC 2948	CR 2948			Rx	
PC 2949	CR 2949			XNIM/84	3
PC 2950	CR 2950			XNIM/84	3
PC 2951	CR 2951			XNIM/84	3
PC 2952	CR 2952			Rx	
PC 2953	CR 2953			Rx	
PC 2954	CR 2954			Rx	
PC 2955	CR 2955			Rx	
PC 2956	CR 2956			XCRH/87	
PC 2957	CR 2957			XCRH/87	
PC 2958	CR 2958			XCRH/87	
PC 2959	CR 2959			XCRH/87	
PC 2960	CR 2960			XCRH/87	
PC 2961	CR 2961			XCRH/87	
PC 2962	CR 2962			XCRH/87	
PC 2963	CR 2963			XCRH/87	
PC 2964	CR 2964			XCRH/87	
PC 2965	CR 2965			XCRH/87	
PC 2966	CR 2966			XCRH/87	
PC 2967	CR 2967			XCRH/87	
PC 2968	CR 2968			XCRH/87	
PC 2969	CR 2969			XCRH/87	
PC 2970	CR 2970			XCRH/87	

Notes:
1) All CR U33B's retired by 6/86.
2) CR 2890, 2892/94/97/98/2901-2908/2910-2913, 2915 to Chrome Crankshaft, Silvis, IL, in 1984.
3) CR 2938/43/44/47/49/50/51 to Naporano Iron & Metal for scrap 7/84.
4) CR 2916, 2919 and 2925 to B&M 190-192 8/84. B&M 190 repainted GTI Waterville 10/84. To GE 3/88 for Super 7 program; to Pielet Bros. for scrap 11/91. B&M 191 to GE 3/88 via MS&A for Super 7 program; to Pielet Bros. for scrap 11/91. B&M 192 to Lackawanna Valley 903 3/88; then to Reading & Blue Mountain 3303.
5) CR 2917, 2918, 2920, 2922 and 2924 leased to D&H 8/84 by ITEL; restencilled D&H in CR paint. CR 2923 rejected by D&H.
6) CR 2895 to Moxahala Valley 2895 2/84; then to Reading & Blue Mountain 3300.
7) CR 2896 to Panther Valley 2896 1/84 to replace ex-CR 2882 transferred to MOXV; then to Reading & Blue Mountain 3301.
8) CR 2893 leased to Iowa RR 1/84 via Chrome Loco. to Pielet for scrap 6/86.
9) CR 2930 to Lackawanna Valley in 1986; then to Reading & Blue Mountain 3304.
10) CR 2914 to Knox & Kane 29 in 1983; to LVAL in 1988, then to Reading & Blue Mountain 3302.

Rock Island

U33B	Serial	Built	Options/Notes
190-199	37128-37137	5/69	
285-289	36969-36973	1/69	
290-299	36822-36831	7/68-9/68	

Original Road No.	Status	Notes
RI 190	X	1
RI 191	X	1
RI 192	X	1
RI 193	X	1
RI 194	X	1
RI 195	X	1
RI 196	X	1
RI 197	X	1
RI 198	X	1
RI 199	X	1
RI 285	XNIM/83	1
RI 286	XNIM/83	1
RI 287	XNIM/83	1, 2
RI 288	XNIM/83	1, 2
RI 289	XNIM/83	1, 2
RI 290	XNIM/83	1, 2
RI 291	XNIM/83	1, 2
RI 292	XNIM/83	1, 2
RI 293	XNIM/83	1, 2
RI 294	XNIM/83	1, 2
RI 295	XNIM/83	1, 2
RI 296	XNIM/83	1, 2
RI 297	XNIM/83	1, 2
RI 298	XNIM/83	1, 2
RI 299	XNIM/83	1, 2

Notes:
1) RI 190-199, 285-299 returned to lessor after RI shut down and scrapped. RI 190-199 presumed scrapped by Chrome Locomotive at ex-RI shops, Silvis, IL., RI 285-299 to NI&M for scrap.
2) RI 287-299 modified to operate with road slugs in 1977.

Seaboard Coast Line

U33B	Serial	Built	Options/Notes
1719-1734	36467-36482	12/67-1/68	Blomberg trucks
1735-1747	36837-36849	1/69-2/69	Blomberg trucks

Original Road No.	SBD Road No.	CSX Road No.	Post CSX Road No.	Status & Notes	
SCL 1719				Slug	1
SCL 1720	SBD 5600	CSX 5600		XWC/87	
SCL 1721	SBD 5601	CSX 5601		R	
SCL 1722	SBD 5602	CSX 5602		Rx/87	
SCL 1723	SBD 5603	CSX 5603		R	
SCL 1724	SBD 5604	CSX 5604		R12/86	
SCL 1725	SBD 5605	CSX 5605		XGC	2
SCL 1726	SBD 5606	CSX 5606		XCIM/87	
SCL 1727	SBD 5607	CSX 5607		XSPC/87	
SCL 1728	SBD 5608	CSX 5608		R	
SCL 1729	SBD 5609	CSX 5609	GC 1015	R	
SCL 1730	SBD 5610	CSX 5610		XSPC/87	
SCL 1731	SBD 5611			XCIM/87	
SCL 1732	SBD 5612	CSX 5612		R	
SCL 1733	SBD 5613	CSX 5613		R	
SCL 1734	SBD 5614	CSX 5614		XGC	2
SCL 1735	SBD 5615	CSX 5615		R	
SCL 1736	SBD 5616			XCIM/87	
SCL 1737	SBD 5617	CSX 5617		R	
SCL 1738	SBD 5618	CSX 5618		R	
SCL 1739	SBD 5619	CSX 5619	GC 1016		2
SCL 1740	SBD 5620	CSX 5620		R	
SCL 1741	SBD 5621	CSX 5621	GC 1013		2
SCL 1742	SBD 5622	CSX 5622		R	
SCL 1743	SBD 5623	CSX 5623		R	
SCL 1744	SBD 5624	CSX 5624		R	
SCL 1745	SBD 5625	CSX 5625	GC 1014		2
SCL 1746	SBD 5626	CSX 5626	GC 1012		2
SCL 1747	SBD 5627	CSX 5627		R	

Notes:
1) SCL 1719 wrecked Biloxi, MS. 3/21/74. Unit derailed into Gulf of Mexico after span of L&N Biloxi Bay bridge knocked out by tug boat. To IMS, Hammond, IN., 9/74, then to RI. Rebuilt RI Silvis (IL) shops to road slug RI 282; re# RI 50.
2) Sold to Georgia Central; CSX 5605 and 5614 cannibalized for parts at Lyons, GA.

U33C

Atchison, Topeka & Santa Fe

U33C	Serial	Built	Options/Notes
8500-8524	37073-37097	6/69- 8/69	

Original Road No.	Status	Notes
ATSF 8500	XPNC/85	1
ATSF 8501	XPNC/85	1
ATSF 8502	XPNC/85	1
ATSF 8503	XPNC/85	1
ATSF 8504	XPNC/85	1
ATSF 8505	XPNC/85	1
ATSF 8506	XPNC/85	1
ATSF 8507	XPNC/85	1
ATSF 8508	XPNC/85	1
ATSF 8509	XPNC/85	1
ATSF 8510	XPNC/85	1
ATSF 8511	XPNC/85	1
ATSF 8512	XPNC/85	1
ATSF 8513	XPNC/85	1
ATSF 8514	XPNC/85	1
ATSF 8515	XPNC/85	1
ATSF 8516	XPNC/85	1
ATSF 8517	XPNC/85	1
ATSF 8518	XPNC/85	1
ATSF 8519	XPNC/85	1
ATSF 8520	XPNC/85	1
ATSF 8521	XPNC/85	1
ATSF 8522	XPNC/85	1
ATSF 8523	XPNC/85	1
ATSF 8524	XPNC/85	1

Notes:
1) ATSF 8500-8524 returned to lessor 12/84 and scrapped by PNC.

Burlington Northern

U33C	Serial	Built	Options/Notes
5725-5734	37685-37694	2/71-3/71	
5735-5763	37972-38000	7/71-9/71	

Original Road No.	Resale Road No.	Status	Notes
BN 5725		XSL/87	1, 2
BN 5726		XSL/87	1, 2
BN 5727		XSL/87	1, 2
BN 5728		XSL/87	1, 2
BN 5729		XSL/87	2
BN 5730		XSL/87	2
BN 5731		XSL/87	2
BN 5732		XSL/87	2
BN 5733		XSL/87	2
BN 5734		XSL/87	2
BN 5735		XSL/87	2
BN 5736		XSL/87	2
BN 5737		XSL/87	2
BN 5738		XSL/87	2
BN 5739		XSL/87	2
BN 5740		XSL/87	2
BN 5741		XSL/87	2
BN 5742		XSL/87	2
BN 5743		XSL/87	2
BN 5744		XSL/87	2
BN 5745		XSL/87	2
BN 5746		XSL/87	2
BN 5747		XSL/87	2
BN 5748		XSL/87	2
BN 5749		XSL/87	2
BN 5750		XSL/87	2
BN 5751		XSL/87	2
BN 5752	SqCr 5752		3
BN 5753		XSL/87	2
BN 5754		XSL/87	2
BN 5755		XSL/87	2
BN 5756		XSL/87	2
BN 5757		XSL/87	2
BN 5758		XSL/87	2
BN 5759		XSL/87	2
BN 5760		XSL/87	2
BN 5761		XSL/87	2
BN 5762		XSL/87	2
BN 5763		XSL/87	2

Notes:
1) BN 5725-5728 ordered as CB&Q 578-581; delivered as BN.
2) BN 5725-5763 retired 2-7/86. All but 5752 to St. Louis Auto Shredding for scrap in 1986-87.
3) BN 5752 retired 2/86, sold to Squaw Creek Coal 5752 12/86 for use at Ayrshire Mine, Chandler, IN.

Delaware & Hudson

U33C	Serial	Built	Options/Notes
754-762	37616-37624	9/70-12/70	

Original Road No.	2nd Road No.	3rd Road No.	4th Road No.	Status & Notes		Super 7 Rebuild	Super 7 Shop/Date
D&H 754				GE	3		
D&H 755							
D&H 756				GE	3		
D&H 757				R/88	1		
D&H 758	D&H 653	D&H 668	D&H 658		4	FNM 14021	MTL 12/89
D&H 759	D&H 654	D&H 669	D&H 659		5	FNM 14020	MTL 12/89
D&H 760				XDH/89	2		
D&H 761	D&H 652	D&H 661		XPL/91	3		
D&H 762	D&H 662			GE	3,6		

Notes:
1) D&H 757 Burned in Binghamton, NY roundhouse fire 10/6/74; rebuilt Morrison-Knudsen 9/75.
2) D&H 760 ran away & wrecked Lanesboro, PA 5/10/74. Rebuilt Morrison-Knudsen 12/74.
3) To GE for Super 7 program via MS&A 3/88.
4) D&H 658 To GE; rebuilt GE Montreal 12/89 to C30-Super 7 FNM 14021.
5) D&H 659 To GE; rebuilt GE Montreal 12/89 to C30-Super 7 FNM 14020.
6) D&H 762 to GE for Super 7 program via MS&A 3/88. To GE Montreal for Super 7 rebuild.

Erie Lackawanna

U33C	Serial	Built	Options/Notes
3300-3305	36785-36789	7/68	
3306-3315	37054-37062	8/69	

Original Road No.	D&H Road No.	CR	1979 Re#	Status & Notes	
EL 3301	D&H 751	CR 6564	CR 6869	XCRH/87	1,2
EL 3302	D&H 752	CR 6565	CR 6870	XCRH/87	1,2
EL 3303	D&H 753	CR 6566	CR 6871	XCRH/87	1,2
EL 3304		CR 6567	CR 6872	XCRH/87	1
EL 3305		CR 6568	CR 6873	XCRH/87	1
EL 3306		CR 6569	CR 6874	TGX/85	1
EL 3307		CR 6570	CR 6875	TGX/85	1
EL 3308		CR 6571	CR 6876	TGX/85	1
EL 3309		CR 6572	CR 6877	TGX/85	1
EL 3310		CR 6573	CR 6878	TGX/85	1
EL 3311		CR 6574	CR 6879	TaiBao	1,3
EL 3312		CR 6575	CR 6880	TaiBao	1,3
EL 3313		CR 6576	CR 6881	TaiBao	1,3
EL 3314		CR 6577	CR 6882	TGX/85	1
EL 3315		CR 6578	CR 6883	TGX/85	1

Notes:
1) EL 3301-3315 financed by N&W (Dereco) for EL, returned to N&W as CR 6869-6883 10/84 on expiration of lease. Traded in to GE by N&W 3/85.
2) EL U33C's 3301-3303 traded to D&H for SD45's 801-803 in March 1969. Units returned 12/75 in anticipation of Conrail.
3) CR (N&W) 6879-6881 rebuilt GE-Cleveland 8/87 as cabless, remote- controlled, 1800 hp., Cummins-powered mine engines for use at An Tai Bao, China coal mine. Numbered 1-3.

Great Northern

U33C	Serial	Built	Options/Notes
2530-2538	36776-36784	5/68-7/68	
2539-2544	37026-37031	4/69	

Original Road No.	BN Road No.	Status	Notes
GN 2530	BN 5700	Rx	1
GN 2531	BN 5701	WX/71	2
GN 2532	BN 5702	Rx	1
GN 2533	BN 5703	Rx	1
GN 2534	BN 5704	Rx	1
GN 2535	BN 5705	Rx	1
GN 2536	BN 5706	Rx	1
GN 2537	BN 5707	Rx	1
GN 2538	BN 5708	Rx	1
GN 2539	BN 5709	NRE/84	3
GN 2540	BN 5710	NRE/84	3
GN 2541	BN 5711	XAZ/85	4
GN 2542	BN 5712	NRE/84	3
GN 2543	BN 5713	NRE/84	3
GN 2544	BN 5714	NRE/84	3

Notes:
1) Returned to lessor 12/83.
2) BN 5701 wrecked and scrapped in 1971.
3) BN 5709, 5710, 5712 and 5714 retired 7/84 and sold to National Railway Equipment for scrap.
4) BN 5711 sold to NRE 2/85; to Azcon for scrap.

Illinois Central

U33C	Serial	Built	Options/Notes
5050-5059	36690-36699	4/68-5/68	

Original Road No.	ICG	Status	Notes
IC 5050	ICG 5050	XPNC/84	1,3
IC 5051	ICG 5051	XPNC/84	3
IC 5052	ICG 5052	XPNC/84	3
IC 5053	ICG 5053	XPNC/84	3
IC 5054	ICG 5054	XPNC/84	3
IC 5055		WX/69	2
IC 5056	ICG 5056	XPNC/84	3
IC 5057	ICG 5057	XPNC/84	3
IC 5058	ICG 5058	XPNC/84	3
IC 5059	ICG 5059	XPNC/84	3

Notes:
1) ICG 5050 wrecked in head-on Cobden IL, 12/2/73. Repaired Paducah 1974.
2) IC 9239, 9086 and 5055 wrecked Riverdale, IL, 9/69 in rear-end collision with coal train. IC 5055 retired and scrapped.
3) ICG 5050-5054, 5056-5059 retired May 18, 1984; sold to PNC and scrapped.

Milwaukee Road

U33C	Serial	Built	Options/Notes
8000-8003	36504-36507	1/68-2/68	

Original Road No.	1973 Re#	Status	Notes
MILW 8000	MILW 5700	WX/81	1
MILW 8001	MILW 5701	Rx	
MILW 8002	MILW 5702	XCCS/84	
MILW 8003	MILW 5703	Rx	

Notes:
1) MILW 8000 first U33C built; wrecked as 5700 and scrapped West Milwaukee 1/81.

Northern Pacific

U33C	Serial	Built	Options/Notes
3300-3309	37118-37127	7/69	

Original Road No.	BN Road No.	Status	Notes
NP 3300	BN 5715	XPNC/84	2
NP 3301	BN 5716	XPNC/84	2
NP 3302	BN 5717	XPNC/84	2
NP 3303	BN 5718	XPNC/84	2
NP 3304	BN 5719	XPNC/84	2
NP 3305	BN 5720	WX/78	1
NP 3306	BN 5721	XPNC/84	2
NP 3307	BN 5722	XPNC/84	2
NP 3308	BN 5723	XPNC/84	2
NP 3309	BN 5724	XPNC/84	2

Notes:
1) BN 5720 wrecked 12/78; scrapped 7/79.
2) BN 5715-5719; 5721-5724 retired 7/84 and sold to PNC for scrap.

Penn Central

U33C	Serial	Built	Options/Notes
6540-6559	36670-36689	2/68-4/68	
6560-6563	36864-36867	8/68	

Original Road No.	CR	1979 Re#	D&H	Status & Notes		Super 7 Rebuild
PC 6540	CR 6540	CR 6845	D&H 650	W/87	1,3,7	
PC 6541	CR 6541	CR 6846			1	
PC 6542	CR 6542	CR 6847			1	
PC 6543	CR 6543	CR 6848			1	
PC 6544	CR 6544	CR 6849			1	
PC 6545	CR 6545	CR 6850			1	
PC 6546	CR 6546	CR 6851			1	
PC 6547	CR 6547	CR 6852			1	
PC 6548	CR 6548	CR 6853			1	
PC 6549	CR 6549	CR 6854			1	
PC 6550	CR 6550	CR 6855			1	
PC 6551	CR 6551	CR 6856	D&H 651		1,3,4	
PC 6552	CR 6552	CR 6857			1	
PC 6553	CR 6553	CR 6858			1	
PC 6554	CR 6554	CR 6859			1	
PC 6555	CR 6555	CR 6860	D&H 652		1,2	
PC 6556	CR 6556	CR 6861		XPL/86	1,2	
PC 6557	CR 6557	CR 6862	D&H 653		1,2,4	
PC 6558	CR 6558	CR 6863		XPL/86	1,2	
PC 6559	CR 6559	CR 6864	D&H 654		1,5	FNM 14022
PC 6560	CR 6560	CR 6865	D&H 655		2	
PC 6561	CR 6561	CR 6866	D&H 656		2	
PC 6562	CR 6562	CR 6867		XPL/86	2,6	
PC 6563	CR 6563	CR 6868			2	

Notes:
1) PC 6540-6559 ordered by PRR, delivered as Penn Central.
2) CR 6860-6868 to Chrome Crankshaft 1984 on expiration of lease; 6860, 6862, 6864-6866 to D&H 652-656 in 8/85. D&H 652-656 to GE via MS&A 3/88 for Super 7 program.
3) CR 6845, 6856 to D&H 650, 651 via Naporano Iron & Metal.
4) D&H 651, 652, 653 repainted GTI colors; to MS&A 3/88; to GE for Super 7 program. D&H 652 to GE-Montreal (MLW) in 1990.
5) CR 6864 to D&H 654 via Chrome Crankshaft 1984. D&H 654 to GE via MS&A 3/88. To GE Montreal (MLW) 9/89 and rebuilt to C30-Super 7 FNM 14022 12/89.
6) CR 6867 to Iowa RR. for parts via Chrome Crankshaft; scrapped Pielet Bros. 1986.
7) GTI train POSE, engines ST 617, B&M 313, D&H 650, ST 638 derailed at Elnora, NY, 6/7/87. D&H 650 heavily damaged.

S.J. Groves

U33C	Serial	Built	Options/Notes
507-508	37366-37367	10/69	

Original Road No.	BN	Status	Notes
SJG 507	BN 5764	XSL/86	1, 2
SJG 508	BN 5765	XSL/87	1, 2

Notes:
1) S.J. Groves & Sons Construction U33C's purchased for use on Interstate 280 construction project between Roseland and West Orange, NJ. Sold to BN 5764-5765 1/73 (reportedly for $300,000) after completion of their work on the project.
2) BN 5764-5765 retired 7/86 and 11/86; to St. Louis Auto Shredders for scrap 12/86 and 3/87.

Southern

U33C	Serial	Built	Options/Notes
3805-3809	37388-37392	4/70	High nose
3810-3814	38213-38217	1/72	High nose

Original Road No.	2nd Road No.	Status & Notes		Super 7 Rebuild	Super 7 Shop/Date
SOU 3805		TGE	1,2		
SOU 3806		TGE	2		
SOU 3807		TGE	2		
SOU 3808		TGE	2		
SOU 3809	SqCr 3809		2,3		
SOU 3810	GE 405		4,6		
SOU 3811		TGE	4,5	GECX 3000	MK 5/89
SOU 3812		TGE	4,5	GECX 3001	MK 5/89
SOU 3813		TGE	4		
SOU 3814	GE 404		4, 6		

Notes:
1) SOU 3800 and 3805 severely damaged in wreck at Atlanta, GA, 7/73; both repaired GE-Chamblee, GA.
2) Traded-in to GE
3) Rebuilt GE Cleveland Apparatus Shop and sold to Squaw Creek Coal 3809 for use at Ayrshire Mine, Chandler, IN, chop-nosed c.1992.
4) Retired 2/87 and traded-in to GE on C39-8's.
5) SOU 3811 and 3812 rebuilt Morrison Knudsen Boise, ID, 5/89 to Super 7 C30's GECX 3000 and 3001.
6) SOU 3810 and 3814 reconditioned and repainted to GE 405 and 404 for use as load engines on GE Erie, PA., test track.

Southern Pacific

U33C	Serial	Built	Options/Notes
8585-8599	39753-39767	12/74-1/75	
8600-8629	36899-36928	1/69-4/69	
8630-8644	37032-37046	4/69-5/69	
8645-8646	37179-37180	10/69	
8647-8687	37181-37221	2/70-6/70	
8688-8713	38095-38120	10/71-12/71	
8714-8737	38121-38144	12/71-5/72	
8738-8767	38320-38349	2/72-5/72	

U33C	Serial	Built	Options/Notes
8768-8777	38785-38794	1/73-2/73	
8778-8785	39297-39304	6/73-7/73	
8786-8796	39733-39743	2/74-4/74	

Original Road No.	2nd Road No.	Status	Notes
SP 8585		XSW/87	
SP 8586		XSW/87	
SP 8587			
SP 8588		R/86	
SP 8589		XSW/87	
SP 8590		XLM/87	
SP 8591		XSW/87	
SP 8592		XSW/87	
SP 8593		XSW/87	
SP 8594		XSW/87	
SP 8595		XSW/87	
SP 8596		XSW/87	
SP 8597		XSW/87	
SP 8598		XLM/87	
SP 8599		XLM/87	
SP 8600		XCC/85	
SP 8601		XCC/85	
SP 8602		Rx	
SP 8603		Rx	
SP 8604		Rx	
SP 8605		Rx	
SP 8606		XCC/85	
SP 8607		XCC/85 .	
SP 8608		XCC/85	
SP 8609		Rx	
SP 8610		XCC/85	
SP 8611		XCC/85	
SP 8612		Rx	
SP 8613		XCC/85	
SP 8614		Rx	
SP 8615		Rx	
SP 8616		Rx	
SP 8617		Rx	
SP 8618		XCC/85	
SP 8619		Rx	
SP 8620		XCC/85	
SP 8621		Rx	
SP 8622		XCC/85	
SP 8623		XCC/85	
SP 8624		XCC/85	
SP 8625		Rx	
SP 8626		ATSF 144	2
SP 8627		Rx	
SP 8628		XCC/85	
SP 8629		XCC/85	
SP 8630		XCC/85	
SP 8631		XCC/85	
SP 8632		Rx	
SP 8633		Rx	
SP 8634		Rx	
SP 8635		XCC/85	
SP 8636		XCC/85	
SP 8637		XCC/85	
SP 8638		Rx	
SP 8639		Rx	
SP 8640		XCC/85	
SP 8641		Rx	
SP 8642		WX/69	3
SP 8643		XCC/85	
SP 8644		ATSF 143	2
SP 8645		Rx	
SP 8646		XCC/85	
SP 8647		XLM/86	
SP 8648		XLM/86	
SP 8649		XLM/86	
SP 8650		XLM/86	
SP 8651		XLM/86	
SP 8652		XLM/86	
SP 8653			7
SP 8654		Rx	
SP 8655		XSW/86	
SP 8656		XCC/85	
SP 8657		XCC/85	
SP 8658		XLM/86	
SP 8659		XLM/86	
SP 8660		WX/NdeM	5
SP 8661		XSW/86	
SP 8662		XSW/87	
SP 8663		XSW/87	
SP 8664		XSW/87	
SP 8665		XSW/87	
SP 8666		XSW/87	
SP 8667		XSW/87	
SP 8668		XSW/87	
SP 8669			7
SP 8670		XSW/86	
SP 8671		XLM/86	
SP 8672		XLM/86	
SP 8673		XSW/87	
SP 8674		XSW/86	
SP 8675		XLM/86	
SP 8676		XSW/86	
SP 8677		XSW/86	
SP 8678		XSW/86	
SP 8679		XSW/86	
SP 8680		XSW/86	
SP 8681		XSW/86	
SP 8682		XLM/86	
SP 8683		XLM/86	
SP 8684		XSW/86	4
SP 8685		XLM/86	
SP 8686		Rx	
SP 8687		XSW/86	
SP 8688		XSW/87	
SP 8689		GE/88	6
SP 8690		XSW/87	
SP 8691		Rx	
SP 8692		XSW/87	
SP 8693		XSW/87	
SP 8694		Rx	
SP 8695		XSW/87	
SP 8696		XSW/87	
SP 8697		XSW/87	
SP 8698		XSW/87	
SP 8699		XSW/87	
SP 8700		Rx/86	
SP 8701		XSW/87	
SP 8702		XSW/87	
SP 8703		XLM/87	
SP 8704		XSW/87	
SP 8705		XSW/87	
SP 8706		XSW/87	
SP 8707		XSW/87	
SP 8708		XSW/87	
SP 8709		XSW/87	
SP 8710		XSW/87	
SP 8711		XSW/87	
SP 8712		XSW/87	
SP 8713		XSW/87	
SP 8714		XSW/87	
SP 8715		XSW/87	
SP 8716		XSW/87	
SP 8717		GE/88	6
SP 8718	NdeM 8987		5
SP 8719		XSW/87	
SP 8720		Rx4/88	
SP 8721		Rx	
SP 8722		XSW/87	
SP 8723		XSW/87	
SP 8724		XLS/87	
SP 8725		Rx	
SP 8726		Rx/86	
SP 8727		GE/88	6
SP 8728		XSW/87	
SP 8729		XSW/87	
SP 8730		XSW/87	
SP 8731		XSW/87	
SP 8732		XSW/87	
SP 8733		XSW/87	
SP 8734		Rx	
SP 8735		XSW/87	
SP 8736		XSW/87	
SP 8737		XSW/87	
SP 8738		XSW/87	
SP 8739		XSW/87	
SP 8740		XSW/87	
SP 8741		XSW/87	
SP 8742		XSW/87	
SP 8743		XSW/87	
SP 8744		XSW/87	
SP 8745		XSW/87	
SP 8746		XSW/87	
SP 8747		Rx/86	
SP 8748		XSW/87	
SP 8749		XSW/87	5
SP 8750		XPRI/88	
SP 8751		XGS/87	
SP 8752		XLS	
SP 8753		XLS	
SP 8754		GE/88	6, 8
SP 8755		XSW/87	
SP 8756		GE/88	
SP 8757		XSW/87	
SP 8758		XSW/87	
SP 8759		XSW/87	
SP 8760		XLM/87	
SP 8761		XSW/87	
SP 8762		XSW/87	
SP 8763		XSW/87	
SP 8764		XSW/87	
SP 8765		XSW/87	
SP 8766		XSW/87	
SP 8767		XSW/87	
SP 8768		XSW/87	
SP 8769		XSW/87	
SP 8770		GE/88	
SP 8771		GE/88	
SP 8772		GE/88	6
SP 8773		XMPI/87	
SP 8774		XLS/87	
SP 8775		R/86	
SP 8776		XLS/87	
SP 8777		R4/88	
SP 8778		XSW/87	
SP 8779		XSW/87	
SP 8780		XNMP/87	
SP 8781		XSW/87	
SP 8782		XSW/87	
SP 8783		Rx	
SP 8784		XSW/87	
SP 8785		XSW/87	
SP 8786		Rx/86	

Original Road No.	2nd Road No.	Status	Notes
SP 8787		XSW/87	
SP 8788		XSW/87	
SP 8789		XSW/87	
SP 8790		XSW/87	
SP 8791		XSW/87	
SP 8792		XSW/87	
SP 8793		XSW/87	
SP 8794		XSW/87	
SP 8795		XSW/87	
SP 8796		XSW/87	

Notes:
1) All SP U33C's built with L-shaped windshield on engineer's side.
2) SP 8626 and 8644 to CC San Bernardino, CA 1985; to ATSF 3/88. Rebuilt as slugs ATSF 143 and 144.
3) SP 8642 wrecked in tunnel near San Luis Obispo, CA, 9/25/69; cut up on site. Scrapped after only 91 days of service.
4) SP 8684 repainted blue and red while on lease to NdeM; returned 9/81 and repainted in standard colors.
5) SP 8660 and 8718 wrecked while leased to NdeM; acquired by NdeM and reblt 2/86 to U36C 8987; SP 8660 acquired by NdeM and scrapped at Empalme, Sonora.
6) SP 8772 to Southwest Railroad Car Parts for scrap; resold to GE for Super 7 program in 9/88.
7) For several years after retirement, SP 8653 and 8669 for standby electrical power at West Colton, CA. Units derelict at West Colton in February 1994.
8) SP 8754 last operating U33C on Southern Pacific; failed 11/88 in pool service on Norfolk Southern.

U23B

Atchison, Topeka & Santa Fe

U23B	Serial	Built	Options/Notes
6300-6348	37491-37539	6/70-2/71	GT581/D.C.

Original Road No.	2nd/3rd Road No.	Status & Notes	Super 7 Rebuild	Super 7 Rebuild
ATSF 6300		XPL/91	2	
ATSF 6301		TG/83	1	
ATSF 6302		TG/83	1	
ATSF 6303		TG/83	1	
ATSF 6304		XPL/92	2	
ATSF 6305		GE	2	
ATSF 6306		TG/83	1	
ATSF 6307		TG/83	1	
ATSF 6308		TG/83	1	
ATSF 6309		GE/MTL	2	
ATSF 6310		GE/MTL	1,7	
ATSF 6311		GE/MTL	2	
ATSF 6312		TG/83	1	
ATSF 6313		GE	2	
ATSF 6314		XPL/91	2	
ATSF 6315		XPL/91	2	
ATSF 6316		GE	2	
ATSF 6317		GE	2	
ATSF 6318		GE	2	
ATSF 6319		XPL/92	2	
ATSF 6320		TG/83	1	
ATSF 6321		WX/83	3	
ATSF 6322		GE	2	
ATSF 6323		GE	2	
ATSF 6324		TG/83	1, 7	
ATSF 6325		GE	2	
ATSF 6326		GE	2	
ATSF 6327		GE	2	
ATSF 6328		XPL/91	2, 7	
ATSF 6329		GE	2	
ATSF 6330		GE	2	
ATSF 6331		TG/83	1	
ATSF 6332	7200 6419		4	
ATSF 6333		XPL/91	2	
ATSF 6334		XPL/92	2	
ATSF 6335		GE/MTL	2	
ATSF 6336		XPL/91	2	
ATSF 6337			5	R&S 50	MTL 6/90
ATSF 6338			5	R&S 51	MTL 12/90
ATSF 6339		TG/83	1	
ATSF 6340		XPL/91	2	
ATSF 6341	GE 26-1		6	
ATSF 6342		GE	2,7	
ATSF 6343		GE	2	
ATSF 6344		XPL/91	2	
ATSF 6345		GE/MTL	2	
ATSF 6346		TG/83	1	
ATSF 6347		XPL/91	2	
ATSF 6348		XPL/91	2	

Notes:
1) Retired 6/1/83 and traded in to GE on C30-7's 8153-8166. Held for Super 7 program.
2) Sold to GE 9/88 for Super 7 Program. ATSF 6309, 6311, 6329, 6337, 6338 to GE-Montreal (MLW) rest stored at Erie.
3) ATSF 6321 wrecked 3/19/83 in Texas on grain train and scrapped.
4) ATSF 6332 wrecked and rebuilt Cleburne (TX) shops 9/87 to 3000 hp SF30B as pilot for U23B rebuild program. No other rebuilds done. ATSF 7200 renumbered 6419 and derated to 2500 h.p. in 1989.

Notes Cont.
5) ATSF 6337 and 6338 rebuilt GE-Montreal (MLW) to Super 7-B23's R&S 50 and 51 in 19/90. R&S 50 has builders plate reading serial number 37511 in error.
6) ATSF 6341 traded in to GE 6/83. Transferred to Building 26 for use as switcher etc. Repainted grey and white, numbered 26-1 and named "Cristine."
7) ATSF 6310, 6324, 6328 and 6342 were loaned to BN for use as GE horsepower /hour guarantee units in 1989.

Chesapeake & Ohio

U23B	Serial	Built	Options/Notes
2300-2329	37228-37257	9/69-10/69	GTA-11/A.C.; Blombergs

Original Road No.	CSX	Status	Notes
C&O 2300	CSX 3200	R	
C&O 2301		XPLJ/85	
C&O 2302		XPLJ/85	
C&O 2303	CSX 3203	R	
C&O 2304	CSX 3204	R	
C&O 2305	CSX 3205	R	
C&O 2306		XPLJ/85	
C&O 2307		XPLJ/85	
C&O 2308		XPLJ/85	
C&O 2309	CSX 3209	R	
C&O 2310	CSX 3210	XSPC/93	
C&O 2311	CSX 3211	R/92	
C&O 2312		XPLJ/85	
C&O 2313		XPLJ/85	
C&O 2314		XPLJ/85	
C&O 2315		XPLJ/85	
C&O 2316		XPLJ/85	
C&O 2317		XPLJ/85	
C&O 2318	CSX 3218	R/93	
C&O 2319		XPLJ/85	
C&O 2320		R	
C&O 2321	CSX 3221	R	
C&O 2322	CSX 3222	R	
C&O 2323	CSX 3223	R	
C&O 2324		XPLJ/85	
C&O 2325	CSX 3225	R	
C&O 2326		XPLJ/85	
C&O 2327		XPLJ/85	
C&O 2328		XPLJ/85	
C&O 2329	CSX 3229	R	

Conrail

U23B	Serial	Built	Options/Notes
2789-2798	41584-41593	5/77-6/77	GTA-11/A.C.

Original Road No.	Post-CR	Status	Notes
CR 2789	R&N 2397		3
CR 2790	P&W 2205		4
CR 2791	R&N 2399		3
CR 2792	P&W 2202		4
CR 2793	R&N 2398		3
CR 2794	P&W 2208		4
CR 2795	P&W 2204		4
CR 2796	P&W 2207		4
CR 2797	P&W 2206		4
CR 2798	P&W 2203		1,4

Notes:
1) CR 2798 last domestic U-boat built.
2) All retired 4/91; returned to service 11/92.
3) Sold to Reading & Northern in 1992.
4) Sold to Providence & Worcester 1992-1993.

Delaware & Hudson

U23B	Serial	Built	Options/Notes
301-316	36803-36818	8/68-9/68	GT581/D.C.

Original Road No.	1973 Re#	1975 Re#	MEC	Status	& Notes
D&H 301	D&H 2301		MEC 280		1
D&H 302	D&H 2302		MEC 281		1
D&H 303	D&H 2303		MEC 282	FX/86	1,2
D&H 304	D&H 2304		MEC 283	XPL/91	3
D&H 305	D&H 2305		MEC 284	XMEC/88	4
D&H 306	D&H 2306		MEC 285		
D&H 307	D&H 2307		MEC 286	GE/88	3
D&H 308	D&H 2308		MEC 287	GE/88	3
D&H 309	D&H 2309		MEC 288	OS/93	
D&H 310	D&H 2310		MEC 289	GE/88	
D&H 311	D&H 2311		MEC 290	XPL/91	3
D&H 312	D&H 2312	D&H 1776	MEC 291	XMEC/88	5
D&H 313	D&H 2313		MEC 292	W/87	6
D&H 314	D&H 2314		MEC 293	XMEC/88	4
D&H 315				WX/68	7
D&H 316	D&H 2316		MEC 294	SoPC 15	8

Notes:
1) D&H 2301-2314, 2316 to MEC 280-294 6/83.
2) MEC 282 burned on D&H at Sanitaria Springs, NY., 11/86. Scrapped Waterville, ME., 1988.
3) To GE for Super 7 program via MS&A 3/88.

Delaware & Hudson U23B Notes Cont.

4) Scrapped at Waterville, ME, shops by MS&A spring/88.
5) D&H 2312 painted red-white-and-blue and lettered for Preamble Express 7/74. Renumbered D&H 1776 (still in Bicentennial paint) 3/75. Repainted D&H blue & yellow 1/78. Renumbered 2312 c./77.
6) MEC 292 wrecked Bangor, ME, 4/10/87 and scrapped.
7) D&H 315 wrecked in runaway at Colonie, NY, 11/29/68 and scrapped.
8) MEC 294 traded to Morrison-Knudsen 8/86 for N&W (ex-IT) SD39 2966. Rebuilt 2/87 as South Peru Copper 15 and shipped to Cuajone, Peru, for service.

Ferrocarril del Pacifico

U23B	Serial	Built	Options/Notes
537-546	40820-40829	8/75-9/75	1800 h.p.; GT581/D.C.

Original Road No.	FNM	Status	Notes
FCP 537		OS/93	2
FCP 538			
FCP 539			
FCP 540	FNM 540		
FCP 541		OS/93	2
FCP 542	FNM 542		4
FCP 543		OS/93	3
FCP 544		OS/93	2
FCP 545		OS/93	2
FCP 546			

Notes:
1) Rated at 1800 h.p. and indicated as such on builder's plates.
2) Derelict at Empalme, Sonora 2/73 in grey and red.
3) Derelict at Empalme, Sonora 2/73 in original paint.
4) FCP 542 rebuilt overhauled Empalme 2/93 as FNM 542.

Lehigh Valley

U23B	Serial	Built	Options/Notes
501-512	40098-40109	11/74	GT581/D.C.

Original Road No.	CR	Resale	Status	Notes
LV 501	CR 2777		R/91	
LV 502	CR 2778		R/91	
LV 503	CR 2779		R/91	
LV 504	CR 2780		R/91	
LV 505	CR 2781		R/91	1
LV 506	CR 2782		R/91	TGX/94
LV 507	CR 2783		R/91	3
LV 508	CR 2784		R/91	
LV 509	CR 2785		R/91	
LV 510	CR 2786		R/91	
LV 511	CR 2787		R/91	
LV 512	CR 2788		R/91	3

Notes:
1) CR 2781 wreck received B23-7 nose in wreck repairs.
2) CR 2777-2788 retired 4/91.
3) Reactivated late 1992, retired c./93.

Louisville & Nashville

U23B	Serial	Built	Options/Notes
2708-2727	38765-38784	1/73-4/73	GT581/D.C.; FB2
2728-2752	39257-39281	6/73-9/73	GTA-11/A.C.; FB2
2753-2772	39508-39527	2/74-4/74	GTA-11/A.C.; FB2
2800-2824	40110-40134	12/74-3/75	GTA-11/A.C.; FB2

Original Road No.	2nd L&N	SBD	CSX	Status & Notes
L&N 2708		SBD 3238	CSX 3238	
L&N 2709		SBD 3239	CSX 3239	R/93
L&N 2710		SBD 3240	CSX 3240	R
L&N 2711		SBD 3241	CSX 3241	R/92
L&N 2712		SBD 3242	CSX 3242	
L&N 2713		SBD 3243	CSX 3243	R
L&N 2714		SBD 3244	CSX 3244	
L&N 2715		SBD 3245	CSX 3245	XWC/90
L&N 2716		SBD 3246	CSX 3246	
L&N 2717		SBD 3247	CSX 3247	XSPC/93
L&N 2718				WX/77 1
L&N 2719		SBD 3248	CSX 3248	R
L&N 2720		SBD 3249	CSX 3249	XWC/88
L&N 2721		SBD 3250	CSX 3250	R
L&N 2722		SBD 3251	CSX 3251	
L&N 2723		SBD 3252	CSX 3252	XSPC/93
L&N 2724		SBD 3253	CSX 3253	XSPC/93
L&N 2725		SBD 3254	CSX 3254	XSPC/93
L&N 2726		SBD 3255	CSX 3255	R/93
L&N 2727		SBD 3256	CSX 3256	R
L&N 2728		SBD 3257	CSX 3257	
L&N 2729		SBD 3258	CSX 3258	R
L&N 2730		SBD 3259	CSX 3259	
L&N 2731		SBD 3260	CSX 3260	R
L&N 2732		SBD 3261	CSX 3261	
L&N 2733		SBD 3262	CSX 3262	R/92
L&N 2734		SBD 3263	CSX 3263	
L&N 2735		SBD 3264	CSX 3264	
L&N 2736		SBD 3265	CSX 3265	
L&N 2737		SBD 3266	CSX 3266	
L&N 2738		SBD 3267	CSX 3267	R/92
L&N 2739		SBD 3268	CSX 3268	XSPC/93
L&N 2740		SBD 3269	CSX 3269	
L&N 2741		SBD 3270	CSX 3270	
L&N 2742		SBD 3271	CSX 3271	R
L&N 2743		SBD 3272	CSX 3272	R
L&N 2744		SBD 3273	CSX 3273	R
L&N 2745		SBD 3274	CSX 3274	R
L&N 2746		SBD 3275	CSX 3275	R
L&N 2747		SBD 3276	CSX 3276	XSPC/93
L&N 2748		SBD 3277	CSX 3277	
L&N 2749		SBD 3278	CSX 3278	R
L&N 2750		SBD 3279	CSX 3279	XSPC/93
L&N 2751		SBD 3280	CSX 3280	XSPC/93
L&N 2752		SBD 3281	CSX 3281	
L&N 2753		SBD 3282	CSX 3282	R
L&N 2754		SBD 3283	CSX 3283	
L&N 2755		SBD 3284	CSX 3284	R
L&N 2756		SBD 3285	CSX 3285	XSPC/93
L&N 2757		SBD 3286	CSX 3286	XSPC/93
L&N 2758		SBD 3287	CSX 3287	XSPC/93
L&N 2759		SBD 3288	CSX 3288	
L&N 2760		SBD 3289	CSX 3289	R/92
L&N 2761		SBD 3290	CSX 3290	
L&N 2762		SBD 3291	CSX 3291	R
L&N 2763		SBD 3292	CSX 3292	
L&N 2764		SBD 3293		R/84
L&N 2765		SBD 3294	CSX 3294	
L&N 2766		SBD 3295	CSX 3295	
L&N 2767		SBD 3296	CSX 3296	R/92
L&N 2768		SBD 3297	CSX 3297	
L&N 2769		SBD 3298	CSX 3298	R
L&N 2770		SBD 3299	CSX 3299	
L&N 2771				WX/80 2
L&N 2772		SBD 3300	CSX 3300	R/93
L&N 2800		SBD 3301	CSX 3301	
L&N 2801		SBD 3302	CSX 3302	
L&N 2802		SBD 3303	CSX 3303	
L&N 2803	L&N 2818			WX/78 3
L&N 2804		SBD 3305	CSX 3305	
L&N 2805		SBD 3306	CSX 3306	R
L&N 2806		SBD 3307	CSX 3307	R
L&N 2807		SBD 3308	CSX 3308	
L&N 2808		SBD 3309	CSX 3309	
L&N 2809		SBD 3310	CSX 3310	
L&N 2810		SBD 3311	CSX 3311	
L&N 2811		SBD 3312	CSX 3312	R
L&N 2812		SBD 3313	CSX 3313	
L&N 2813		SBD 3314	CSX 3314	
L&N 2814		SBD 3315	CSX 3315	R
L&N 2815		SBD 3316	CSX 3316	
L&N 2816		SBD 3317	CSX 3317	
L&N 2817		SBD 3318	CSX 3318	
L&N 2818	L&N 2803	SBD 3304	CSX 3304	XWC/90 3
L&N 2819		SBD 3319	CSX 3319	R
L&N 2820		SBD 3320	CSX 3320	R/93
L&N 2821		SBD 3321	CSX 3321	R
L&N 2822		SBD 3322	CSX 3322	
L&N 2823		SBD 3323	CSX 3323	
L&N 2824		SBD 3324	CSX 3324	

Notes:
1) L&N 2718 wrecked Kennesaw, GA, 9/28/77. Retired 11/15/77 and scrapped.
2) L&N 2771 wrecked in head-on collision on SCL at Hamlet, NC, 4/2/80. Retired 5/21/80 and scrapped.
3) L&N 3008, 2505, 2818 wrecked in collision with standing cars at Franklin, TN, 8/6/78. L&N 2803 wrecked at Lawrenceburg, TN 7/6/78. L&N 2818 repaired and renumbered 2803 (2nd); outshopped from South Louisville (KY) shops in Family Lines paint with special lettering celebrating shop's 75th anniversary. Original L&N 2803 renumbered 2818 (2nd), retired 8/16/78 and scrapped.

Milwaukee Road

U23B	Serial	Built	Options/Notes
4800-4804	38772-38776	6/73	GT581/D.C.; FB2

Original Road No.	1973 Re#	Status	Notes
MILW 4800	MILW 5000	GE	2
MILW 4801	MILW 5001	XEH/84	
MILW 4802	MILW 5002	XEH/84	
MILW 4803	MILW 5003	GE	2
MILW 4804	MILW 5004	XPL/91	2

Notes:
1) All retired by 1980.
2) MILW 5000, 5003, 5004 to GE 9/88 for Super 7 program.

Missouri-Kansas-Texas

U23B	Serial	Built	Options/Notes
350-352	39225-39227	5/73	GT581/D.C.

Original Road No.	Status	Notes
MKT 350	XPL/84	1
MKT 351	XPL/84	1
MKT 352	XPL/84	1

Notes:
1) MKT 350-352 traded in to EMD in 1983 on GP39-2's; scrapped 2/84 at Pielet Bros.

Missouri Pacific

U23B	Serial	Built	Options/Notes
668-674	38758-38764	1/73-2/73	GTA-11/A.C.
2257-2267	39905-39915	10/74-11/74	GTA-11/A.C.; FB2
2268-2273	40356-40361	3/75	GTA-11/A.C.; FB2
2274-2278	40920-40924	6/76	GTA-11/A.C.; FB2
2279-2288	41523-41532	12/76-1/77	GTA-11/A.C.; FB2

Original Road No.	1974 Re#	1980 Re#	Resale	Re#	Status/Notes
MP 668	MP 2250	MP 4500	CMGN 8903		
MP 669	MP 2251	MP 4501	CMGN 8904		
MP 670	MP 2252	MP 4502	CMGN 4502		
MP 671	MP 2253	MP 4503			GE/90
MP 672	MP 2254	MP 4504	CMGN/DM 4504	CMGN 8905	3
MP 673	MP 2255	MP 4505	CMGN 4505		
MP 674	MP 2256	MP 4506	CMGN 8902		1, 2

Notes:
1) MP 2256 rebuilt with EMD cab during wreck repairs.
2) To Central Michigan in 1989, via NRE. MP 4505 for parts only.
3) CMGN 4504 stencilled D&M (Detroit & Mackinac); stored in MP blue at Tawas City 6/93; to CMGN 8905.

Original Road No.	UP/ 1980 Re#	Resale	Status/Notes		Super 7 Rebuild	Super 7 Shop/Date
MP 2257	MP 4507		XSW/90			
MP 2258	MP 4508	UP 542	NRE 542			
MP 2259	MP 4509		NRE 4509	2		
MP 2260	MP 4510		GE	4, 7		
MP 2261	MP 4511	UP 545	TUGX	6		
MP 2262	MP 4512	UP 546	TGE/90			
MP 2263	MP 4513	UP 547	NRE 547			
MP 2264	MP 4514	UP 548				
MP 2265	MP 4515	NRE 4515		2		
MP 2266	MP 4516		GE	4, 7		
MP 2267	MP 4517	UP 551	XAZ/90			
MP 2268	MP 4518		XSW/88			
MP 2269	MP 4519		XSW/88			
MP 2270	MP 4520		XSW/88			
MP 2271			WX/78	3		
MP 2272	MP 4521		XPL/92	1,4		
MP 2273	MP 4522		TGE/90			
MP 2274	MP 4523	UP 557				
MP 2275	MP 4524	UP 558				
MP 2276	MP 4525		XAZ/91			
MP 2277	MP 4526	UP 560				
MP 2278	MP 4527	UP 561				
MP 2279	MP 4528		GE	1, 4		
MP 2280	MP 4529	UP 563	GE	4		
MP 2281	MP 4530		GE	4, 7		
MP 2282	MP 4531	UP 565	GE	1,4		
MP 2283	MP 4532	UP 566	GE	4		
MP 2284	MP 4533		GE	4		
MP 2285	MP 4534	UP 568	GE	1, 5		
MP 2286	MP 4535	UP 569		4	R&S 52	MTL 2/91
MP 2287	MP 4536	UP 570	GE	4		
MP 2288	MP 4537	UP 571	XAZ/91	4		

Notes:
1) Rebuilt with EMD cab during wreck repairs.
2) Retired 1/91 and sold to NRE. Leased to IAIS fall/91. [UP 542, 545, 547, 548 and 551 retired 1/91 and returned to lessor GATX. To NRE 1991. NRE 542, 547 leased to IAIS fall/91.
3) MP 2271 wrecked on Austin Division 10/78. Retired 11/30/78 and scrapped.
4) To GE for Super 7 program. UP 546, 563, 565, 566, 568 and 569 to GE-Montreal (MLW) for rebuilding. UP 569 rebuilt to B23 Super 7 Roberval & Saguenay 52.
5) UP 546, 565, 568 to GE MTL. 90-91 for Super 7 rebuild.
6) UP 545 retired 01/91; to Texas Utilities, Beckville, TX via NRE 2/91.
7) MP 4510, 4516 and 4530 shipped to Conrail Juniata shops Altoona, PA, c./93 to provide trucks for GE ex-ATSF B36-6 lease units.

Monon

U23B	Serial	Built	Options/Notes
601-608	37293-37300	3/70-5/70	GT581/D.C.

Original Road No.	L&N	CSX	Status	Notes
MON 601	L&N 2700	CSX 3230	R	
MON 602	L&N 2701	CSX 3231	R/93	
MON 603	L&N 2702	CSX 3232	XSPC/93	
MON 604	L&N 2703	CSX 3233	XSPC/93	
MON 605	L&N 2704	CSX 3234	XSPC/93	
MON 606	L&N 2705	CSX 3235	R	
MON 607	L&N 2706	CSX 3236		
MON 608	L&N 2707	CSX 3237	R	

Nacionales de Mexico

U23B	Serial	Built	Options/Notes
9100-9113	40326-40339	3/75	GT581/D.C.; FB2
9114-9121	40340-40347	3/75-5/75	GT581/D.C.
9122-9129	40348-40355	5/75-6/75	GT581/D.C.; FB2

Original Road No.	Status	Notes
NdeM 9100		
NdeM 9101		
NdeM 9102		
NdeM 9103	R/82	
NdeM 9104		
NdeM 9105		
NdeM 9106		
NdeM 9107		
NdeM 9108		
NdeM 9109	R	
NdeM 9110		
NdeM 9111		
NdeM 9112		
NdeM 9113		
NdeM 9114		
NdeM 9115		
NdeM 9116	R	
NdeM 9117		
NdeM 9118	R	
NdeM 9119		
NdeM 9120		
NdeM 9121		
NdeM 9122		
NdeM 9123		
NdeM 9124		
NdeM 9125	OS 2/93	
NdeM 9126		
NdeM 9127		
NdeM 9128		
NdeM 9129		

Penn Central

U23B	Serial	Built	Options/Notes
2700-2749	38506-38555	8/72-10/72	GT581/D.C.
2750-2776	39305-39331	8/73-10/73	GT581/D.C.

Original Road No.	CR	Resale	Status	Notes
PC 2700	CR 2700		TGE/94	
PC 2701	CR 2701		R	
PC 2702	CR 2702		R	
PC 2703	CR 2703		TGE/94	
PC 2704	CR 2704		R	
PC 2705	CR 2705		TGE/94	
PC 2706	CR 2706		R	2
PC 2707	CR 2707		R	2
PC 2708	CR 2708		R	2
PC 2709	CR 2709		R	
PC 2710	CR 2710		R	
PC 2711	CR 2711		R	
PC 2712	CR 2712		R	
PC 2713	CR 2713		R	
PC 2714	CR 2714		TGE/94	
PC 2715	CR 2715		R	
PC 2716	CR 2716		R	
PC 2717	CR 2717	CSKR 2717		3
PC 2718	CR 2718		R	
PC 2719	CR 2719		R	
PC 2720	CR 2720		R	
PC 2721	CR 2721		R	
PC 2722	CR 2722		R	
PC 2723	CR 2723		TGE/94	
PC 2724	CR 2724		R	
PC 2725	CR 2725		TGE/94	
PC 2726	CR 2726		R	
PC 2727	CR 2727		R	
PC 2728	CR 2728		R	
PC 2729	CR 2729		R	
PC 2730	CR 2730		R	
PC 2731	CR 2731		R	
PC 2732	CR 2732		WX/85	
PC 2733	CR 2733		R	
PC 2734	CR 2734		R	
PC 2735	CR 2735		R	
PC 2736	CR 2736		R	
PC 2737	CR 2737		R	
PC 2738	CR 2738		R	2
PC 2739	CR 2739		WX/85	
PC 2740	CR 2740		TGE/94	
PC 2741	CR 2741		R	
PC 2742	CR 2742		R	
PC 2743	CR 2743		R	
PC 2744	CR 2744		R	
PC 2745	CR 2745		R	
PC 2746	CR 2746		R	
PC 2747	CR 2747		R	
PC 2748	CR 2748		R	
PC 2749	CR 2749		R	
PC 2750	CR 2750		R	
PC 2751	CR 2751		R	
PC 2752	CR 2752		R	
PC 2753	CR 2753		R	
PC 2754	CR 2754		R	
PC 2755	CR 2755		R	
PC 2756	CR 2756		R	
PC 2757	CR 2757		R	
PC 2758	CR 2758		TGX/94	
PC 2759	CR 2759		R	
PC 2760	CR 2760		R	
PC 2761	CR 2761		R	

Penn Central U23B Cont.

Original Road No.	CR	Resale	Status	Notes
PC 2762	CR 2762		R	
PC 2763	CR 2763		R	
PC 2764	CR 2764		R	
PC 2765	CR 2765		R	
PC 2766	CR 2766		R	
PC 2767	CR 2767		R	
PC 2768	CR 2768		R	
PC 2769	CR 2769		R	
PC 2770	CR 2770		R	2
PC 2771	CR 2771		R	
PC 2772	CR 2772		TGE/94	
PC 2773	CR 2773		R	
PC 2774	CR 2774		R	
PC 2775	CR 2775		TGE/94	
PC 2776	CR 2776		TGE/94	

Notes:
1) CR 2700-2731, 2733-38, 2740-76 retired 4/91.
2) Reactivated late 1992, retired again in 1993.
3) Sold in 1994 to Al Luedtke for use on Carbon & Schuykill.

Southern

U23B	Serial	Built	Options/Notes
3900-3904	38392-38396	5/72	GTA-11/A.C.; High nose
3905-3914	39215-39224	5/73-6/73	GTA-11/A.C.; High nose
3915-3934	39621-39640	5/74	GTA-11/A.C.; High nose
3935-3954	40078-40097	5/75-7/75	GTA-11/A.C.; High nose; FB2
3955-3969	41508-41522	11/76-2/77	GTA-11/A.C.; High nose; FB2

Original Road No.	Status	Notes
SOU 3900		
SOU 3901		
SOU 3902		
SOU 3903		
SOU 3904		
NS 3905		1
CG 3906		2
CG 3907		2
CG 3908		2
CG 3909		2
CG 3910		2
GSF 3911		3
GSF 3912		3
GSF 3913		3
INT 3914		4
SOU 3915		
SOU 3916		
SOU 3917		
SOU 3918		
SOU 3919		
SOU 3920		
SOU 3921		
SOU 3922		
SOU 3923		
SOU 3924		
SOU 3925		
SOU 3926		
SOU 3927		
SOU 3928		
SOU 3929		
SOU 3930		
SOU 3931		
SOU 3932		
SOU 3933		
SOU 3934		
SOU 3935		
SOU 3936		
SOU 3937		
SOU 3938		
SOU 3939		
SOU 3940	WX/81	5
SOU 3941		
SOU 3942		
SOU 3943		
SOU 3944		
SOU 3945		
SOU 3946		
SOU 3947		
SOU 3948		
SOU 3949		
SOU 3950		
SOU 3951	R	
SOU 3952		
SOU 3953		
SOU 3954		
SOU 3955		
SOU 3956		
SOU 3957		
SOU 3958		
SOU 3959		
SOU 3960		
SOU 3961		
SOU 3962		
SOU 3963	R	
SOU 3964		
SOU 3965		

Original Road No.	Status	Notes
SOU 3966		
SOU 3967	WX/79	6
SOU 3968		
SOU 3969		

Notes:
1) Sublettered NS for (original) Norfolk Southern.
2) Sublettered CofG
3) Sublettered GSF
4) Sublettered INT
5) SOU 3940 wrecked 9/14/81 in collision with log truck Sugar Valley, GA, and scrapped.
6) SOU 3967 wrecked and burned Centerville, AL, 6/25/79. Scrapped.

Southern Peru Copper Corporation

U23B	Serial	Built	Options/Notes
40-45	40372-40377	10/75-11/75	GT581/D.C.; FB2 trucks
50-57	40362-40369	3/75-5/75	GT581/D.C.; FB2 trucks
58-59	40370-40371	10/75-11/75	GT581/D.C.; FB2 trucks

Original Road No.	Status	Notes
SPCC 40		1
SPCC 41		1
SPCC 42		1
SPCC 43		1
SPCC 44		1
SPCC 45		1
SPCC 50		2
SPCC 51		2
SPCC 52		2
SPCC 53		2
SPCC 54		2
SPCC 55		2
SPCC 56		2
SPCC 57		2
SPCC 58		2
SPCC 59		2

Notes:
1) SPCC 40-45 road units for Ilo-Cuajone, Peru, ore movements. Extra equipment blower radiators for extended dynamic brake operation.
2) SPCC 50-59 built for use at Cuajone, Peru, mine; equipped for remote control operation.

Texas Utilities

U23B	Serial	Built	Options/Notes
103	40719	5/75	GT581/D.C.

Original Road No.	2nd No.	Serial	Built	Status	Notes
TUGX 103	TUGX 3305	40719	5/75		1

Notes:
1) Remote control

Western Pacific

U23B	Serial	Built	Options/Notes
2251-2265	38397-38411	5/72-6/72	GT581/D.C.; Blombergs Dual Controls

Original Road No.	Super 7 Rebuild	Resale	Super 7 Rebuild	Status & Notes
WP 2251	GECX 2001	MGA 2306	M-K 3/89	1,2,6
WP 2252	MGA 2302		MTL 11/89	7
WP 2253	MGA 2304		MTL 12/89	7
WP 2254	MGA 2300		MTL 9/89	7
WP 2255	MGA 2301		MTL 10/89	7
WP 2256			WX/79	3
WP 2257	GECX 2002		M-K 3/89	6
WP 2258	MGA 2303		MTL 11/89	7
WP 2259			WX/81	4
WP 2260	MGA 2308		MTL 2/90	7
WP 2261	MGA 2309		MTL 2/90	7
WP 2262	MGA 2307		MTL 2/90	7
WP 2263	GECX 2000		GE 3/89	5
WP 2264	MGA 2305		MTL 12/89	7
WP 2265	MGA 2310		MTL 3/90	7

Notes:
1) All surviving WP U23B's stored by UP by late 1983 and retired 11/87. Traded in to GE on UP Dash 8-40C's 2/88.
2) GECX 2001 sold to Monongahela 2/90.
3) WP 2256 wrecked on UP at Devil's Slide, UT, 11/17/79. Wreck purchased by UP in settlement; stripped for parts and scrapped 7/81.
4) WP 2259 wrecked near Deeth, NV, 9/12/81 and scrapped on site.
5) Rebuilt to Super 7-B23 prototype at GE Erie, PA, 3/89.
6) Rebuilt to Super 7-B23 by Morrison-Knudsen, Boise, ID.
7) Rebuilt to Super 7-B23 by GE Montreal, Quebec, at former Montreal Locomotive Works.

U23C

Atchison, Topeka & Santa Fe

U23C	Serial	Built	Options/Notes
7500-7519	37098-37117	6/69-7/69	

Original Road No.	Status	Notes
ATSF 7500	XPNC/85	1
ATSF 7501	XPNC/85	1
ATSF 7502	XPNC/85	1
ATSF 7503	XPNC/85	1
ATSF 7504	XPNC/85	1
ATSF 7505	XPNC/85	1
ATSF 7506	XPNC/85	1
ATSF 7507	XPNC/85	1
ATSF 7508	XPNC/85	1
ATSF 7509	XPNC/85	1
ATSF 7510	XPNC/85	1
ATSF 7511	XPNC/85	1
ATSF 7512	XPNC/85	1
ATSF 7513	XPNC/85	1
ATSF 7514	XPNC/85	1
ATSF 7515	XPNC/85	1
ATSF 7516	XPNC/85	1
ATSF 7517	XPNC/85	1
ATSF 7518	XPNC/85	1
ATSF 7519	XPNC/85	1

Notes:
1) ATSF 7500-7519 returned to lessor 12/84 and scrapped by PNC.

Chicago, Burlington & Quincy

U23C	Serial	Built	Options/Notes
460-468	36988-36996	4/69	A

Original Road No.	BN	Status	Notes
CB&Q 460	BN 5200	XAZ/84	
CB&Q 461	BN 5201	XAZ/84	
CB&Q 462	BN 5202	XAZ/84	
CB&Q 463	BN 5203	XAZ/84	
CB&Q 464	BN 5204	XAZ/84	
CB&Q 465	BN 5205	XAZ/84	
CB&Q 466	BN 5206	XAZ/84	
CB&Q 467	BN 5207	XAZ/84	
CB&Q 468	BN 5208	XAZ/84	

Notes:
A) CB&Q 460-468 delivered in BN colors prior to merger; lettered only "Burlington."
1) BN 5200-5208 retired 7/84 and sold to NRE; scrapped by Azcon.

Lake Superior & Ishpeming

U23C	Serial	Built	Options/Notes
2300-2301	36706-36707	3/68-4/68	
2302	37138	9/69	
2303-2304	37572-37573	9/70	

Original Road No.	Resale	Status	Notes
LS&I 2300	W&M 2300		1, 2
LS&I 2301	W&M 2301		2
LS&I 2302	W&M 2302		2
LS&I 2303	W&M 2303		2
LS&I 2304	W&M 2304		2

Notes:
1) LS&I 2300 first U23C built.
2) LS&I 2300-2304 stored in 1989 after purchase of ex-BN U30C's. Sold to Wisconsin & Michigan 2300-2304 in 1993.

Penn Central

U23C	Serial	Built	Options/Notes
6700-6718	37540-37558	10/70-11/70	

Original Road No.	CR	1983 Re#	Status	Notes
PC 6700	CR 6700	CR 6900		
PC 6701	CR 6701	CR 6901		
PC 6702	CR 6702	CR 6902		
PC 6703	CR 6703	CR 6903		
PC 6704	CR 6704	CR 6904	OS/94	3
PC 6705	CR 6705	CR 6905	OS/94	3
PC 6706	CR 6706	CR 6906	OS/94	3
PC 6707	CR 6707	CR 6907		
PC 6708	CR 6708	CR 6908		
PC 6709	CR 6709	CR 6909		
PC 6710	CR 6710	CR 6910		
PC 6711	CR 6711	CR 6911		
PC 6712	CR 6712	CR 6912		
PC 6713	CR 6713	CR 6913	WX/85	1
PC 6714	CR 6714	CR 6914		
PC 6715	CR 6715	CR 6915		
PC 6716	CR 6716	CR 6916		
PC 6717	CR 6717	CR 6917		
PC 6718	CR 6718	CR 6918		

Notes:
1) CR 6713 wrecked Selkirk, NY, 3/3/85.
2) Renumbered to 6900's in 1983 to accommodate SD50's 6700-6739.
3) CR 6904, 6905, 6906 frost damaged at Allentown, PA, winter 1994.

Rede Ferroviaria Federal S. A.*

U23C	Serial	Built	Options/Notes
3801-3880	2500247-2500326	12/72-8/74	1
3901-3920	2500603-2500622 (40608-40627)	11/75-1/76	2
3921-3990	2500623-2500692	1974-1976	1

*Federal Railways of Brazil

Notes:
1) RFFSA 3801-3880 and 3921-3990 were assembled by GE do Brasil's Campinas, Sao Paulo plant.
2) RFFSA 3901-3920 were built at Erie without trucks and completed by GE do Brasil at Campinas, Sao Paulo, using Brazilian truck castings and Erie-supplied traction motors. Units assigned serial numbers by Erie and GE do Brasil, but carry only GE do Brasil builders plates.

U36B

Auto Train

U36B	Serial	Built	Options/Notes
4000-4004	38031-38035	11/71	Blomberg trucks
4005-4009	38744-38748	12/72	Blomberg trucks
4010-4012	39845-39847	5/74	Blomberg trucks
4013-4016	40064-40067	12/74	Built but not delivered

Original Road No.	Status	Notes
AT 4000	XSL/85	5
AT 4001	WX/73	2
AT 4002	XSL/85	5
AT 4003	XSL/85	5
AT 4004	WX/73	2,3
AT 4005	XSL/85	5
AT 4006	XSL/85	5
AT 4007	XSL/85	5
AT 4008	XSL/85	5
AT 4009	XSL/85	5
AT 4010	XSL/85	5
AT 4011	XSL/85	5
AT 4012	XSL/85	5
[AT 4013]	CR 2971	TGE/94	4
[AT 4014]	CR 2972	TGE/94	4
[AT 4015]	CR 2973	TGE/94	4
[AT 4016]	CR 2974	TGE/94	4

Notes:
1) All Auto Train U36B's built to SCL specifications.
2) AT 4001 and 4004 Wrecked in crossing collision Hortense, GA, 3/13/73 and scrapped.
3) AT 4004 equipped with experimental FB2 trucks 1972.
4) AT 4013-4016 built but never delivered. Stored at GE Erie in full Auto Train paint until sold to Conrail 9/76. Reconditioned, re-trucked with AAR-B's and outshopped as CR 2971-2974.
5) Auto-Train shut down 5/81. All surviving AT U36B's: 4000, 4002-4003, 4005-4012 returned to lessor by 5/81; most stored at C&NW Oelwein, IA by Mar/83. All scrapped at SLAS, St. Louis 1984-1985.

Conrail

U36B	Serial	Built	Options/Notes
2971-2974	40064-40067	12/74	

Original Road No.	[Built As]	Status	Notes
CR 2971	[AT 4013]	TGE/94	1,2
CR 2972	[AT 4014]	TGE/94	1,2
CR 2973	[AT 4015]	TGE/94	1,2
CR 2974	[AT 4016]	TGE/94	1,2

Notes:
1) CR 2971-2974 built 12/74 to SCL specifications (including Blomberg trucks) as Auto Train 4013-4016 but not delivered. Stored at GE Erie and sold 9/76 to Conrail. Blomberg trucks changed to AAR-B's at Conrail request.
2) CR 2971-2974 retired 4/91, still on property 4/94.

Seaboard Coast Line

U36B	Serial	Built	Options/Notes
1748-1777	37411-37440	5/70-8/70	Blomberg trucks
1776:2	37799	6/71	Blomberg trucks
1778-1812	37774-37809	3/71-8/71	Blomberg trucks
(1813) 1776:1	37439	8/70	Blomberg trucks
1814-1834	38036-38056	9/71-12/71	Blomberg trucks
1835-1855	38278-38298	1/72-3/72	Blomberg trucks

Original Road No.	SBD	CSX	Resale	Status	Notes
SCL 1748	SBD 5700	CSX 5700		XSPC/93	
SCL 1749	SBD 5701	CSX 5701		R	
SCL 1750	SBD 5702	CSX 5702		R	
SCL 1751	SBD 5703	CSX 5703		R	
SCL 1752	SBD 5704	CSX 5704		R	
SCL 1753	SBD 5705	CSX 5705		R	
SCL 1754	SBD 5706	CSX 5706		XIBS/92	
SCL 1755	SBD 5707	CSX 5707		R	
SCL 1756	SBD 5708	CSX 5708		XSPC/93	
SCL 1757	SBD 5709	CSX 5709		R	
SCL 1758	SBD 5710	CSX 5710		XSPC/93	
SCL 1759	SBD 5711	CSX 5711		R	
SCL 1760	SBD 5712	CSX 5712		R	
SCL 1761	SBD 5713	CSX 5713		R	
SCL 1762	SBD 5714	CSX 5714		R	
SCL 1763	SBD 5715	CSX 5715	BITY 361		6
SCL 1764	SBD 5716	CSX 5716		R	
SCL 1765	SBD 5717	CSX 5717		R	
SCL 1766	SBD 5718	CSX 5718		R	
SCL 1767	SBD 5719	CSX 5719		R	
SCL 1768	SBD 5720	CSX 5720		R	
SCL 1769	SBD 5721	CSX 5721		R	
SCL 1770	SBD 5722	CSX 5722		R	
SCL 1771	SBD 5723	CSX 5723		R	
SCL 1772	SBD 5724	CSX 5724		R	
SCL 1773	SBD 5725	CSX 5725		R	
SCL 1774	SBD 5726	CSX 5726		R	
SCL 1775	SBD 5727	CSX 5727			
SCL 1776:1	SBD 5763	CSX 5763		SCL 1813	1
SCL 1776:2	SBD 5728	CSX 5728		R	1
SCL 1777	SBD 5729	CSX 5729		R	
SCL 1778	SBD 5730	CSX 5730		R/93	
SCL 1779	SBD 5731	CSX 5731		R	
SCL 1780	SBD 5732	CSX 5732			
SCL 1781	SBD 5733	CSX 5733		OS/92	
SCL 1782	SBD 5734	CSX 5734		XSPC/93	
SCL 1783	SBD 5735	CSX 5735		R	
SCL 1784	SBD 5736	CSX 5736		XIBS/92	
SCL 1785	SBD 5737	CSX 5737		R	
SCL 1786	SBD 5738	CSX 5738		R	
SCL 1787	SBD 5739	CSX 5739		R	
SCL 1788	SBD 5740	CSX 5740		XIBS/92	
SCL 1789	SBD 5741	CSX 5741		R	
SCL 1790	SBD 5742	CSX 5742		NRE/91	
SCL 1791	SBD 5743	CSX 5743		R	
SCL 1792	SBD 5744	CSX 5744		R	
SCL 1793	SBD 5745	CSX 5745		R	
SCL 1794	SBD 5746	CSX 5746		R	
SCL 1795	SBD 5747	CSX 5747		R	
SCL 1796	SBD 5748	CSX 5748		R	
SCL 1797	SBD 5749	CSX 5749		R	
SCL 1798	SBD 5750	CSX 5750		R	
SCL 1799	SBD 5751	CSX 5751		R	
SCL 1800	SBD 5752	CSX 5752		XSPC/93	
SCL 1801				WX	3
SCL 1802	SBD 5753	CSX 5753		R	2, 5
SCL 1803	SBD 5754	CSX 5754		R	2
SCL 1804	SBD 5755	CSX 5755		R	2
SCL 1805	SBD 5756	CSX 5756		R	2
SCL 1806	SBD 5757	CSX 5757		R	2
SCL 1807	SBD 5758	CSX 5758			2
SCL 1808	SBD 5759	CSX 5759		XSPC/93	2
SCL 1809	SBD 5760	CSX 5760			2
SCL 1810	SBD 5761	CSX 5761		XSPC/93	2
SCL 1811	SBD 5762	CSX 5762			2
SCL 1812				WX	2,3
SCL 1813*	SBD 5763	CSX 5763			
SCL 1814	SBD 5764	CSX 5764			
SCL 1815	SBD 5765	CSX 5765		XPL/91	
SCL 1816	SBD 5766	CSX 5766		R	
SCL 1817	SBD 5767	CSX 5767			
SCL 1818	SBD 5768	CSX 5768		R	
SCL 1819	SBD 5769	CSX 5769		R	
SCL 1820	SBD 5770	CSX 5770		R/93	
SCL 1821	SBD 5771	CSX 5771		CSKR 5771	7
SCL 1822	SBD 5772	CSX 5772		R/93	
SCL 1823	SBD 5773	CSX 5773		R	
SCL 1824	SBD 5774	CSX 5774		R	
SCL 1825	SBD 5775	CSX 5775		R	
SCL 1826	SBD 5776	CSX 5776		R	
SCL 1827	SBD 5777	CSX 5777		R	
SCL 1828	SBD 5778	CSX 5778		R	
SCL 1829	SBD 5779	CSX 5779			
SCL 1830	SBD 5780	CSX 5780			
SCL 1831	SBD 5781	CSX 5781		R	
SCL 1832	SBD 5782	CSX 5782		R	
SCL 1833	SBD 5783	CSX 5783		R	
SCL 1834	SBD 5784	CSX 5784		R	
SCL 1835	SBD 5785	CSX 5785		R	2
SCL 1836	SBD 5786	CSX 5786			2
SCL 1837	SBD 5787	CSX 5787		R	2
SCL 1838	SBD 5788	CSX 5788		R	2
SCL 1839	SBD 5789	CSX 5789		R	2
SCL 1840	SBD 5790	CSX 5790			2
SCL 1841	SBD 5791	CSX 5791			2
SCL 1842	SBD 5792	CSX 5792		R	2
SCL 1843	SBD 5793	CSX 5793			2
SCL 1844	SBD 5794	CSX 5794		XSPC/93	2
SCL 1845	SBD 5795	CSX 5795		R/93	2
SCL 1846	SBD 5796	CSX 5796			2
SCL 1847	SBD 5797	CSX 5797			2
SCL 1848	SBD 5798	CSX 5798		R	2
SCL 1849	SBD 5799	CSX 5799		XIBS/92	2
SCL 1850	SBD 5800	CSX 5800		XSPC/93	2
SCL 1851	SBD 5801	CSX 5801		R	2,4
SCL 1852	SBD 5802	CSX 5802		R	2
SCL 1853	SBD 5803	CSX 5803		R	2
SCL 1854	SBD 5804	CSX 5804			2
SCL 1855	SBD 5805	CSX 5805		R	2,4

Notes:
1) SCL 1776 (first) renumbered SCL 1813 in 1971; SCL 1776 (second) delivered 6/71 in red-white-and-blue Bicentennial paint. Repainted in Family Lines paint 3/80.
2) SCL 1802-1812, 1835-1855 equipped to operate with MATE-4 road slugs 3200-3204.
3) SCL 1801 and 1812 wrecked and scrapped.
4) SCL 1851 "Mate" road slug 3215 and 1855 tested extensively on SP in 1977.
5) CSX 5753 rebuilt at Waycross (GA) shops in 1989 as prototype for planned U36B rebuild program. No other units done.
6) CSX 5715 to Bristol Industrial Terminal Railway 361 in 1993.
7) CSX 5771 to Carbon & Schuykill 5771 in 1993.

U36C

Atchison, Topeka & Santa Fe

U36C	Serial	Built	Options/Notes
8700-8714	38455-38469	6/72-7/72	
8715-8735	38877-38897	2/73-4/73	
8736-8762	39686-39712	6/74-7/74	
8763-8799	40007-40043	11/74-2/75	

Original Road No.	SF30C	ReBlt	Status	Notes
ATSF 8700	ATSF 9507	10/85		
ATSF 8701	ATSF 9505	10/85		
ATSF 8702	ATSF 9529	2/86		
ATSF 8703	ATSF 9513	11/85		
ATSF 8704	ATSF 9526	2/86		
ATSF 8705	ATSF 9515	12/85		
ATSF 8706			WX/81	2
ATSF 8707	ATSF 9511	11/85		
ATSF 8708	ATSF 9527	2/86		
ATSF 8709	ATSF 9517	12/85		
ATSF 8710	ATSF 9522	1/86		
ATSF 8711	ATSF 9525	2/86		
ATSF 8712	ATSF 9523	1/86		
ATSF 8713	ATSF 9502	9/85		
ATSF 8714	ATSF 9518	12/85		
ATSF 8715	ATSF 9514	12/85		
ATSF 8716	ATSF 9528	2/86		
ATSF 8717	ATSF 9516	12/85		
ATSF 8718	ATSF 9506	10/85		
ATSF 8719	ATSF 9504	10/85		
ATSF 8720	ATSF 9521	1/86		
ATSF 8721	ATSF 9500	4/85		3
ATSF 8722			WX/77	4
ATSF 8723	ATSF 9509	11/85		
ATSF 8724	ATSF 9512	11/85		
ATSF 8725	ATSF 9510	11/85		
ATSF 8726	ATSF 9530	3/86		
ATSF 8727	ATSF 9520	1/86		
ATSF 8728	ATSF 9501	9/85		
ATSF 8729	ATSF 9508	11/85		
ATSF 8730	ATSF 9524	1/86		
ATSF 8731	ATSF 9531	3/86		
ATSF 8732	ATSF 9532	3/86		
ATSF 8733	ATSF 9503	10/85		
ATSF 8734	ATSF 9519	1/86		
ATSF 8735	ATSF 9533	3/86		
ATSF 8736			XPL/92	
ATSF 8737			XPL/92	
ATSF 8738			XPL/92	
ATSF 8739			XPL/92	
ATSF 8740			XPL/92	
ATSF 8741			XPL/92	
ATSF 8742			XPL/92	
ATSF 8743			XPL/92	
ATSF 8744			XPL/92	
ATSF 8745			XPL/92	
ATSF 8746			XPL/92	
ATSF 8747			XPL/92	
ATSF 8748			XPL/92	
ATSF 8749			XPL/92	
ATSF 8750			XPL/92	
ATSF 8751			XPL/92	
ATSF 8752			XPL/92	
ATSF 8753			XPL/92	
ATSF 8754			XPRI/92	
ATSF 8755			XPL/92	
ATSF 8756			XPL/92	
ATSF 8757			XPL/92	
ATSF 8758			XPL/92	
ATSF 8759			XPL/92	
ATSF 8760			XPRI/92	
ATSF 8761			XPL/92	
ATSF 8762			XPL/92	
ATSF 8763			WX/78	5
ATSF 8764	ATSF 9539	4/86		
ATSF 8765	ATSF 9534	3/86		
ATSF 8766	ATSF 9535	3/86		
ATSF 8767	ATSF 9536	3/86		
ATSF 8768	ATSF 9537	4/86		
ATSF 8769	ATSF 9538	4/86		
ATSF 8770	ATSF 9562	9/86		
ATSF 8771	ATSF 9548	6/86		
ATSF 8772	ATSF 9544	5/86		
ATSF 8773	ATSF 9545	5/86		
ATSF 8774	ATSF 9546	5/86		
ATSF 8775	ATSF 9542	5/86		
ATSF 8776	ATSF 9559	9/86		
ATSF 8777	ATSF 9549	6/86		
ATSF 8778	ATSF 9547	6/86		
ATSF 8779	ATSF 9550	6/86		
ATSF 8780	ATSF 9566	10/86		
ATSF 8781	ATSF 9555	7/86		
ATSF 8782	ATSF 9556	8/86		
ATSF 8783	ATSF 9554	7/86		
ATSF 8784	ATSF 9553	7/86		
ATSF 8785	ATSF 9552	7/86		
ATSF 8786	ATSF 9563	10/86		
ATSF 8787	ATSF 9567	10/86		
ATSF 8788	ATSF 9568	10/86		
ATSF 8789	ATSF 9564	10/86		
ATSF 8790	ATSF 9540	4/86		
ATSF 8791	ATSF 9557	8/86		
ATSF 8792	ATSF 9560	9/86		
ATSF 8793	ATSF 9551	7/86		
ATSF 8794	ATSF 9558	8/86		
ATSF 8795	ATSF 9565	10/86		
ATSF 8796	ATSF 9543	5/86		
ATSF 8797	ATSF 9541	4/86		
ATSF 8798	ATSF 9561	9/86		
ATSF 8799	ATSF 9569	10/86		

Notes:
1) All SF30C rebuilds done at ATSF Cleburne (TX) shops.
2) ATSF 8706 wrecked and scrapped 1981.
3) ATSF 8721 wrecked off line 6/81; Rebuilt as SF30C 9500 4/85.
4) ATSF 8722 wrecked at Kingman, AZ, 11/23/77 and scrapped by Marathon Steel, Tempe, AZ.
5) ATSF 8763 wrecked and burned with ATSF 5037, 5011 and 5610 in washout near Summit, CA, 3/6/78. Scrapped.

Clinchfield

U36C	Serial	Built	Options/Notes
3600-3606	38228-38234	10/71-11/71	

Original Road No.	SCL	SBD	CSX	Status/ Notes
CRR 3600	SCL 2125	SBD 7300	CSX 7300	XNIM/91
CRR 3601	SCL 2126	SBD 7301	CSX 7301	R
CRR 3602	SCL 2127	SBD 7302	CSX 7302	XNIM/91
CRR 3603	SCL 2128	SBD 7303	CSX 7303	R
CRR 3604	SCL 2129	SBD 7304	CSX 7304	R
CRR 3605	SCL 2130	SBD 7305	CSX 7305	R
CRR 3606	SCL 2131	SBD 7306	CSX 7306	R

Notes:
1) Clinchfield 3600 first U36C built.
2) Clinchfield U36C's 3600-3606 traded to SCL for SD45's 2038-2044 (to CRR 3625-3631) in August 1977.

Erie Lackawanna

U36C	Serial	Built	Options/Notes
3316-3328	38586-38598	10/72	

Original Road No.	CR	1979 Re#	Status	Notes
EL 3316	CR 6587	CR 6884	XCRH/92	
EL 3317	CR 6588	CR 6885	R 12/87	
EL 3318	CR 6589	CR 6886	XCRH/92	
EL 3319	CR 6590	CR 6887	R 12/87	
EL 3320	CR 6591	CR 6888	R 12/87	
EL 3321	CR 6592	CR 6889	XCRH/92	
EL 3322	CR 6593	CR 6890	R 12/87	
EL 3323	CR 6594	CR 6891	XCRH/92	
EL 3324	CR 6595	CR 6892	XCRH/92	
EL 3325	CR 6596	CR 6893	R 12/87	
EL 3326	CR 6597	CR 6894	R 12/87	
EL 3327	CR 6598	CR 6895	XCRH/92	
EL 3328	CR 6599	CR 6896	XCRH/92	

Notes:
1) CR 6884-6896 retired 12/87.

Ferrocarril Del Pacifico

U36C	Serial	Built	Options/Notes
409-418	40316-40325	3/75	

Original Road No.	Super 7 Rebuild	Super 7 Shop/Date	Status	Notes
FCP 409	FNM 14086	EMP/92		
FCP 410			WX/82	
FCP 411				2
FCP 412	FNM 14056	EMP/92		
FCP 413	FNM 14055	EMP/92		
FCP 414				2
FCP 415	FNM 14097	EMP/93		1
FCP 416	FNM 14058	EMP/92		
FCP 417	FNM 14087	EMP/92		
FCP 418	FNM 14057	EMP/92		1

Notes:
1) Rebuilt to Super 7-30C at FNM Empalme, Sonora, shops.
2) FCP 411, 414 stripped to frame Empalme 2/93 for Super 7 rebuild.

Milwaukee Road

U36C	Serial	Built	Options/Notes
8500-8503	38388-38391	6/72	

Original Road No.	1973 Re#	Status	Notes	Super 7 Rebuild	Super 7 Shop/Date
MILW 8500	MILW 5800	GE/MTL	1		
MILW 8501	MILW 5801	XEH/84	2		
MILW 8502	MILW 5802		1	GECX 3009	MTL 10/90
MILW 8503	MILW 5803	GE/MTL	1		

Notes:
1) MILW 8500, 8502,8503 to GE-Montreal 9/88 for Super 7 program.

Nacionales de Mexico

U36C	Serial	Built	Options/Notes
8900-8937	39350-39387	7/73-11/73	
8958-8986	39768-39796	1/74-3/74	
8987*	38125	12/71	*ex-SP U33C 8718
9300-9316	40240-40256	1/75-2/75	

Original Road No.	Status	Notes	Super 7 Rebuild	Super 7 Rebuild
NdeM 8900				
NdeM 8901	R			
NdeM 8902				
NdeM 8903		2	FNM 14010	SLP/90
NdeM 8904		2	FNM 14034	SLP/90
NdeM 8905				
NdeM 8906	OS			
NdeM 8907		2	FNM 14014	SLP/90
NdeM 8908		2	FNM 14011	SLP/90
NdeM 8909				
NdeM 8910	R			
NdeM 8911	R			
NdeM 8912	OS			
NdeM 8913	R		FNM 14004	
NdeM 8914				
NdeM 8915				
NdeM 8916				
NdeM 8917				
NdeM 8918	OS			
NdeM 8919	OS	1		
NdeM 8920	OS	1		
NdeM 8921	OS	1		
NdeM 8922		3	FNM 14002	AGS/90
NdeM 8923		4	FNM 14024	CON/90
NdeM 8924	OS			
NdeM 8925	OS			
NdeM 8926		3	FNM 14006	AGS/90
NdeM 8927		4	FNM 14023	CON/90
NdeM 8928	R			
NdeM 8929				
NdeM 8930	OS			
NdeM 8931	OS			
NdeM 8932	OS			
NdeM 8933				
NdeM 8934				
NdeM 8935	OS			
NdeM 8936	OS			
NdeM 8937				
NdeM 8958				
NdeM 8959				
NdeM 8960				
NdeM 8961		3	FNM 14009	AGS/90
NdeM 8962				
NdeM 8963				
NdeM 8964		3	FNM 14008	AGS/90
NdeM 8965				
NdeM 8966		4	FNM 14028	CON/90
NdeM 8967		3	FNM 14005	AGS/90
NdeM 8968				
NdeM 8969		3	FNM 14003	AGS/90
NdeM 8970	OS			
NdeM 8971	OS			
NdeM 8972				
NdeM 8973				

Nacionales de Mexico U36C Cont.

Original Road No.	Status	Notes	Super 7 Rebuild	Super 7 Rebuild
NdeM 8974	OS			
NdeM 8975				
NdeM 8976				
NdeM 8977				
NdeM 8978			FNM 14064	5/92
NdeM 8979	OS			
NdeM 8980				
NdeM 8981				
NdeM 8982				
NdeM 8983	OS			
NdeM 8984		3	FNM 14007	AGS/90
NdeM 8985		3	FNM 14001	AGS/90
NdeM 8986		3	FNM 14000	AGS/90
NdeM 8987*		6		
NdeM 9300		5	FNM 14012	SLP/90
NdeM 9301				
NdeM 9302	OS			
NdeM 9303				
NdeM 9304				
NdeM 9305				
NdeM 9306	OS			
NdeM 9307				
NdeM 9308				
NdeM 9309				
NdeM 9310		5	FNM 14030	SLP/90
NdeM 9311				
NdeM 9312				
NdeM 9313				
NdeM 9314	OS			
NdeM 9315				
NdeM 9316				

Notes:
1) NdeM 8919, 8920 and 8921 repowered with Alco 251 engines.
2) NdeM 8903, 8904, 8907, 8908 rebuilt to Super 7-C30's at FNM San Luis Potosi shops 1990.
3) NdeM 8913, 8922, 8926, 8961, 8964, 8967, 8969, 8984-8986 rebuilt to Super 7-C30's at FNM Aguascalientes shops 1990.
4) NdeM 8923, 8927, 8966, rebuilt to Super 7-C30's at FNM Concarrel shops 1990.
5) NdeM 9300, 9310 rebuilt to Super 7-C30's at FNM San Luis Potosi shops 1990.
6) NdeM 8987 rebuilt 2/86 from wreck damaged SP U33C 8718 acquired after being wrecked while on lease to NdeM.

U36CG

Nacionales de Mexico

U36CG	Serial	Built	Options/Notes
8938-8957	39797-39816	4/74-5/74	Steam generator

Original Road No.	Status	Notes	Super 7 Rebuild	Super 7 Shop/Date
NdeM 8938				
NdeM 8939		2	FNM 14025	CON/90
NdeM 8940				
NdeM 8941				
NdeM 8942				
NdeM 8943		2	FNM 14026	CON/90
NdeM 8944	OS			
NdeM 8945	OS			
NdeM 8946		1		
NdeM 8947	OS	1		
NdeM 8948				
NdeM 8949	OS			
NdeM 8950				
NdeM 8951		2	FNM 14027	CON/90
NdeM 8952				
NdeM 8953	OS			
NdeM 8954		1		
NdeM 8955				
NdeM 8956				
NdeM 8957				

Notes:
1) NdeM 8946, 8947 and 8954 repowered with Alco 251 engines.
2) NdeM 8939, 8943 and 8951 rebuilt FNM Concarrel 1990 to Super 7-C30's 14025-14027.

U34CH

Erie Lackawanna/NJ DOT

U34CH	Serial	Built	Options/Notes
3351-3356	37625-37630	10/70-12/70	
3357-3373	37935-37951	3/71-5/71	
3374-3382	38749-38757	12/72-1/73	

Original Road No.	1976 Re#	NJT	Status	Notes
EL 3351	CR 1776	NJT 4151		1
EL 3352		NJT 4152		2
EL 3353		NJT 4153		
EL 3354		NJT 4154		2
EL 3355		NJT 4155		
EL 3356		NJT 4156		
EL 3357		NJT 4157		
EL 3358		NJT 4158		2
EL 3359		NJT 4159		
EL 3360		NJT 4160		
EL 3361		NJT 4161		
EL 3362		NJT 4162		
EL 3363		NJT 4163		
EL 3364		NJT 4164		
EL 3365		NJT 4165		
EL 3366		NJT 4166		
EL 3367		NJT 4167		
EL 3368		NJT 4168		
EL 3369		NJT 4169		
EL 3370		NJT 4170		
EL 3371		NJT 4171		
EL 3372		NJT 4172		
EL 3373		NJT 4173		
EL 3374		NJT 4174		
EL 3375		NJT 4175		
EL 3376		NJT 4176		
EL 3377		NJT 4177		
EL 3378		NJT 4178		
EL 3379		NJT 4179		
EL 3380		NJT 4180		
EL 3381		NJT 4181		
EL 3382		NJT 4182		

Notes:
1) EL/NJDOT 3351 wrecked 7/8/74 at Belleville, NJ. Rebuilt GE Apparatus Shop, Cleveland, Ohio. Outshopped 3/20/76 in primer and painted in Bicentennial colors as Conrail/NJDOT 1776 at Hoboken, NJ. 6/76. Renumbered NJT 4151 in March 1978 and later repainted to standard NJT colors.
2) NJT 4152, 4154 and 4158 leased to Southeastern Pennsylvania Transportation Authority in April 1993 for SEPTA work train and commuter service during RailWorks project. NJT 4154, repainted dark blue and relettered SEPTA, failed 8/9/93 in SEPTA service and returned to NJT.

Metro-North Commuter Railroad

U34CH	Serial	Built	Options/Notes
4183	42017	10/78	From C&NW 934

Original Road No.	MNCR	Status	Notes
C&NW 934	MNCR 4183		1

Notes:
1) C&NW U30C 934 (serial 36654 Blt 2/68) rebuilt GE Pittsburg 8-10/78 to Metro-North Commuter Railroad U34CH 4183 and assigned new serial number by GE. Joined NJDOT U34CH fleet in service out of Hoboken as MNCR's contribution to Hoboken, New Jersey-Port Jervis, NY, "West of Hudson" commuter service.

U50C

Union Pacific

U50C	Serial	Built	Options/Notes
5000-5002	37139-37141	10/69-11/69	
5003-5011	37142-37150	3/70-5/70	
5012-5016	37151-37155	11/70-12/70	
5017-5019	37156-37158	1/71-2/71	
5020-5039	37273-37292	5/71-11/71	

Road No.	Status	Notes
UP 5000	XEH/77	5
UP 5001	XEH/77	5,2
UP 5002	XEH/77	5
UP 5003	XEH/77	5
UP 5004	XEH/77	5
UP 5005	WX/77	5
UP 5006	XEH/77	5
UP 5007	XEH/77	5
UP 5008	XEH/77	5
UP 5009	XEH/77	5
UP 5010	XEH/77	5
UP 5011	XEH/77	5
UP 5012	XEH/77	5
UP 5013	XEH/77	5
UP 5014	XEH/77	5
UP 5015	XEH/77	5
UP 5016	XEH/77	5
UP 5017	XEH/77	5,4
UP 5018	XEH/78	6
UP 5019	XEH/78	6,4
UP 5020	XEH/78	6
UP 5021	XEH/78	6
UP 5022	XEH/78	6
UP 5023	XEH/78	6
UP 5024	XEH/78	6
UP 5025	XEH/78	6
UP 5026	XEH/78	6,5
UP 5027	XEH/78	6,5
UP 5028	XEH/78	6
UP 5029	XEH/78	6
UP 5030	XEH/78	6
UP 5031	XEH/78	6
UP 5032	XEH/78	6
UP 5033	XEH/78	6
UP 5034	XEH/78	6
UP 5035	XEH/78	6
UP 5036	XEH/78	6
UP 5037	XEH/78	6
UP 5038	XEH/78	6
UP 5039	XEH/78	6,5

Notes:
1) UP 5000-5039 built on trade-in trucks from UP turbines 1-30.
2) UP 5001 tested on EL Buffalo-Secaucus, N.J., in flat grey primer as GE 5001 for several weeks.
3) All U50C's out of service by 1976.
4) UP 5019 and 5027 leased to Ford Motor Co. Lorain, OH, 2/78 to provide auxiliary electric power during coal strike; UP 5039 to FMC Indianapolis, IN; 5017 and 5026 to Ford Motor, Hazelwood, MO for same service. All returned to storage on UP.
5) UP 5000-5017 retired March 8, 1977; sold for scrap to Erman-Howell, Turner, KS. Wreck-damaged 5005 cut up at Omaha, NE.
6) UP 5018-5039 retired Feb. 23, 1978 after lengthy period in storage; sold for scrap to Erman-Howell, Turner, KS.

U18B

Maine Central

U18B	Serial	Built	Options/Notes
400-409	40720-40729	5/75	Blomberg trucks, A

Original Road No.	"Independence Class" Name	Status	Notes
MEC 400	General Henry Knox		
MEC 401	Hannah Weston	OS/90	1
MEC 402	General John Stark	OS/93	1
MEC 403	General Peleg Wadsworth	OS/90	1
MEC 404	Kenneth Roberts		
MEC 405	Arundel	OS/93	1
MEC 406	Colonel John Anderson		
MEC 407	Unity		
MEC 408	Battle of Bagaduce	OS/89	
MEC 409	Ethan Allen	OS/89	1

Notes:
A) MEC "Independence Class" U18B's carried names until repainted in Guilford colors.
1) Out of service at Waterville, ME, still in MEC yellow.

Nacionales de Mexico

U18B	Serial	Built	Options/Notes
9000-9044	39641-39685	1/74-10/74	AAR-B trucks

Original Road No.	Status	Notes
NdeM 9000		
NdeM 9001		
NdeM 9002		
NdeM 9003		
NdeM 9004		
NdeM 9005		
NdeM 9006	R	
NdeM 9007		
NdeM 9008		
NdeM 9009		
NdeM 9010		
NdeM 9011	R	
NdeM 9012		
NdeM 9013	R	
NdeM 9014		
NdeM 9015		
NdeM 9016	R	
NdeM 9017		
NdeM 9018	W/80	
NdeM 9019		
NdeM 9020		
NdeM 9021	W/80	
NdeM 9022		
NdeM 9023	R	
NdeM 9024		
NdeM 9025		
NdeM 9026		
NdeM 9027		
NdeM 9028		
NdeM 9029		
NdeM 9030		
NdeM 9031		
NdeM 9032		
NdeM 9033		
NdeM 9034		
NdeM 9035	W/80	
NdeM 9036		
NdeM 9037		
NdeM 9038	R	
NdeM 9039		
NdeM 9040		
NdeM 9041	R	
NdeM 9042	R	
NdeM 9043		
NdeM 9044		

Providence & Worcester

U18B	Serial	Built	Options/Notes
1801	41482	10/76	FB2 trucks

Original Road No.	Status	Notes
P&W 1801		1

Notes:
1) P&W 1801 retrucked in 1981 with AAR-B's from P&W RS3 1501 (ex-MEC 553).

Seaboard Coast Line

U18B	Serial	Built	Options/Notes
250-261	39407-39418	12/73	FB2 trucks/lightweight
300-324	38847-38871	3/73-5/73	FB2 trucks
325-343	39388-39406	11/73-1/73	Blomberg trucks
344-392	39852-39900	8/74-11/74	Blomberg trucks

Original Road No.	SBD	CSX	Post CSX	Status	Notes
SCL 250	SBD 1888	CSX 1888			1
SCL 251	SBD 1889	CSX 1889			
SCL 252	SBD 1890	CSX 1890		R	1
SCL 253	SBD 1891	CSX 1891		R/93	1
SCL 254	SBD 1892	CSX 1892		XNIM/93	1
SCL 255	SBD 1893	CSX 1893		XSPC/93	1
SCL 256	SBD 1894	CSX 1894			1
SCL 257	SBD 1895	CSX 1895		R/92	1
SCL 258	SBD 1896	CSX 1896			1
SCL 259	SBD 1897	CSX 1897		R	1
SCL 260	SBD 1898	CSX 1898		R/93	1
SCL 261	SBD 1899	CSX 1899		R	1
SCL 300	SBD 1900	CSX 1900			
SCL 301	SBD 1901	CSX 1901		Sold	4
SCL 302	SBD 1902	CSX 1902		XSPC/93	
SCL 303	SBD 1903	CSX 1903		R	
SCL 304	SBD 1904	CSX 1904		R/93	
SCL 305				WX/82	2
SCL 306	SBD 1905	CSX 1905			
SCL 307	SBD 1906	CSX 1906		R	
SCL 308	SBD 1907	CSX 1907		R	
SCL 309	SBD 1908	CSX 1908		R/92	
SCL 310	SBD 1909	CSX 1909		R/93	
SCL 311	SBD 1910	CSX 1910		R	
SCL 312	SBD 1911	CSX 1911		R/93	
SCL 313				WX/	3
SCL 314	SBD 1912	CSX 1912			
SCL 315	SBD 1913	CSX 1913		R	
SCL 316	SBD 1914	CSX 1914			
SCL 317	SBD 1915	CSX 1915		R/92	
SCL 318	SBD 1916	CSX 1916		R/92	
SCL 319	SBD 1917	CSX 1917		XSPC/93	
SCL 320	SBD 1918	CSX 1918			
SCL 321	SBD 1919	CSX 1919		XSPC/93	
SCL 322	SBD 1920	CSX 1920		R/92	
SCL 323	SBD 1921	CSX 1921			
SCL 324	SBD 1922	CSX 1922		R	
SCL 325	SBD 1923	CSX 1923		R/92	
SCL 326	SBD 1924	CSX 1924		R/92	
SCL 327	SBD 1925	CSX 1925		R	
SCL 328	SBD 1926	CSX 1926			
SCL 329	SBD 1927	CSX 1927			
SCL 330	SBD 1928	CSX 1928		R	
SCL 331	SBD 1929	CSX 1929		R/92	
SCL 332	SBD 1930	CSX 1930		R/93	
SCL 333	SBD 1931	CSX 1931		R	
SCL 334	SBD 1932	CSX 1932			
SCL 335	SBD 1933	CSX 1933			
SCL 336	SBD 1934	CSX 1934			
SCL 337	SBD 1935	CSX 1935		R	
SCL 338	SBD 1936	CSX 1936			
SCL 339	SBD 1937	CSX 1937		R/92	
SCL 340	SBD 1938	CSX 1938			
SCL 341	SBD 1939	CSX 1939			
SCL 342	SBD 1940	CSX 1940			
SCL 343	SBD 1941	CSX 1941			
SCL 344	SBD 1942	CSX 1942			
SCL 345	SBD 1943	CSX 1943		R	
SCL 346	SBD 1944	CSX 1944		R	
SCL 347	SBD 1945	CSX 1945			
SCL 348	SBD 1946	CSX 1946			
SCL 349	SBD 1947	CSX 1947			
SCL 350	SBD 1948	CSX 1948			
SCL 351	SBD 1949	CSX 1949			
SCL 352	SBD 1950	CSX 1950			
SCL 353	SBD 1951	CSX 1951			
SCL 354	SBD 1952	CSX 1952		XPL/93	
SCL 355	SBD 1953	CSX 1953		R	
SCL 356	SBD 1954	CSX 1954		R/92	
SCL 357	SBD 1955	CSX 1955			

Seaboard Coast Line U18B Cont.

Original Road No.	SBD	CSX	Post CSX	Status	Notes
SCL 358	SBD 1956	CSX 1956			
SCL 359	SBD 1957	CSX 1957		XPL/93	
SCL 360	SBD 1958	CSX 1958			
SCL 361	SBD 1959	CSX 1959		R	
SCL 362	SBD 1960	CSX 1960			
SCL 363	SBD 1961	CSX 1961		R/93	
SCL 364	SBD 1962	CSX 1962			
SCL 365	SBD 1963	CSX 1963			
SCL 366	SBD 1964	CSX 1964			
SCL 367	SBD 1965	CSX 1965			
SCL 368	SBD 1966	CSX 1966		XSPC/93	
SCL 369	SBD 1967	CSX 1967			
SCL 370	SBD 1968	CSX 1968		R/92	
SCL 371	SBD 1969	CSX 1969		R/93	
SCL 372	SBD 1970	CSX 1970		R/93	
SCL 373	SBD 1971	CSX 1971		XSPC/93	
SCL 374	SBD 1972	CSX 1972		R/93	
SCL 375	SBD 1973	CSX 1973			
SCL 376	SBD 1974	CSX 1974		R/93	
SCL 377	SBD 1975	CSX 1975			
SCL 378	SBD 1976	CSX 1976		R/93	
SCL 379	SBD 1977	CSX 1977			
SCL 380	SBD 1978	CSX 1978		R	
SCL 381	SBD 1979	CSX 1979			
SCL 382	SBD 1980	CSX 1980		R/92	
SCL 383	SBD 1981	CSX 1981			
SCL 384	SBD 1982	CSX 1982		R/92	
SCL 385	SBD 1983	CSX 1983			
SCL 386	SBD 1984	CSX 1984			
SCL 387	SBD 1985	CSX 1985		R/92	
SCL 388	SBD 1986	CSX 1986			
SCL 389	SBD 1987	CSX 1987			
SCL 390	SBD 1988	CSX 1988		R	
SCL 391	SBD 1989	CSX 1989		R/92	
SCL 392	SBD 1990	CSX 1990		R	

Notes:
1) SCL 250-261 are light-weight, 111-ton U18B's with 1200-gallon fuel tanks.
2) SCL 305 wrecked c./82 and sold to Chrome Crankshaft 9/82.
3) SCL 313 wrecked and scrapped.
4) CSX 1901 painted "Illinois Southern" 1901 and used with ex-N&W GP30 536 in filming "The Fugitive" on Great Smoky Mountain Railway in 1993.

Texas Utilities

U18B	Serial	Built	Options/Notes
101-102	39506-39507	2/74	AAR-B trucks

Original Road No.		Status	Notes
TUGX 101	TUGX 2301	GE/91	1
TUGX 102	TUGX 2302		1

Notes:
1) Equipped for remote control operation.

P30CH

Amtrak

P30CH	Serial	Built	Options/Notes
700-724	40694-40718	8/75-12/75	

Original Road No.	Status	Notes
AMTK 700	R8/91	
AMTK 701	R8/91	
AMTK 702	R8/91	
AMTK 703	R8/91	
AMTK 704	R8/91	
AMTK 705	R	
AMTK 706	XNIM/92	
AMTK 707	R	
AMTK 708	XNIM/92	
AMTK 709	R8/91	
AMTK 710	R8/91	
AMTK 711	XNIM/92	
AMTK 712	R	
AMTK 713	WX/77	1
AMTK 714	XNIM/92	
AMTK 715	WX/79	2
AMTK 716	XNIM/92	
AMTK 717	XNIM/92	
AMTK 718	R8/91	
AMTK 719	XNIM/92	
AMTK 720	XNIM/92	
AMTK 721	XNIM/92	
AMTK 722	XNIM/92	
AMTK 723	R	
AMTK 724	R8/91	

Notes:
1) Amtrak 713 wrecked 12/77 and scrapped.
2) Amtrak 715, leading northbound Shawnee, totalled in head-on collision with ICG piggyback train #51 (GP40's 3000, 3029, +1) at Harvey, IL, 10/29/79.

APPENDIX

Although the demand for used U-boats has never been strong, several railroads acquired significant groups of hand-me-down GE's. Fleets of three or more second-hand U-boats not acquired through merger are listed below.

Boston & Maine

Road No.	Original Road No.	Subsequent Road Nos.	Model	Status	Notes
B&M 190	PC 2916	CR 2916	U33B	XPL/91	1
B&M 191	PC 2919	CR 2919	U33B	XPL/91	1
B&M 192	PC 2925	CR 2925 RBMR 3303	U33B		2
B&M 663	DE 012	B&M 640	U30C		3

Notes:
1) To B&M 8/84. Retired by 1988 and sold to GE for Super 7 program via MS&A 3/88. To Pielet Bros. for scrap 11/91.
2) To B&M 8/84. To Al Luedtke for Lackawanna Valley 3/88, then to Reading & Blue Mountain.
3) Detroit Edison 012 to B&M 640 via Helm 2/86.

Central Michigan

Road No.	Original Road No.	Subsequent Road Nos.	Model	Notes
CMGN 8902	MP 674	MP 2256 MP 4506	U23B	1,2
CMGN 8903	MP 668	MP 2250 MP 4500	U23B	2
CMGN 8904	MP 669	MP 2251 MP 4501	U23B	2
CMGN 8905	MP 672	MP 2254 MP 4504 CMGN/DM 4504	U23B	2, 3
CMGN 4502	MP 670	MP 2252 MP 4502	U23B	2
CMGN 4505	MP 673	MP 2255 MP 4505	U23B	2

Notes:
1) MP 2256 rebuilt with EMD cab during wreck repairs.
2) To Central Michigan in 1989, via NRE. MP 4505 for parts only.
3) CMGN 4504 stencilled D&M (Detroit & Mackinac); stored in MP blue at Tawas City 6/93; to CMGN 8905.

Delaware & Hudson

Road No.	Original Road No.	Subsequent Road Nos.	Model	Status	Notes
D&H 650	PC 6540	CR 6540 CR 6845	U33C	W/87	1,3
D&H 651	PC 6551	CR 6551 CR 6856	U33C		1
D&H 652	PC 6555	CR 6555 CR 6860	U33C		2,4
D&H 653	PC 6557	CR 6557 CR 6862	U33C		2,4
D&H 654	PC 6559	CR 6559 CR 6864	U33C	FNM 14022	2,4
D&H 655	PC 6560	CR 6560 CR 6865	U33C		2,4
D&H 656	PC 6561	CR 6561 CR 6866	U33C		2,4
D&H 2917	PC 2917	CR 2917	U33B	XNIM/86	5
D&H 2918	PC 2918	CR 2918	U33B	XNIM/86	5
D&H 2920	PC 2920	CR 2920	U33B	XNIM/86	5
D&H 2922	PC 2922	CR 2922	U33B	XNIM/86	5
D&H 2924	PC 2924	CR 2924	U33B	XNIM/86	5

Notes:
1) To D&H via Naporano Iron & Metal 8/85.
2) To D&H via Chrome Crankshaft 8/85.
3) GTI train POSE, engines ST 617, B&M 313, D&H 650 derailed at Elnora, NY, 6/7/87. D&H 650 heavily damaged.
4) To GE for Super 7 program via MS&A 3/88. D&H 654 rebuilt GE Montreal, Quebec 12/89 to Super 7-C30 FNM 14022.
5) Leased to D&H by ITEL in 8/84. In CR paint, but restencilled D&H. CR 2923 rejected by D&H. All returned by 1986 and sold for scrap.

General Electric

Road No.	Original Road No.	Subsequent Road Nos.	Model	Status	Notes
GE 26-1	ATSF 6341		U23B		1
GE 404	SOU 3814		U33C		2
GE 405	SOU 3810		U33C		2

Notes:
1) ATSF 6341 traded-in to GE 6/83. Transferred to Building 26 for use as switcher etc. Repainted gray-and-white, numbered 26-1 and named "Cristine."
2) Retired 2/87 and traded-in to GE on C39-8's. Reconditioned and repainted to GE 404 and 405 for use as load engines on GE Erie, PA, test track.

Georgia Central

Road No.	Original Road No.	Subsequent Road Nos.	Model	Status Notes
GC 1001	SAL 801	SCL 1705 SBD 5522 CSX 5305	U30B	
GC 1002	C&O 8221	CSX 5349	U30B	
GC 1003	C&O 8222	CSX 5350	U30B	
GC 1004	L&N 2501	SBD 5537 CSX 5320	U28B	1
GC 1005	GE 302	C&O 8223 CSX 5351	U30B	2
GC 1006	C&O 8204	CSX 5332	U30B	
GC 1007	C&O 8230	CSX 5358	U30B	
GC 1008	C&O 8232	CSX 5360	U30B	
GC 1009	L&N 2506	SBD 5541 CSX 5324	U30B	
GC 1010	C&O 8213	CSX 5341	U30B	
GC 1011	C&O 8219	CSX 5347	U30B	
GC 1012	SCL 1746	SBD 5626 CSX 5626	U33B	
GC 1013	SCL 1741	SBD 5621 CSX 5621	U33B	
GC 1014	SCL 1745	SBD 5625 CSX 5625	U33B	
GC 1015	SCL 1729	SBD 5609 CSX 5609	U33B	
GC 1016	SCL 1739	SBD 5619 CSX 5619	U33B	

Notes:
1) Upgraded to U30B specs by L&N.
2) Built as GE 302, U30B demonstrator/test bed. Rebuilt to U33B 7/67. Upgraded to U36B specs in 1968 and operated until 12/70. Rebuilt to U30B standards and sold to C&O in 1972.
3) All to GC 9-11/90.

Kyle Railroad

Road No.	Original Road No.	Subsequent Road Nos.	Model	Status	Notes
KYLE 5794	SL-SF 857	BN 5794	U30B		1
KYLE 5795	SL-SF 858	BN 5795	U30B		1
KYLE 5796	SL-SF 859	BN 5796	U30B		1
KYLE 5799	SL-SF 862	BN 5799	U30B		1
KYLE 5321	BN 5321		U30C		2
KYLE 5322	BN 5322		U30C		2
KYLE 5331	BN 5331		U30C		2
KYLE 5332	BN 5332		U30C		2
KYLE 5808	BN 5808		U30C		2
KYLE 5810	BN 5810		U30C		2
KYLE 5819	BN 5819		U30C		2
KYLE 5820	BN 5820		U30C		2
KYLE 5821	BN 5821		U30C		2
KYLE 5918	BN 5918		U30C		2
KYLE 5925	BN 5925		U30C		2
KYLE 5928	BN 5928		U30C		2

Notes:
1) BN 5794, 5795, 5796, 5799 to KYLE 5/91 via Pielet Bros.
2) To Kyle via Pielet Bros. 12/90-1/91.

Lake Superior & Ishpeming

Road No.	Original Road No.	Subsequent Road Nos.	Model	Status	Notes
LS&I 3000	BN 5931		U30C		1
LS&I 3001	BN 5828		U30C		1
LS&I 3002	BN 5830		U30C		1
LS&I 3003	BN 5937		U30C		1
LS&I 3004	BN 5825		U30C		1
LS&I 3005	BN 5929		U30C		1
LS&I 3006	BN 5932		U30C		1
LS&I 3007	BN 5934		U30C		1
LS&I 3008	BN 5832		U30C		1
LS&I 3050	BN 5827		U30C		1
LS&I 3051	BN 5930		U30C		1
LS&I 3052	BN 5936		U30C		1
LS&I 3053	BN 5938		U30C		1

Notes:
1) Returned to lessor 4/89 and sold to LS&I.

Maine Central

Road No.	Original Road No.	Model	Status	Notes
MEC 225	RI 225	U25B	XMSA/88	1
MEC 226	RI 226	U25B	XMEC/91	1
[MEC 227]	RI 227	U25B	X/MEC	2
MEC 228	RI 228	U25B	XMSA/88	1
MEC 229	RI 229	U25B	XMSA/88	1
MEC 230	RI 230	U25B	XMEC/88	1
MEC 231	RI 231	U25B	WX/87	1,4
MEC 232	RI 232	U25B	XMEC/88	1
[MEC 233]	RI 233	U25B	XMEC	2
MEC 234	RI 234	U25B	XMSA/88	1,3
[MEC 235]	RI 235	U25B	X/MEC	2
[MEC 236]	RI 236	U25B	XMCB/83	2
[MEC 237]	RI 237	U25B	XMCB/83	2
MEC 238	RI 238	U25B	XMSA/88	1

Notes:
1) Sold by lessor to MEC 6/80.
2) Sold by lessor to MEC 6/80, cannibalized for parts; never operated by MEC.
3) MEC 234 operated in full ROCK blue-and-white until repainted MEC orange in late/82.
4) MEC 231 wrecked in three-train collision at Fitchburg, MA, 1/27/87 and scrapped.

Nacionales de Mexico

Road No.	Original Road No.	Subsequent Road Nos.	Model	Status	Notes
DH 701	D&H 701		U30C	OS	1, 2
DH 702	D&H 702		U30C	OS	1, 3
DH 703	D&H 703		U30C	OS	1
DH 704	D&H 704		U30C	OS	1, 3
DH 705	D&H 705		U30C	OS	1
DH 706	D&H 706		U30C	OS	1, 2
DH 707	D&H 707		U30C	OS	1
DH 708	D&H 708		U30C	OS	1
DH 709	D&H 709		U30C	OS	1
DH 710	D&H 710		U30C	OS	1
DH 711	D&H 711		U30C	OS	1, 3
DH 712	D&H 712		U30C	OS	1
NdeM 930	C&NW 930		U30C	OS	2
NdeM 931	C&NW 931		U30C	OS	2
NdeM 932	C&NW 932		U30C	OS	2
NdeM 933	C&NW 933		U30C	OS	2
NdeM 935	C&NW 935		U30C	OS	2
NdeM 936	C&NW 936		U30C	OS	2
NdeM 6900	N&W 1904		U28B	OS	3
NdeM 6901	N&W 1905		U28B	OS	3
NdeM 6902	N&W 1906		U28B	OS	3
NdeM 6903	N&W 1909		U28B	OS	3
NdeM 6904	N&W 1923		U28B	OS	3
NdeM 6905	N&W 1924		U28B	OS	3
NdeM 6906	N&W 1926		U28B	OS	3
NdeM 7600	C&O 2500	C&O 8100	U25B	OS	4
NdeM 7601	C&O 2503	C&O 8103	U25B	OS	4
NdeM 7602	C&O 2505	C&O 8105	U25B	OS	4
NdeM 7603	C&O 2506	C&O 8106	U25B	OS	4
NdeM 7604	C&O 2513	C&O 8113	U25B	OS	4
NdeM 7605	C&O 2516	C&O 8116	U25B	OS	4
NdeM 7606	C&O 2521	C&O 8121	U25B	OS	4
NdeM 7607	C&O 2522	C&O 8122	U25B	OS	4
NdeM 7608	C&O 2525	C&O 8125	U25B	OS	4
NdeM 7609	C&O 2527	C&O 8127	U25B	OS	4
NdeM 7610	C&O 2528	C&O 8128	U25B	OS	4
NdeM 7611	C&O 2529	C&O 8129	U25B	OS	4
NdeM 7612	C&O 2532	C&O 8132	U25B	OS	4
NdeM 7613	C&O 2533	C&O 8133	U25B	OS	4
NdeM 7614	C&O 2537	C&O 8137	U25B	OS	4
NdeM 7700	ACL 3000	SCL 2100	U25C	OS	5
NdeM 7701	ACL 3001	SCL 2101	U25C	OS	5
NdeM 7702	ACL 3002	SCL 2102	U25C	OS	5
NdeM 7703	ACL 3003	SCL 2103	U25C	OS	5
NdeM 7704	ACL 3004	SCL 2104	U25C	OS	5
NdeM 7705	ACL 3005	SCL 2105	U25C	OS	5
NdeM 7706	ACL 3006	SCL 2106	U25C	OS	5
NdeM 7707	ACL 3007	SCL 2107	U25C	OS	5
NdeM 7708	ACL 3008	SCL 2108	U25C	OS	5
NdeM 7710	ACL 3010	SCL 2110	U25C	OS	5
NdeM 7711	ACL 3014	SCL 2114	U25C	OS	5
NdeM 7712	ACL 3015	SCL 2115	U25C	WX	5
NdeM 7713	ACL 3016	SCL 2116	U25C	OS	5
NdeM 7714	ACL 3017	SCL 2117	U25C	OS	5
NdeM 7715	ACL 3018	SCL 2118	U25C	OS	5
NdeM 7716	ACL 3019	SCL 2119	U25C	OS	5
NdeM 7800	ACL 3011	SCL 2111	U25C	OS	5,6
NdeM 7801	ACL 3012	SCL 2112	U25C	OS	5,6
NdeM 7802	ACL 3013	SCL 2113	U25C	OS	5,6
NdeM 8987	SP 8718		U33C		7
NdeM 9700	N&W 1931		U30B	OS	8
NdeM 9701	N&W 1933		U30B	OS	8
NdeM 9702	N&W 1940		U30B	OS	8
NdeM 9703	N&W 1941		U30B	OS	8
NdeM 9704	N&W 1944		U30B	OS	8
NdeM 9705	N&W 1953		U30B	OS	8
NdeM 9706	N&W 1956		U30B	OS	8
NdeM 9707	N&W 1957		U30B	OS	8
NdeM 9708	N&W 8466		U30B	OS	8
NdeM 9709	N&W 8470		U30B	OS	8
NdeM 9710	N&W 8471		U30B	OS	8
NdeM 9711	N&W 8472		U30B	OS	8
NdeM 9712	N&W 8478		U30B	OS	8
NdeM 9713	N&W 8479		U30B	OS	8
NdeM 9714	N&W 8482		U30B	OS	8
NdeM 9715	N&W 8489		U30B	OS	8
NdeM 9716	N&W 8491		U30B	OS	8